YOUNG AMERICANS ABROAD

Contributors ▪ Joseph Lelyveld

Christopher T. Rand

N. N.

Reuel Wilson

Jane O'Reilly Jencks

Christopher Jencks

Smith Hempstone

Julian Mayfield

Shepard L. Forman

James W. Rowe

Edited by Roger H. Klein

YOUNG

AMERICANS

ABROAD

HARPER & ROW, PUBLISHERS

NEW YORK,

EVANSTON,

AND LONDON

Parts of the essay entitled "Some Burmese Days" by Joseph Lelyveld originally appeared in the Columbia University *Forum,* Volume V, Number 3, under the title " 'One to Speak, Another to Hear': Burmese Encounters."

Contents

vii   Preface
       ROGER KLEIN

  1   Some Burmese Days
       JOSEPH LELYVELD

 36   Debate Without End (Iran)
       CHRISTOPHER T. RAND

 62   You Do Your Job, I'll Do Mine (Russia)
       N.N.

 92   Some Polish Impressions
       REUEL WILSON

107   The Lonely Queue (England)
       JANE O'REILLY JENCKS AND
       CHRISTOPHER JENCKS

138   An Expatriate in Africa (Keyna)
       SMITH HEMPSTONE

v

176 Ghanaian Sketches
       JULIAN MAYFIELD

205 Up from the Parrot's Perch (Brazil)
       SHEPARD L. FORMAN

232 What Ever Happened to the Happy Lands? (Argentina)
       JAMES W. ROWE

Preface

Thirty years ago it was by no means uncommon for Americans to go abroad, but "abroad" invariably meant Europe. A graduate student could choose between Oxford, Cambridge, Heidelberg, Paris, Bologna, and some other ancient towns, but it was rare indeed to find any American at the universities of Teheran, Rio de Janeiro, or Cracow. A novelist wanting a change of scene might follow well-worn paths to Italy or England or the south of France. Very few ever went to Ghana.

As this book shows, the situation has changed drastically since those days. For the first time in our history, many young Americans are traveling to all corners of the earth—to teach, study, set up businesses, write, work with the government and, lately, with the much publicized Peace Corps. The most obvious reason for this global burgeoning of contacts is political. Countries that had previously seemed provincial (because colonial) backwaters are now beginning to edge toward the center of the stage. The Cold War inevitably makes each of these countries important as ally, foe, or neutral. Thus anyone who reads the papers is continually aware of the revolutionary transformations taking place on all sides and must be curious to know what it is like to set up a life in these countries. At least I was very curious, which gave me the idea for this book.

I asked ten young Americans, between the ages of 25 and 35, to describe their recent stays, lasting from one to as many as six years, in a foreign country. Unlike members of the Peace Corps or other government-sponsored groups, these individuals went on their own and were thus able to speak freely without fear of saying something that went against official policy. Their youth was an advantage in the sense that it allowed them to enter more easily into the everyday life and habits of their particular locality and to form friendships. I hoped that each essay would indicate, in actual and vivid cases, how much of value could come from such exchanges; how persons of different nationalities might overcome, or fail to surmount, the barriers of a different speech, way of life, and outlook—in other words, to tell how much or how little they had in common.

Though some of the contributors are highly trained political observers, it was not the book's purpose to give up-to-the-minute "inside information" on changes in Asia, Africa, Europe, and Latin America. Rather, each author was asked to describe the working and living conditions he had seen and experienced, the political climate as it appeared from conversations with friends and acquaintances and, most particularly, the general problems of youth that he had witnessed: the difficulties of getting a good education, adapting to the demands of a changing society, the search for roots and tradition, and the conflict of loyalties to past and future. Whenever the authors did go into the recent history of a country in some detail, they did so to make the people of that country more vivid to us as they responded to their changing world, not in order to appear as pundits.

Nonetheless, the political opinions expressed in this book may be of interest in their own right, as they represent in varying degrees the outlook of what was once known as "the silent generation." That generation, whether it really was silent or not, is now coming into its own, and its point of view, shaped by years of hot and cold war, as well as affluence, will inevitably differ in many ways from the viewpoint of the older generation. Conservative or radical, the contributors indicate the new political feelings of today.

Hopefully, from this personal method of writing will come the reader's intimate sense of what it means to be a young American abroad, participating in one of the most exciting and encouraging developments of the last years.

I am grateful to Richard H. Nolte of the Institute of Current World Affairs, to Emmi Baum, and to Pat M. Holt, for suggesting contributors to this book, and to Genevieve Young for help in times of trouble.

ROGER H. KLEIN

YOUNG AMERICANS ABROAD

JOSEPH LELYVELD

■

Some Burmese Days

Why Burma? I heard the question for months. (*Asia . . . how wonderful! But why Burma?*) I had a number of answers, some academic, others in terms of a career I could dimly see ahead—all, however, excuses after the idea took hold. Not until the journey was irrevocable, on the last leg of our long flight to Rangoon, did I put the question to myself. Then it hurt. My stock answers seemed paltry. I had a moment of near-panic reviewing what I knew about the country: a disjointed series of names, facts, and dates plus the first line of the Lord's Prayer in Burmese, conned from the language manuals for missionaries.

I remember staring out fixedly into the woolly darkness, trying to imagine what it covered. It gave back no hints. Still I stared on, rigid and unnerved, until the big plane began to float down like a puppet on wires and I could make out some lights. A moment later and they were all there, strewn across the blackness of the night. There were no garishly flashing signs, no moving auto

---

Joseph Lelyveld graduated summa cum laude from Harvard in 1958 and has since done graduate work at Harvard and the Columbia School of Journalism. He is presently on the staff of the *New York Times* and has contributed articles on Burma to various magazines.

beams, nothing but this breathtaking, glimmering stillness. I felt good again.

I have felt good about Burma ever since but still do not know just why I wanted to go there. The too-simple truth is that I went to Burma to find out why. My avowed aim was to study political attitudes. That Burma had been fairly inconspicuous on the international scene made it seem all the more attractive, a kind of byway on which the traffic would be less heavy and therefore easier to observe clearly. Choice and chance connive to keep the country out of the way. The hills and jungles along its borders serve as buffers, making what we call "neutrality" easy and practical. They also make good homes for bandits and rebels, and after fifteen years of skirmishing there are still rebels in the hills, some of whom are called Communists. Because of the remoteness of the terrain they cannot be readily extirpated; but on the same count it is possible to take them fairly casually. China, Laos, Thailand, Pakistan, and India have sectors of the border, but this does not make them neighbors. One travels to Rangoon from Bangkok or Calcutta by plane or boat only—mostly by plane. Thus the cold war arrives abruptly, the way my wife and I did. Magazines, books, diplomats, journalists, land in Rangoon full of the names of far-off places: Cuba, the Congo, Russia, America . . . China, Laos, India. All are somehow equally far and equally near.

We were traveling light. What I had learned in twenty-three years about being an American in America had helped to set me in motion; I was not preparing to be a skilled American-in-the-world. Our trip was to be a test of our readiness to come to terms with something new and make it matter in our lives. Why Burma? An empty question—we were there.

I had been told my first impressions would be decisive and was resolved to fill reams of paper with stunning accounts and reflections. I never did. The excitement I felt during our first days in Rangoon was nearly stifling, like the excitement of a feverish dream.

In a hurry to slough my feeling of newness in the place, I

walked and walked, up and down narrow streets spilling over with bare-bottom boys and little girls with shaved heads, past dark doorways where toothless old crones hunkered down to enjoy their cheroots, and along the crowded main avenues where side-walk hawkers spread out their wares—plastic gadgets mostly, such as toys, flashlights, ballpoint pens. Pretty schoolgirls, neat and composed, hurried by, fresh flowers in their tightly braided hair, their dark eyes shining. Young orange-robed monks roamed the streets as I did, apparently still involved in the flux of this world; while in the pagodas women, young and old, lovingly washed down images of the Buddha to gain merit. Half-naked Indian coolies strained under enormous loads. Indian mothers dispatched timid tots after me to cry for *baksheesh*. Scraggly pariah dogs, the most despised creatures on earth, yelped and whimpered from one garbage bin to another. Long lines hugged the walls of movie theaters for shade or cover from rain, and at nearly every corner there was a teashop where men and boys sat chatting quietly. Chinese, Moslems, and Sikhs, Englishmen in white ducks and cassocked missionaries, hastened down the streets through the ambling crowds. Nearly everyone carried an um-brella, for the monsoon season had just begun.

It rained every day, but not all day. The rain came in torrents; then, almost before the pavements could cool, the hot sun was bearing down again on the city. After a few hours heavy dark clouds blew in to cover it and the rains returned. But again they passed, and the sun fought its way back and usually won the day, throwing an astonishing sheet of crimson over the sky as it sank down—just before the evening rains. It was not an easy rhythm to get used to. I had the feeling my brain was getting addled and flushed by turns each day.

When I had sweated through my raincoat several times, I learned to carry an umbrella. When I had ruined a pair of shoes, I learned to wear sandals. In the bazaar I found myself a *longyi*, one of the brightly colored wrap-around skirts Burmese men wear; though I rarely had the gumption to wear it out of the house, it was for me a mark of my Burmanization. My walks continued, but I was no longer walking off my newness. Already my wife Carolyn was calling it "our Rangoon."

Newness was not the only reason for our malaise during our first weeks, however. Several nights after we arrived we were taken to a meeting of the Burma-America Association—a promotion of the embassy's designed to encourage cultural exchange or some such thing. There we made our debut in Rangoon's little America. Carolyn was briefed by some ladies on the handling of servants, the avoidance of mildew and dysentery, shopping at the commissary, and the advantages of getting to Bangkok as often as possible—the favorite conversational gambits of American ladies in Rangoon. We were hit with advice from all sides and lugubriously assured that Rangoon was really not so bad, not if you played bridge, had a good stock of booze, took out membership in the clubs, and possessed air-conditioning, a car, a chauffeur, and an iron stomach. When we said we liked Rangoon and expected to be very happy there, the Burmese (who had all been to America) were flattered and incredulous; the Americans, amused and tolerant.

The next day I was toured through the embassy. The officials I met all seemed uniformly boyish in manner, whatever their age, and they all had a way of talking out of the corners of their mouths as if anything they had to say must be said in strict confidence. They understood I would be making a study of the Burmese press. They had plenty of trouble with the papers. I would not find many that took a responsible attitude to world affairs. Burma was a strange country, very strange, they said. Nearly everyone offered the gratuitous assurance that there were no ugly Americans in Rangoon. I asked one man what his work was.

"What do we do?" he said, swiveling back in his chair and gesturing to a map of Asia over his head, his finger vaguely tracing the serpentine curves of China's long border, as if it alone, this charmed American digit, was keeping the great blot of red from streaming over the varicolored patchwork below. "Why, we're just trying to hold the line in Asia."

Once we got on the party circuit our troubles were compounded. I have a way of feeling out of place at parties, and this was never more true than in Burma. We found that the invitations we received were all, in effect, to the same party. The settings changed, but the faces remained the same. If it was a social evening, the Burmese there danced, talked golf, knew what martinis were and liked them dry—uncommonly sybaritic tastes for Burma. If it was an official function, the Burmese guests were people in whom the embassy was "interested," mostly officials and journalists. The hurt, sullen expressions I saw at these parties were my first clues to the difficulty of being the kind of Burmese in whom an embassy might be interested.

Finally, having had our fill of talk about dysentery, we managed to extricate ourselves from this society. It had been a bad false start. The time had come to venture out of the nest. We never did join the Burma-America Association—a small treason —figuring that since we were lucky enough to be in Burma we did not require its auspices to meet Burmese. Carolyn enrolled at the university. I got down to work, too.

I call it "work" but am not sure I should, since all I was doing then was hanging around the newspapers, talking to their editors, and watching how they went about their business. There are over twenty dailies in Rangoon. The average circulation is not much more than three thousand, so the destitute papers must live off their editors' vanity or inertia or hope.

Deliberate distortion of the news is rare, though in some cases this is simply because editorial practices are not disciplined enough for such purposeful maneuvering of copy. However, the smaller organs have the daily vexation of having to fill up spaces left for ads that have failed to materialize, so it sometimes happens that anti-Communist publications pick up dispatches from Tass to use as fillers, while their pro-Red opposite numbers run U.S.I.S. handouts for the same reasons. The embassies (the one I knew best, in particular) often ascribed great significance to such quirks and solemnly interpreted them.

On the well-edited papers, however, news is segregated from editorial remarks, which are, as a safety precaution, restrained in direct proportion to the closeness of the matter at hand to the newspaper itself. Editorials steaming like brimstone could be tossed off on items out of Washington or London. But if the story emanated from Rangoon, the editors approached it the way they might be expected to approach a snarling, rabid dog.

Most of the papers, as a matter of good business, are at least mildly in favor of whatever they expect their readers to support strongly. But they prefer to suggest that the government consider some course of action rather than to demand it—which is more than good business, since quite a number of newsmen have at one time or another been favored with subpoenas, if not always with the right of habeas corpus. Naturally, however, they care most deeply about what happens in Rangoon and draw up their fuming declarations on events in remote parts fairly casually, almost as a way of relieving their pent-up feelings about the close-at-hand, though they know that such pieces do not excite their readers very much.

Before long I had friends at most of the presses. One of the earliest and best of these friends was Soe Min, the first boy my age I got to know well in Burma. He was working on the *Htoon Daily*, a paper defined and distinguished by the many animosities of its editor, U Tun Pe, a brilliant, slightly daft man, a pioneer journalist, and an ex-cabinet minister with a gift for sibylline utterances and a fierce need to vent them. He was a Burmese Mencken—a contradiction in terms that whipped him up to astonishing peaks of fury and expressiveness without, unfortunately, bringing him many readers.

After introducing me to his chief, Soe Min modestly retired to his desk. I talked to U Tun Pe for about an hour. He sat bundled in an English trench coat on a shabby beach chair. The room, a dimly lit section of a musty old loft, having maybe five chairs and three tables, was fairly typical of Burmese newspaper offices.

He told me with a mixture of pride and resentment of the schooling he had gotten as a boy from English missionaries—how he had to amalgamate a Western name to his own, study the history of Britain but not Burma, and learn of Christ but not the

Buddha. Then, still provoked by my Westernness, he recalled his trip as a cabinet minister to Britain and America. New York, he said, is "the epitome of modernity . . . the epitome of modernity." He repeated the phrase several times, pleased with it, but using it, I thought, to exorcise the memory, the note of bitterness getting stronger on each repetition. Finally he brought me back to Burma, speaking with passion of his country, people, and Buddha, pointing to the limitations—which I as a Westerner would see—and the richness—which I as a Westerner needed to experience. The Burmese, he said, are a superstitious people, easy prey for cynical politicians. Such men would ruin the country. To survive, Burma needed to abandon the rituals of Buddhism for the teachings of the Buddha, to accept Western science but not Western ways, to purify its language and art, which had become corrupt and derivative, and to be first of all truly Burmese.

I listened, overwhelmed by the way he fitted together the hard little nuggets of his thinking. "I never search for words," he said, "I find the image I need and squeeze it out of my head." It was a notable head, too—large, with decisive features that looked as if they had been sculptured, steel-gray hair, and dark eyes that burned like disks of lava. He was called, but never to his face, *gaung-gyi*, "big head."

After U Tun Pe left, Soe Min and I sat and talked in the office. Then he took me to a small cane-juice shop, where a fat Moslem in *longyi* and tee-shirt ran the long stalks through a press until the last fragrant drops had been crunched out into an old slop bucket.

His family, Soe Min told me, lived in a village where his father was the headman. He had accepted their Buddhism until he came to the university in Rangoon; then he had put it aside. It was a superstition of the village, he believed, which was holding Burma back. From U Tun Pe's revolutionary generation he had inherited a sweeping hostility to the West, which could be expressed more fully and confidently since most of his contacts with the West had been secondhand through his elders. His hostility was, in fact, so impersonal that he could talk of it to me without applying it to me, approaching me with an ingenuous curiosity that a man like U Tun Pe could never manage. He considered U Tun Pe eccentric, yet he was devoted to him and, in many ways, his disciple. His broad face showed the difference between them, a difference in years and character. As remarkable in its way as U Tun Pe's, a cupid's face, open and gentle, both knowing and innocent.

That night, I realized, I was talking altogether earnestly about politics for the first time in a long time. At home our opinions and the opinions of our friends had been too tepid and similar to support much discussion. We neither followed a line nor held an independent point of view. All we had was a general sense of reservation. We would have liked, I think, to have been radicals, but could find no radicalism that had not been so submerged in the bottomless complacency of America as to appear cruel, futile, or bizarre. Certainly there was enough to oppose—poverty, affluence, bigotry, fake good will, totalitarians of all sorts, the bomb, those who enjoyed its power and even some who feared it. But, more than anything else, we mistrusted enthusiasm. However big and mighty our country, we seemed too small to count for much.

Soe Min, on the other hand, from a far smaller, weaker country, cared deeply and believed it mattered that he cared. Listening, I felt older and worldlier. I wanted to tell him he was missing the point, that his and my words would count for little; but I said nothing because I envied him. We were on a conversational reconnaissance. I had no idea what a Burmese boy my age might say; he probably never before thought there were American students who worried about the kind of things he did. He knew Americans to be rich, powerful and distant, and it was phenomenal to be talking to one in a cane-juice shop. He said so. It was phenomenal all round.

Soon after I met him, Soe Min found a job on a paper called *Oway* ("the Peacock.") He worked there during the day and then, with only a tea break, went to his job as night editor on the *Htoon*. There he was given a place to sleep as his pay, consisting of a cot in a dark corner of the editorial room just above the clanking old flat-bed presses, which reverberated in his ears all night long. *Oway* promised a small salary, but he was never sure when he would get it. The new job did at least lend him a measure of prestige, and he was experiencing the subtle metamorphosis reflected in the Burmese system of titles. He had been Ko Soe Min when we met him, *Ko* being roughly the pupil's designation. Now he was emerging into full manhood as an *U*.

Occasionally, when he could get away from his two papers, Soe Min would take me to meet people he knew in leftist circles. In part, he did this to make mischief. He would introduce me, guide me through the exchange of pleasantries, ask a leading question, and sit back to enjoy a debate. More seriously, he wanted me to meet these people for my own sake, so that I would get to understand them.

One rainy afternoon he took me to meet the general-secretary of the National United Front, a coalition of the major near-Communist and aboveground Communist groups in the country. The headquarters of the N.U.F. was a small damp room on the top floor of a decrepit building on a side street. Cuttings from Soviet magazines were the only decorations on the unpainted walls. At one end of the room there was a mimeograph machine; at the other, a desk. Between the two was a long table at which two girls were sorting some freshly mimeographed sheets. The odor of ink filled the room.

Behind the desk sat U Aung Than, the general-secretary, a young man with a round, earnest face that came to an abrupt point at the chin, giving the whole something of the configuration of a question mark. He peered out at me from behind his large glasses, raising his heavy eyelids now and then as Soe Min made his way through an elaborate introduction in Burmese to assure him I was a student and not a spy. Then he shifted his weight and turned to me.

"Let us not talk politics," he began. "We would disagree too much. Let us talk philosophy only."

He asked me what I thought of the Burmese. I said I found them generous, proud, spirited, and sometimes, in the presence of foreigners like myself, a bit on the defensive.

"In a word, nationalistic," the G.S. said, thumping his desk.

I replied, too glibly, that I had not been talking politics.

"What would you think," he asked, "of a country that increased its armaments in order to increase world tensions?"

"I would condemn such a country. Do you have any particular country in mind?"

"Your country is such a country."

I said my country wanted peace and armed itself only to counter the threat of Soviet power.

"And what about your bases?"

I said our military men deemed these necessary to deter the forces poised along the vast borders of the Communist world. "After all, there are Russian forces stationed in the nations of Eastern Europe, aren't there?"

"Do you imply that the Socialist nations are all Soviet?"

"Well, the Russian troops there are all Russians."

We continued in this vein for some time, until finally U Aung Than smiled and, spreading his hands palms-down on his desk, said, "Let us leave these disagreeable points of philosophy aside and agree that all the peoples of the world want peace."

I agreed, but said that more than that would have to be agreed on if there was ever to be real peace. He held his smile.

"The youth of the world must stand solidly together for peace," he said, warming to his theme. "Let us all work for peace in our own ways. I trust I will meet you one day at the winning post. Meanwhile, let our joint communiqué mention our mutual desire for peace." Then, ringing my hand with both of his, he ushered us to the door. As we started down the dark stairs, he tried to turn on the light, but it was dead.

Outside, it was still raining, a fine, cold rain. "I knew you would argue," Soe Min said with a satisfied laugh.

We walked a few blocks and stopped. An ancient Chinese

woman was lighting candles on the street for her dead. The smoke and smell of burning wax hung in the air and the drippings sizzled on the wet pavement. Soe Min clapped his hands in a special rhythm, telling me this was a signal for a friend. The sounds of a saxophone drifted incongruously from a window nearby. The harmony of these notes with the softly falling rain and the sizzling wax held me transfixed. I was tired of talking to dedicated men in offices. It was better to stand in the rain and listen.

"Do you like Francis Powers?" a voice asked abruptly, snapping off my musing. For a moment I hated that voice the way you hate the ring of an alarm clock.

"I do not like what he did," I said after Soe Min had introduced me to his friend, a lean, smiling boy, "but the United States didn't invent espionage."

"The people of Burma hope that Kennedy will be elected," the boy raced on. "He will end the Eisenhower policy of espionage and work for peace with Khrushchev."

"How can you talk for the people of Burma?" Soe Min asked him, laughing condescendingly. "You are only saying what your friends at the university say."

"But I know the people of Burma are for Kennedy," the boy said. Soe Min just laughed.

By the time we reached a teashop, I was hanging on the ropes. The boy kept after me, though always with a smile. He said Khrushchev wanted peace and there would be peace if the United States would only accept the Five Principles of Peaceful Coexistence. I said the Five Principles were fine but China had already violated them in India, with whom she first proclaimed them, and this showed it was not enough merely to say the word in order to have peace. He said he was for peace. I argued that the United States was prepared to sign an agreement on disarmament and that Russia's fear of checks prevented it. He said he was for peace. I said that peace could only come when each side had confidence in the other's intentions. He said he was for peace. I said that for real peace to exist, the Communist nations would have to give up their efforts to press their system on the other nations of the world. He was still for peace. Finally I said I was for peace, too. On this we shook hands and parted.

That afternoon scared me. I knew I had been sanctimonious, intent only on staking out my position and holding it. I had meant what I said but had never felt I was really the one who was speaking or being spoken to. This was not a rare feeling for me. I had it in Washington just before we left, sitting through the dismal sessions of an "orientation" I received at the hands of the State Department. Over and over we were told that we would be ambassadors for our country; and however it was said, I squirmed. "You will be considered as a representative of the United States," the President explained once to some departing teachers. "Your values will be considered as its values; your words as its words."

Of course, I was normally introduced to people in Burma as an American and addressed as one. But I was not an archetype, a tiny chunk of one nation encountering another nation; I was simply one person encountering others—by chance, not appointment. So long as I played the ambassador, I had to use the rhetoric of nations. So long as I worried that my words might be taken as the words of the United States, they were always beside the point, the shell and not the meat of the snail. It was not that I had been too impressionable in Washington, just that I was not impressionable enough once I reached Rangoon. An ambassador is like a priest, an intercessor between a unique power and the mass of men; he must take his rituals and virtues seriously. I had no reason to play at being superior.

At about this time, we became friendly with U Thaung, the editor of a jazzy tabloid called *Kyemon* (the Mirror).

I had heard of U Thaung first at the American Embassy, where the mere mention of his name was normally a good pretext for a debate. The editor of the most successful paper in the country, he was both the apple of the embassy's eye and the mote in it. He was considered anti-American, unreasonably so, but potentially pliable, and so he was plied—usually by being invited to cocktail parties where he would drink limeades and scout for news tips. I met him at one of these, a party given by the man from whom I had first heard his name.

"Of course I enjoy arguing with U Thaung," he had said. "But it does no good. You cannot make him understand. He's sly. He acts as if he does not want to understand. He is the kind of person who will always be a great threat to us, unless we can make him see the light."

With that to go on, I was surprised when we were introduced. If there was anything sly about him, it did not show in his face, which was young, full, and unlined. He spoke softly but confidently, smiled often, and laughed easily. I liked him at once.

He invited us to visit him at his press. We did—the next night—and became regular visitors there until our last night in Burma. When we came in, we would sit down by U Khin Maung Ye, the night editor, a wiry man with straight dark hair and laughing eyes. I would scan the evening's wire bulletins while he worked. Carolyn would sit with us or go into U Thaung's flat in the rear to talk to his lovely young wife, Daw Mya Mya Sein.

Pointing to one item or another, I would say, "This is bad," or "This is good." U Khin Maung Ye would look up, suck on his ivory cigarette holder, which was carved into the shape of a reclining nude, and, more often than not, disagree with a taunting laugh. Then perhaps we would debate, but just a bit, only until he reached down below his desk for a bottle of Mandalay Pale Ale, a sign that it was perhaps time to leave well enough alone.

After a while I would go back into U Thaung's flat to talk to him. We did not talk much about the priority stories on the wire bulletins. Instead, we talked gravely and quietly about Burma. Our conversations took the shape of a hill, which we climbed from opposite sides, hoping to reach the top together. They were always low-keyed and rambling, never what diplomats call "a frank exchange of views." I knew the terrain of Burmese politics fairly well, the names and histories of the outstanding landmarks. But I had only seen it from a distance. Laughing, shrugging, spoiling for a fight, looking helpless and strong by turns, U Thaung brought me up close to it. The politicians, soldiers, student leaders, and writers I had met or heard of began to take their places in an emotional setting; I learned to identify them by mood rather than creed. Looking through U Thaung's eyes at the vying between the major groups—the army, the politicians, and what may loosely be called the intelligentsia—I realized that they were caught up in a drama of their own.

Their vying is vaguely comparable in its intensity and frustrations to some excruciating rivalry for a woman between, let's say, her lover, her legal spouse, and a callow youth—a good plot for a French film (which would probably be banned in Burma). Each wants to protect her from the other two, from herself, and most of all, from her past, for she was kept a long time by an old roué, a foreigner, who scornfully ignoring them, enjoyed her till he wore himself out.

The lover wants to keep her but on a more certain basis. He finally abducts her. The army in Burma is in somewhat this position, having ruled for a busy year and a half and then made way of its own accord for U Nu's civil government, only to recoup after two years. More than its rivals, it is determined to see the country forge ahead to Western goals of political unity and economic progress, improvising on Western methods for strictly nationalist ends.

Next we have the cuckold, who would like to put aside his gnawing memories and settle down with the comforts and respect to which his position entitles him. This is the conservative force, the politicians, who are mostly identified with U Nu. Ideally they would like to revive the halcyon precolonial past and forget the West—the whole non-Burmese world, in fact. What they can't forget they try to ignore.

Finally there is the youth, so noble and inept, who wants to rescue the woman from her lover, whom he considers dissolute, and from her husband, whose bland forbearance repels him. Jealous of the success of the one and the erstwhile rights of the other, he longs to purify her without staining himself. He, of course, stands for the intelligentsia, the younger leftists, the vaguest but most intense of the three groups. They love their country but are detached from its life. To end this detachment, they feel they must transform the land—how, they are not sure. They would emulate the West, but the West has given them their greatest grievance. The Communists, who can sweet-talk in the language of nationalism as well as the language of change, sometimes seem to offer the only available model, but taking it would also be taking on a discipline that is, for all the sweet talk, frightening and totally alien. They want to perform great acts but hardly have the chance to carry off small good ones.

U Thaung belonged pretty much to this latter group but was tied to the others by their common grievance and need. He could not hold me responsible for this grievance; yet he could never make light of it in my company. And however complacent I became about my good intentions, I never escaped the feeling that I owed him an apology.

Before I went to Burma, I thought of colonialism as being a six-of-one, half-dozen-of-another affair, represented in my mind by a page of lecture notes divided into two columns: "good effects" and "harmful effects." At any rate, I knew it to be a moribund institution and felt the same bewilderment most Americans feel when speakers from the "emerging" nations rise to denounce it. It is bad form to bring up an old score, and a mark of immaturity. But it is only from the former ruling powers' point of view that colonialism may be considered moribund. Independence did not erase its harmful effects on the colonies.

I had my first glimmering of this fact when I saw the paintings of my friend U Nann Waii, a young man possessed by high ambitions that he will probably never realize. You do not even have to see his paintings to sense the futility about Nann Waii. It is in his face, the face of a tiny waif on the verge of tears. It is in his timid, whimsical conversation, his fear of drinking, and his modest attempts at bravado. He cannot go abroad to study; his government withholds his passport because he once cut a figure in student politics—though Nann Waii has not had a political thought in ten years. Anyway, he would be afraid to go abroad.

He says, like all other Burmese artists, that he could learn nothing outside Burma. "They paint in their way. We paint in ours."

But what is the Burmese way? The storerooms of the Tate Gallery probably hold some clues. Call it middling post-pre-Raphaelite—the aesthetic ideal of the young colonial officers who brought civilization to Burma at the end of the last century. Winston Churchill could be considered its greatest exponent. The colors are the colors of a land that knows autumn and winter; the subjects Burmese in detail only.

Although Nann Waii says his aim is to make his work more and more Burmese, the harder he works to this end, the poorer the results. Nothing in Burma moved or depressed me more than hearing him tell about his one trip to Pagan, the ancient capital. Today Pagan is a deserted thicket of stuccoed brick pagodas, thousands of them—most in ruins, the rest sadly scarred by eight centuries of neglect, decay, and pilferage. Tumbled down and overgrown as they are, it is not easy to imagine what they once were. Yet somehow they still have life. Their original purpose is made even more obvious. They never soared to the heavens but turned inward upon themselves, through half-lit passageways, small recesses, and vaulted chapels, to the image of the Buddha, waiting to be discovered. The point was always the inward turning, the flight from time, so it hardly matters that the Buddha may now be decapitated. A headless Buddha makes the point ironically clearer. You think of yourself long before you think of the humiliated dynasties that inscribed their achievements on the crumbling walls.

But Nann Waii wanted to raise the dead. He made his pilgrimage specifically to master the modes of Burmese art. He copied conscientiously; but when he returned to Rangoon, he found he could do little with what he had: it was all too far removed. And so for a long time he did not paint at all. Nann Waii is like a small bird with a broken wing, hemmed in by the stultifying conventions of Burmese painting, but unable to leave the nest, for that would mean an admission that there is, as yet, no modern

Burmese art. Such an admission would cost too much. Therefore he mopes and waits for the inspiration that is already long overdue.*

The story is much the same for U Thaung in politics. Like Nann Waii, he would like to see Western things accomplished in strictly Burmese ways. But what *is* the Burmese way of investing public capital or organizing the complex structure of the modern state?

"You are poor and underdeveloped. You are weak and threatened. We will raise you up and shield you," we say.

The patient shakes his head; his lips curl into a bitter smile. Something is wrong. "Please don't do me any favors," he says.

"But can't you see you are suffering from economic anemia? You're run down and your borders are exposed. These are dangerous symptoms."

"My poor friend," he says mildly, "when will you realize that you, too, are one of my symptoms?"

We insist. We are certain we understand his predicament better than he does. The way he is carrying on, it can only go from bad to worse.

"You must change your ways," we say. "Follow us. Follow us. . . . Be like us."

He is no longer listening.

---

* Last summer, more than a year after we left Burma, there was a riot at the university in Rangoon. The army, for the first time since independence, fired on the students. According to the official communiqué, fifteen were killed. In fact, the soldiers had fired at random into a large crowd, and there were about forty more who—unofficially—lost their lives. The next day the university was closed and the student union building dynamited by army demolition teams. When I read the news, I thought first of Nann Waii, remembering how we used to sit there sipping tea and talking about painting. Only later did I learn that he had been storing his paintings in the building and that they had all been methodically blown to smithereens. The newspapers here reported that the army was cracking down on Communist agitators. Nann Waii, left with only the clothes on his back, took his loss stoically—so I was told. And though I am one year and half a world away, I know how he took it: I can see him smiling gamely, shrugging his shoulders, waving his cheroot in front of his face, and blinking rapidly—his eyes evasive, swollen, and wet.

Freedom for the Burmese means neither the absence of Communism nor competition between supermarkets. Instead, it has something to do with the preservation and nurturing of their self-esteem, which is injured almost every time it collides with a bloated Western ego. It should go without saying that they don't want to be swallowed alive by China—if it doesn't, consider it said. To deal with the Chinese, they rely on a kind of moral blackmail that has worked pretty well so far. They received a good border settlement and a favorable trading position just by promising not to join any military alliance hostile to China (*i.e.*, SEATO). This cost nothing since they had no such inclination. Now they never miss a chance to celebrate Sino-Burmese solidarity in the most effusive—and evasive—terms, on the theory that the words "good neighbors" make good fences. Their foreign policy is to be as friendly as they can with everyone so that they will not have to get too involved with anyone.

On the whole, I'd say this is a sensible enough approach. The obvious objections to it diminish in the light of the fact that Burma today is more secure than those countries in the area that have relied on our support. But it infuriated many Americans in Rangoon, during my stay, probably because it unmasked the Burmese belief that freedom can be had without the avuncular protection of the land of the free. It was not so much that they thought the Burmese position immoral but rather that Burmese neutrality came as a personal slight. Many Burmese knew this and enjoyed the knowledge. However intimidated they were by the fearful doings in the world, they found themselves a real opportunity for sport. What amused them was knowing they could make someone squirm simply by dropping a casual remark—say, by expressing an admiration for Castro's beard at an American party. It was a kind of gamesmanship that must be salubrious for people who have long known how it feels to wince at the offhand remarks of Westerners.

It is difficult for us to realize how deeply we can be mistrusted simply because we are Americans. But mistrusted we certainly are, not only, I think, because we are from the white West but also because we represent—and insist on representing—the promise of the West, a subject on which these people are permanantly ambivalent. We insist on being conspicuous and will go to any lengths to be taken as seriously as we take ourselves—which we usually are, unfortunately.

One evening at *Kyemon,* U Khin Maung Ye told us he had seen an American aid sticker picturing a strong white hand clasping a feeble yellow one. I was shocked and asked him to show it to me. When he did, I found two identical hands, both colored the same mottled blue and red suggestive of varicosity, one hand looking just as unhealthy as the other. When I showed him he was wrong (very relieved myself to find he was), he said, "Well, of course, they couldn't draw it that way, but that's what they had in mind."

Unreasonable? Very. But can you be absolutely certain that was not "what they had in mind?" I was not. Sure or not, there was no answer I could have offered that would have persuaded him; and even if there had been, the gain would have been small, for he would always find other channels for his resentment. I did not try to knock over his grudges one by one because, first, I often respected them and, second, I wanted him to know that the things of this world that anguished him pained me, too. Our common vulnerability went deeper than any resentment, giving us a solid basis for friendship. There is no way, we learned, to get around mistrust and resentment, no trick or technique that works. The only way across these distances is to reveal the big secret that men suffer in New York as fully and painfully as they do in Rangoon, and to be yourself as honestly as you can.

Guarded words never answer guarded questions. "How would I be treated in New Orleans?" I was asked once by a dark-skinned friend. According to what I learned at my orientation in Washington, I should have used the *yes-but* technique: "*Yes,* there is a small chance that a few people would be rude, *but* most Americans would deplore the rudeness of the few." What I said instead was, "If you ever go there, wear your *longyi.* In Western dress, you'd have a bad time."

It was not a discreet answer, but it was direct and it was true. I offered him as much explanation as he could stand, but my first concern was to be absolutely truthful. I did not want to imply that the problem had been reduced to manageable proportions, or that most Americans took it as a matter of conscience, or even that those who did were then freed from it. I did not want to persuade a man who trusted me that I came from a vibrant, confident democracy, because I was not convinced it was so. The fact of prejudice remains, and I wanted to make it seem large and real. I did not make a Communist of him.

"You are different from other Americans," U Thaung or U Khin Maung Ye would tell us towards the end of an evening at the press, or, later, once the paper had been printed, as we all rode into town together for cow-sway—a noodle dish—or curry in tiny, dim-lit shops or the stalls of the night bazaar, which we would then keep open past their normal closing times.

It was a remark we heard fairly often, one that both pleased and distressed us. It pleased us because it made us feel we had not fallen into the stereotypes many Americans abroad impose on themselves. But it was not entirely pleasant to know that it was meant as a compliment. We pointed out that we had an advantage over other Americans they met in that we were not officials and could therefore speak for ourselves, as representatives of a government cannot always do. They would agree to this but never take it as the last word. "Yes," they said, "but you *are* different. You're more relaxed. You're more like us."

A flock of opinions flapped and rustled between us and U Thaung, but we learned to value them a little less as our friendship grew in spite of them. They could not be ignored, for they sometimes seemed to mock our quiet talks, making us think that we might have to choose between opinions and friendship. But such a choice seemed unreal, an everyday conundrum we could not afford to accept. We liked U Thaung and respected him, so it was more important, we realized finally, that he understand our feelings than that he take them as his own. I could tell him that I didn't like Burmese painting without insulting him, so long as

I told him why. He could describe a satirical play he had written, in which the villains were Americans, without putting us on the defensive. For the most part our talks did not spiral back to cramped, dull disputes but moved ahead to open spaces where we could be at ease. U Thaung would tell us how he wanted to see a theater in Burma that could stage his plays and then would listen closely while we talked about the theater in America. He would take us into his library and show us books he wanted us to read; we would suggest titles to him. We would scheme about meeting in New York, Paris, or Warsaw and plan trips together.

"But not Peking?" he asked once with a twinkle in his eye.

"Yes. Peking, too. Someday perhaps. Why not?"

"You would not mind meeting Communists and talking to them?"

"No. Why should we be afraid of them? If they were good people who could talk openly, we would like it very much."

"I didn't know Americans thought it possible for Communists to be good people," he said, needling us.

"Did you think Americans could be good people?"

"Well, it's a very big country."

At times like this our conversation could go either of two ways: either we would keep on joking and talking, or we would give in to feeling injured, swap wordless apologies, and head out for some good cow-sway.

It was plain that U Thaung's picture of America was a kind of surrealist synthesis of fables, anachronisms, and the grimier truths. But we had not come to Burma to spread the gospel. Besides, the truths we knew were rarely resilient enough for debating purposes. What we could say was limited by what we knew and what he wanted to know. "It takes two to speak the truth," Thoreau wrote, "one to speak and another to hear." Nevertheless, there were times when we got ruffled and accused U Thaung of being as prejudiced and smug as the Westerners whose narrowness offended him. He would look troubled and sad and ask us to understand, saying something like, "You do not know all the things that have happened here."

And that was true, especially during the first months, when we barely knew the colors and sounds and smells of the land. Rangoon was neither here nor there, neither East nor West, like the minds of our friends—real and vivid but tentative. It had been just a small trading post in the delta of the Irrawaddy River, notable only for the great golden stupa of the Shwe Dagon pagoda, when the British took over lower Burma and the portion of the "whiteman's burden" they found there. The heartland of Burma has always been between Pagan and Mandalay along the Irrawaddy. Down through history kings established their capitals there in beautiful places with beautiful names: Pagan, first and southernmost; then, all clustered together, Sagaing, Ava, Amarapura, Mingun; and finally, at the time of our Civil War, Mandalay, less than thirty years before the British sent old King Thibaw into exile in Bengal. The name Mandalay means "the center of the universe"; the city's founding, it is said, fulfilled a prophecy of the Buddha. Today, for all that is not commercial or political or new, Mandalay endures as the real capital. The Burman in Rangoon lives almost as if in an alien world, nearly outnumbered by the foreigners. He is a Gatsby and he knows it. But usually he has his village to which he can and does return, and his trip up-country keeps him Burmese. We knew little until we got an inkling of what he finds there.

Once the rains began to taper off, we were gone from Rangoon, away for seven weeks—perhaps the most memorable seven weeks of my life. Every day still stands out distinct, held in my mind like a well-known song.

Not long after the train left Rangoon, we could feel the difference. We had never been farther than Pegu, just fifty miles out of the capital. The paddy fields were still being turned then, and the landscape had been a monotonous stretch of drab colored earth under the gray monsoon clouds. But now the paddy was swaying and singing in the wind like a thousand violin bows in some gigantic orchestra. Here and there pure white herons— "paddy birds" they are called—danced and glided above the green fields like wind-blown strips of paper. Their dance seemed to be in celebration of the color green, represented and harmonized in its every shade and hue on the soft, endless patchwork of paddy. Along the way, water buffaloes stuck their heavy heads out of stagnant, muddy pools beside the rails, disturbed by the passage of the train, which rippled the surface of the water. The gold on the pagoda stupas caught the sun whenever it peered out from behind great piles of gray fluff in the sky.

Night fell, and traveling third class as we were with no cushions beneath us to absorb the jolts, our backs and backsides got sorer and sorer as the long sleepless hours slowly wore by. All the people around us were snuggled up into cozy little balls. But whenever we found a good way to sit, we were soon jostled out of it, so all we could do was listen to their snoring and stare dully out at the moon-washed paddy—weary, aching, but still happy.

When we left Rangoon, some of our friends wrote letters of introduction to people in Mandalay. One letter was to U Hla, the editor of a paper called *Ludu* ("the People.") Some Americans told me that both the man and the publication were Communist, but I never met a Burman who agreed. *Ludu* was a highly respected paper, and U Hla was held to be one of Burma's best writers. He was set apart not only by his talent but also by the fact that he lived in Mandalay, untempted by the lures of the newer capital. His political ideas were roughly similar to U Thaung's, but the framework in which he held them was surprisingly different. U Thaung, though born near Pagan, never entered a pagoda unless it was to cover a story. U Hla, on the other hand, was committed to everything that could be called Burmese. He was the most conservative "Communist" I ever met.

He was middle-aged and slightly stooped in a way that was almost courtly, as if he were just about to go into a deep bow. He had the look of a man who stays up late studying and writing. Unlike most of our Burmese friends, he did not smile easily or quickly; his smiles came hesitantly, as if they started growing way back in some deep recess of his mind.

We did not talk politics. Instead, we talked mostly about ourselves, about writing, and about newspapers. He said he would like to show us Mandalay and asked what we would most like to see. We asked him to be the judge.

"I thought about you a good deal last night," he said, when we visited him the next day. "I will show you a side of Burma most foreigners never see."

We got into his Skoda and drove out of town, passing through a series of villages, each of which was famous for a particular craft: one carved Buddhas from marble, another wove silk, a third rang with the hammers of silversmiths. After crossing the river, we turned into the round green hills of Sagaing, on the sides of which stand the oldest and most revered monasteries in Burma.

The car followed a winding dirt road up one of the nearer hills, stopping finally at the edge of a grove through which we could make out a number of buildings. Not a sound could be heard and no one was in view. The place seemed deserted. Small points of light penetrated the leafy trees and flecked the earth. As we stepped from the car, we found ourselves talking almost in whispers.

U Hla led us around to a small wooden bungalow with an open porch in front. We sat down with our legs under us. He motioned to Carolyn to pull her skirt further down over her knees.

"I often come here," he said. "This is one of the strictest monasteries in Burma. The *pongyis* here are not even allowed to go into Mandalay because they would have to wear their sandals on the hot pavements and *pongyis* are not supposed to wear sandals outside their monastery."

In several moments the *sayadaw*—the head of the monastery—appeared and sat down opposite us. He was a small, firmly built man with big eyes and a mild, melancholy smile. U Hla told him that Carolyn had been studying Buddhism at the university in Rangoon. He was unimpressed.

"One cannot learn Buddhism by studying it," he said laconically. "You must live according to the teachings of the Buddha. Then you will know they are true and you will be happy."

He was attentive and kind but not at all curious about us,

though certainly he was not used to visits from Americans. We came to him, essentially, in the same circumstances as his other visitors: there is, he knew, only one way.

We met two other *sayadaws* that day. The three of them were impressively alike—their voices soft, not hushed; their faces gentle but firm; their bodies absolutely calm but not languid; and their words simple, not casual, direct but detached. I was not prepared for them, although they suited the images of Buddhist saints I had gotten from books.

"They are simple men," U Hla told us. "They come from the villages and become *pongyis* when they are only boys. They meditate and study, but they are not scholars. They are not learned. Yet those of us who have been to universities believe they know more than we do. They are holy men."

"I am only a simple Burmese *pongyi*," one of them said. U Hla told me he was more than ninety years old; he looked ageless. "But I have been looking at maps lately and I know your country is very far away. I hope you will find peace here."

"Can a Westerner hope to understand Buddhism?" Carolyn asked the third.

"Buddhism is not hard to understand if you give your life to it," he said, speaking in a slow, melodic cadence. "It is the way to true happiness, lasting happiness. The Buddhist dies with a smile on his face. But the happiness you have today will make you sad tomorrow, because it will not last. Once the Buddha took a beautiful queen and aged her in a minute to show her she could not be happy in this world. That is a lesson for you. But you can only understand it by surrendering the things you are most attached to."

I was eying Carolyn anxiously, I confess, by the time he finished speaking.

When U Hla had shown us how to press our foreheads to the ground before the first *sayadaw,* I had felt silly and awkward. But when we left this man, I found myself bowing down unhesitantly in real reverence. I felt lightheaded and unembarrassed.

From his porch we followed a path through a fragrant frangipani grove to the pagoda, a gallery with six archways framing six Buddhas, hewn into the side of the hill. U Hla bought a bunch of white lotuses from each of three women standing there, and we approached the first Buddha together, placing the flowers in vases that were ready to receive them. Then we stepped back and bent over, pressing our foreheads against the cool, smooth tiles. Carolyn, I could see, was flushed and radiant. We felt very close to U Hla.

We moved back to the terrace, which overlooked the calmly flowing river and the soft hills on the other side, showing purple through the late morning haze.

"It is said that when people bow down together before the Buddha, they will be related in the next life," U Hla told us with a benign, fatherly look.

"We would like that," I said.

All day I had a warm feeling of well-being, the kind of feeling you get on a quiet beach or lonely mountaintop. Therefore, it was like a sudden splash of ice water when the third *sayadaw* said, "If Eisenhower and Khrushchev would come here to meditate, there would be no war." He was not, however, talking so much about the world as about his monastery, pointing through the tamarind trees to the placid surface of a lake glistening in the afternoon sun. Nevertheless, as I later told U Hla, I had been startled just to hear the names Eisenhower and Khrushchev there.

"I send him *Ludu*," he explained.

"Well, I hope the chances for peace don't depend on Eisenhower and Khrushchev going into meditation."

"That was not what he meant," U Hla said, obviously annoyed.

"Yes, I know," I offered lamely. "I was just struck by the thought."

There was no point in explaining further, since I had understood the *sayadaw* in the first place. [But I wondered why my remark had annoyed U Hla. It was pretty stale and should have seemed trivial in such a place. It didn't—and that, I concluded, was what had pained him.] Obviously, the question was not whether Eisenhower and Khrushchev could achieve enlightenment in a monastery near Mandalay but, in the world they ruled, whether anyone could—and, perhaps whether anyone should.

"What do you think of Burma now?" U Thaung asked me on our first visit to *Kyemon* after our trip.

I thought in rapid succession of Mweyoegyi, a village we had stayed in; Mandalay; the monasteries of Sagaing; the trip down the Irrawaddy; the ten days at Pagan; the view from Mt. Popa, where the ancient *nat* spirits dwell; the sunsets in Taungyi; the night in the cabin on stilts in the middle of Inlay Lake; the bus trip down the dacoit-infested road to Loikaw; the bazaars of Kayah State; and the sunrise we had seen that morning on our return to Rangoon, which had burnished and tinted the gold on the Shwe Dagon.

"It is a wonderful, wonderful land," I said, feeling very moved.

"But it is a very poor land," U Thaung said.

"That is true," I replied, agreeing with his meaning but unable to apply the word "poor" to Burma. Yet at that moment a spell broke. We had been in what seemed a changeless and timeless world. Now we were back in a world ruled by change and time.

The contrast between city and country colored my feelings for the rest of our stay, bringing me up against history as a force, without any real convictions on the subject. I was an American and had to believe in the efficacy of antibiotics, the balanced diet, turbines, detergents, and colleges. Yet, though I had always had whatever advantages such things give, I did not consider myself significantly better off than my Burmese friends. I did not deny their right to these advantages, or their urgent need, but was awed by the price they would have to pay. I could not help wondering whether that spanking-new Burma of the future could sustain the generous, easygoing life of its impoverished forerunner. I had no conclusions to draw but at least felt closer to understanding their bitter ambivalence.

However carried forward, progress is invariably brutal. Rangoon, the rude creature of world trade, is the emblem of change and progress in Burma. Yet its poverty is infinitely more depressing than the poverty of the villages. The hard outlines of village life are softened by a coherent tradition still intact. The people's needs are matched by their satisfactions.

Refugees from the countryside to the city carry these needs with them but leave the satisfactions behind. As progress strikes the land, more people abandon the country for the city, to work longer hours in a grim, unfamiliar setting. The city teaches them new needs but fails to fill them. Medicine preserves life without providing for it. Education stirs minds without giving them an outlet. The security of the old collapses long before the hoped-for security of the new is experienced. Thus, the greater the progress, the more compelling the need. This melancholy fact gives the rich side of the world no grounds for complacency about the little it has done or is doing.

Since the need for progress invariably outstrips its rate of achievement, a little progress is the best incentive in the world for revolution. Change is the motive and the cue; and the citadels of change—the cities and universities—are the normal centers of revolutionary feeling. This feeling is as endemic to a developing society as its opposites—complacency and despair—are to a developed one.

Early in our stay in Burma, an American who had also just arrived said to me, "This is not at all what I expected. Where is all the ferment? Where are the rising expectations? I don't see them." They were there, I discovered—stuck in the throats of the expectant.

We met Ko Yu about a month before we went upcountry. If we had asked him then, he would have told us he was a Communist. But the morning newspapers had already told us that. He was one of four notorious student agitators who had surrendered themselves to the government the day before after having evaded arrest for more than a year. As fugitives, they had been symbols of defiant radicalism among the students; the government, knowing that prison would only enhance their importance, had not held them. It apparently hoped that they could be belittled by being ignored.

Of the four, Ko Yu was said to be the most intransigent. He was the founder and leader of the Youth Front, a far-out splinter group in the radical student movement. I had no doubt he would be hostile and sullen with us, but I wanted to meet him—once anyway.

Soe Min did the introducing. Ko Yu was a surprise from the start. He was soft-spoken and shy—a most unlikely agitator, I thought. We avoided politics as if we had agreed to do so and talked quietly, first about nothing in particular and then about what I thought of Burma. He hunched forward, his *longyi* tucked between his legs, his sandals clapping on his heels, and his lean face almost squirrel-like as he concentrated on what I was saying. His English was far from perfect but not a bit hesitant; he spoke clearly and forcefully, sometimes hitting on striking combinations of words, as people will who have not quite mastered a language. Though I was used to the questions he asked, I searched myself for the answers as if I was hearing them for the first time. "Do you like Burma?" had always seemed to mean, "Please say nice things about my country." Coming from Ko Yu, it seemed to say, "Tell me what you know that I do not know."

He took in everything I said with slow, serious nods, as though he was storing it away for closer inspection later on. He disputed nothing. It was disconcerting, especially since I could not help talking carelessly. My wife and I were used to exerting enormous care to avoid slang that people would not understand and careless remarks that might cause them pain. In time we had found ourselves able to speak freely to U Thaung, Soe Min, and one or two other Burmese friends. But with Ko Yu, we threw all precautions to the winds at once.

However, when we said good night, we knew little more about him than what we had learned from the papers. Although he answered all our questions directly, there was nothing to link what we thought we knew to the impression he had made on us.

Our doubts did not disappear in a day. But the time did come, before we went up country, when they had been forgotten. Ko Yu by then had assumed a special place in our lives.

There were no sore spots in our friendship that had to be avoided and no need to worry about injured feelings, even when gradually he told us about his political career, which had ended with his surrender to the government. Strangely enough, his background as an agitator made me feel closer to him. It was not just his experiences that impressed me but the way he recounted them. He did not reminisce about his past; he scrutinized it, as if it presented a problem that needed solving. When I tried to understand what that problem was, I realized with surprise that I was close to home.

Explaining this to myself and to Ko Yu was a struggle. I was afraid I would lapse into my usual mock seriousness, but the look of concentration he fastened on me made this impossible. Finally I found myself speaking clumsily in disconnected phrases, blundering along, worried that I was making no sense at all.

I tried to describe the uneasy feeling I got whenever I had to think beyond next week or next month. All the choices that lay before me seemed to be between futility and immolation. I felt forced to choose and unwilling to do so. I could not tell whether this was a matter of politics or pathology or what-have-you; but I did know it was not peculiar to me. I told Ko Yu more about myself and my friends, about the aimless wanderings, real and imagined, which we were forever hoping would lead some-where—"What will you do next?" always being the question, for we could never imagine continuing as we were. The only apparent thread of continuity was the effort, and often it seemed badly frayed.

It was not easy to speak like this and not possible to speak clearly. But Ko Yu followed me, not in mute comprehension but talking about himself, establishing the identification I felt.

He was then twenty-eight, just beginning his thirteenth and final year as an undergraduate at the university. The thirteen years, of course, had not all been passed in classes. In fact, he had spent much more time in jail or fleeing from the police than at his studies.

At one point he led a general strike at the university that ended only when regular army troops were dispatched to the campus. He hid out for eleven months before being captured. Once caught, he was set down in the glare of hot white lights and questioned relentlessly for two sleepless weeks, getting a respite only when he ate or fainted, and then just for as long as it took to be revived. Two weeks—and all he said, over and over, was, "I don't know," even when asked his name. A year later when he was finally released, he called a press conference to describe the treatment he had received; the leading English-language paper ran his picture over the line "Ko Yu, Untamed."

The police had been scouting for certain hard facts—ties to Communist rebels or embassies. These, quite simply, did not exist. Ko Yu was protecting no one, certainly not himself, with his I-don't-knows. For him it was a matter of resistance, not concealment.

"Because they forced me and tortured me, I would not say anything," he explained. "It was my individual pride. I could not. If they had not tried to force me, I might have answered their questions. There was nothing to hide. They already knew everything about me there was to know. But I knew they had no right to examine me this way."

This was not the first time he had been in jail. About six years before, in the country's first year of independence and his first year at the university, he had been picked up in a mass arrest on an odd chance that was to change his life. Then, as on the second occasion, there were no charges or courts to face. With rebels advancing to the outskirts of Rangoon and the government tottering, the university had been closed. Ko Yu, not knowing what to think, was swept up by the eddying fears and resentments. Almost before he knew it, he was in jail.

It was as if a higher authority had endowed him with a political position. Before going to jail, all he had had was a faith in independence, not only as a constitutional fact but as a promise and way of life. It was something he could even feel he had helped to create—despite his age, his bookishness, and his Chinese origins—which we had not at first recognized—for after the war, while the independence movement neared its goal, Ko Yu had been the student president of Rangoon's largest high school. An ardent young prodigy, he had addressed thousands from the speaker's platform at rallies, testifying to the harvest his generation would reap from independence.

Independence should have meant the end of politics, he thought. Instead, the country was in a shambles and he himself in jail. He had gone to the university to become an engineer. What now was the point of studying to take your place in an independent Burma when there were no places to be had? He felt humiliated and baffled. The jail was crowded and filthy, the food vile, and the guards brutal, but his fellow prisoners were kind and encouraging. He found more assurance in their company than he had on the outside. Jail was, all in all, an exciting place to be.

"It was in jail," he said, "that I learned to hate the government. Everyone there claimed to be a Marxist or a Communist. The things they said were new to me. I thought they talked about the more important things in life. I didn't know anyone else who did."

Some six months later, order having been gradually restored, his family managed to arrange his release. He returned to the university, which had just reopened, but his motive for studying had vanished.

"I was not a student any more," he said. "I never went to classes. When I wasn't at home reading Communist books, I was talking about them with my friends in the teashops."

Even when after a while their earnest discussions began to pall, he did not return to classes. If he became an engineer, he would have to go to work for the government, shut out all his new ideas, and lead a safe, conventional life. Such a prospect could not propel him back to his classes. He was not sure the Communists were right, but they were the only alternative he knew to the government, which was static, dreary, and corrupt, the embodiment of everything that needed changing. Inevitably, Ko Yu found his way back into student politics.

Soon his suspicions of the government were bolstered. The leftist students were struggling with a group backed by the ruling party for control of the student union. Ko Yu and some of his friends were offered bribes to quit the campaign, which only strengthened his sense of righteousness. Finally, when the election was held, enough ballots were "lost" to fix the result. It was then that he called the protest strike that closed the university, made him a fugitive, and finally led to his imprisonment the second time.

Two years passed before he returned to the university. By then his friends had won control of the union and he was welcomed back as a hero.

He immediately took his place as a member of the inner circle that ran the union, but was soon unhappy with its program, a strange brew of noise and silence, of strident propaganda and evasion, which only served to intoxicate the leadership. It feigned support for the government and spent most of its time expressing "solidarity" with youth groups in the sundry "people's republics" of the world. All of this seemed extraneous and false to Ko Yu. He was interested only in Burma, not in passing resolutions against the nefarious doings of the "imperialists" in Africa, about which he knew he was ignorant. He believed it was the place of the students to demand justice in their own country, to state and restate their ideals loudly and impatiently until they won their way.

"I realized that the people in the antigovernment camp were just as dishonest as the people in the government," he said. "I knew their line. I dared not sacrifice myself to them."

So he walked out, issuing a dramatic appeal to all students to join him in forming a new organization, the Youth Front. If there was nothing, he reasoned, to be expected from the members of the old order—neither the ones who governed nor the ones who rebelled—a new coalition of old groups would achieve nothing.

What was needed was a fresh start, a new appeal for those who cared most about the future, his peers—not just the students, though naturally they would be the spine of the organization, but all young people, farmers and workers too. Together, he hoped, they would make some headway.

The Youth Front made a lot of noise but very little headway. It had no program; it was a protest organization so possessed by the need to protest that it could not plan beyond it. Its technique was rhetoric and its rhetoric was Ko Yu's—full of anger and hope. He could always draw a large crowd when he called a rally, but that was all. When he went to Moulmein to take a job, the Youth Front withered away in Rangoon. When he returned, it revived there but died out in Moulmein.

He was badly discouraged by the time a military government took over in the fall of 1958. He made a speech attacking the new regime, but his heart was not in it any more. As a result of that speech, however, he had to become a fugitive again. That did it.

"So many things then exhausted my political heart," he said finally. "For ten years I wore myself out saying what I believed, but nothing happened. In the end I did not even know what I believed. The people I joined were as bad and selfish as the people I fought. Maybe worse. I decided I had to stop political life. That is why I surrendered. I thought it would be better to go to jail again and be done with it. I could not continue as I was."

He was speaking slowly. We had been talking and chain-smoking for hours and were both hoarse, tired, and tense.

Those thirteen years were very long from one point of view, but from another they contained the experiences of a century and more. I had only read about such things; and Ko Yu had seen few of the books I had read. Yet somehow, I felt, we had come out at the same point, feeling lonely and too much on our own for comfort.

"I do not feel that I know anything now," Ko Yu said. "I have much need to study. I must consider my life and"—the word did not come easily—"confirm myself."

One day Ko Yu picked up a book I had been reading and began

thumbing through it. It was *The Rebel* by Camus. Then he turned back to the first page.

"Listen to this," he said after a while. He read:

"We can act only in terms of our own time among the people who surround us. We shall know nothing until we know whether we have the right to kill our fellow men, or the right to let them be killed. In that every action today leads to murder, direct or indirect, we cannot act until we know whether or why we have the right to kill."

When he finished, he read the passage to me again, slowly. "That is very good," he said finally. "He asks important questions."

"Yes," I said, deeply moved, and that was all I could say until he started bombarding me with questions about the book and about Camus, of whom he had never heard. The only French author he had ever read, in fact, was Jules Verne.

"What I believe I must say, or say nothing," Ko Yu said to me once. "I am not sure what I believe now, and saying nothing is better than lying."

His words reminded me of a note from Thoreau's journal that has stayed with me ever since I first came upon it: "I have been breaking silence these twenty-three years and have hardly made a rent in it. Silence has no end; speech is but the beginning of it."

CHRISTOPHER T. RAND

■ *IRAN*

Debate Without End

Revolution has been hovering over Iran for the past years, though she was one of the first countries in Asia to have already gone through the experience of modern revolution (1909). In fact, according to many experienced Western observers, the next important revolt will take place in Iran, and some (such as Walter Lippmann, describing his well-known interview with Khrushchev in the spring of 1961) have indicated that the Russians believe this, too, and are trying as best they can to bring down the Shah and his regime. In Soviet eyes, the Shah and his government are degenerate and anachronistic and cannot possibly cope with the misery and poverty spreading through the land. The progressive elements are handcuffed and helpless; the social structure of the country is obsolete, its bureaucracy corrupt, its masses discontented and its economy in chaos.

Yet a revolution may be long in coming. All but the very mildest of the country's progressive elements are carefully con-

Christopher T. Rand took his B.A. at the University of California at Berkeley in 1959 and has attended graduate schools at the Universities of Teheran and Cairo. He is currently doing graduate work in Islamic studies at U.C.L.A.

trolled by the government, which in turn is controlled by the most reactionary elements in the country, which in turn are upheld by the army.

The motives behind this control are obvious. In 1953, when the government of Mohammad Mosaddegh embarked on a program of nationalization and social reform that drew the country away from its alliance with the West and brought it more and more under Soviet influence, it became apparent that no important nonmilitary revolution could keep Iran out of the Communist bloc for long. No bourgeois reformist elements within the country—now or then—could succeed in effecting a nonmilitary revolution without Communist support; and once these bourgeois came to power, they would no longer be able to restrain the Communists because—unlike the Communists—they lack leadership, unity, and coherent, well-thought-out programs (which seems to be the universal problem of the non-Communist left).

Iran borders on Russia and in past years has experienced constant attempts at subversion on the part of Soviet Russia and her agents. Furthermore, her land includes peoples who have struggled for autonomy in the past—notably the Kurds and the Azerbaijanian Turks—and who have received Russian support in those struggles. In 1946 both the Kurdish and the Azerbaijanian governments nearly succeeded in setting up autonomous states within Iran, breaking down the inner strength and cohesion of the Iranian nation, and weakening her resistance against further aggression from Soviet Russia.

The best solution to these problems would be for the government, with the aid of her Western allies, to institute a strong reform program herself. But so much damage has been done to the nation's economy in recent years that the difficulties of instituting reform have become staggering, and the people have grown scornful of any government-proclaimed reformers. In the meantime, a system of suppression continues to spread, bringing moral sickness in its wake and paralyzing the energies of the young and progressive-minded.

As an Asian diplomat recently told me, Mosaddegh was the

last hope for improvement in Iranian domestic affairs, but "the poor fellow was a bit sentimental." In any case, he is now in forced political retirement. Since his demise in 1953, the progressive and active elements of Iranian society have been in a state of near apathy regarding the future of their country. The situation did not change during my two years in Iran, from the fall of 1959 until the fall of 1961.

This condition may surprise most Americans, who know nothing significant about Iran. What little they do know about the country is the result of publicity favorable to its government and irrelevant to its primary problems. Before I went there, I knew very little about it myself. Even if I had known more, I would have been unable, from my distant and comfortable vantage-point in the United States, to understand it any better. It was only when a graduate grant to study Persian allowed me actually to live in Iran that I started to understand the dimension of her troubles.

I went blithely, with the innocence of cocksure youth, assuming that I would master the language with ease, travel widely in the country, make friends with many people, learn a great deal of what went on around me, and return to the United States a lifelong friend of Iran, expert in her affairs and a fine intermediary for interpreting Iran and the United States to one another with unique sensitivity. And all this was to come about simply because I had gone a little out of my way to learn the language and study the country and its people.

When I finally did leave Iran, I had learned the language and gotten to know the people well; I had traveled around the country, made friends, and come to understand the daily life and ways of thought—all as I had planned. I had stayed long enough for that purpose. What I had not expected was that staying longer would only have alienated me from the people of my acquaintance, especially my contemporaries. The longer I stayed, the more I realized that, fundamentally, I had not been able to communicate with them. When I tried to converse with them and hear what they had to say (unless they were the rare misfits who had been brought up in a Western tradition), all they wanted was to force their political sentiments on me and, even more, to force me to agree with them, so that they could convince themselves that they had made me relinquish my entire Western viewpoint. Having learned the approximate limitations of their thought, I wanted to move on.

Every Westerner visiting a country like Iran experiences discomforts and even hostilities. I came expecting life there to be hard and uncomfortable, and found it so. But most physical discomforts are insignificant; one gets used to them and, in fact, forgets them once they have passed. During the dry, hot, glaring Iranian summers I could never remember what a bitter Iranian winter felt like. I could never remember seeing Mashad from a distance, a dull brown, and wondering how the stiff, skeletal, gray sticks around the town and inside its walls could burst aflame with green by summer. I learned to ignore the stones thrown at me in back alleys of provincial towns, the insults snickered on the street here and there, the petty discriminations and embarrassments, the many refusals of merchants to accept the money from me that they would accept from any Iranian, the undue attention people sometimes gave me in public, the annoying teen-agers who seemed to collect around me in every new place, or the agents of the secret police and the uncooperative lower-ranking bureaucrats with their arbitrary use of the law.

As I look back on it, I can remember other annoyances: the scarcity of people one could trust (especially in the cities); the occasions when no friendly people were around, or at least no one accommodating or anxious to talk; the inevitable poverty of congeniality and stimulation. I remember the young Iranians who clustered around me wherever I went, nagging me to speak English—even after I had been in Iran awhile and could speak Persian better than most of them could speak English. They insisted on either speaking English, even the most rudimentary and boring kind, or not speaking at all. On occasion a boy would come up to me on the street and say something in broken English. I would reply in Persian. The boy would say, "Oh, you speak

Persian?" perhaps say a word more, then drift off, shrugging his shoulders.

Sometimes even the friendliness that one craved could be annoying. It was hard to find a reply to the sincerity of the simple, aimless young man who at once said that he liked me very much, insisted that I come to his house, and then, having secured my presence for an elaborate meal by making it impossible for me to excuse myself, sat gaping at me for hours, making small talk about Iranian food and American movie stars, insisting that I be sure to write him a letter soon, and getting my address in America so that he could write me in return. Often I found myself among such people, wondering how to leave them gracefully or how to let them give me their addresses without leading them to expect a reply, or even a return visit.

But all these oddities and annoyances were minor. What mattered was something different, something I had not expected: the hostility of the people whom I had thought I would be close to and with whom I wanted to establish friendships—the educated, the interesting and alive, the future leaders of the country, those looked up to by the common people. In Iran these members of the elite are the ones who not only dislike their country but are genuinely hostile to it—not like the common people, who may gripe and be miserable in their surroundings, but are nonetheless at ease in them. The hostility of intellectuals, of the young and progressive-minded, is really significant, because it is deep, relentless, and malicious. Furthermore it is subtle. One becomes aware of it slowly, distracted at first by the day-to-day aggravations one had thought to be one's main obstacle.

It may have been six months before I started to notice this deep antagonism. At the time I was on a trip to Teheran from Zahidan, a small, fly-ridden government outpost not far from the Pakistani border. On my way I stopped in Kerman and took a bed for the night in a cheap hotel. I entered the room, where there were several beds, and found some young men sitting around a table in the middle, eating roast chicken and freely drinking vodka. We fell into conversation. I told them that I was an American and that I was going to Teheran. One of them gave me a glass of vodka. Shortly someone else offered to give me a ride the rest of the way, which I accepted. For a while we made conversation aimlessly. Then another of the men turned to me and lifted his glass. Squinting, he moved it back and forth slightly until it was pointing at me. "You're an American," he said. "Tell me. Why does your country, the great democracy, act the way it does. Eh?"

"What way?" I asked.

"How do you think the people of Asia feel about the way your country acts? What does your country mean? Talking about democracy, by God—what does your country mean about democracy? It has enslaved half the world. The Asian people know what your country means."

I shrugged my shoulders and muttered that there was no perfect democracy anywhere—what did he want?

"Oh, yes," he went on. "And what about the enslavement of South Korea? And what about Formosa? Is this democracy?" He spoke half-coherently but with bitterness.

Again I shrugged my shoulders and told him to ask the refugees from China and North Korea.

"Hah!" he retorted.

"All right," I went on, "what about Hungary? That's oppression for you. Can a person leave Hungary whenever he wants to, the way somebody can leave Formosa?"

"Hah!" the man repeated. "What we know about Hungary comes from the American press. You tell us, what did the Americans do to Guatemala?" His lips immediately spread into a grin. "Eh? Tell me about Guatemala."

He laughed, and I shrugged my shoulders again. I avoided looking at his grin. The conversation trailed off, and before long we went to bed. The next day I left early, and later joined the man who had offered me the ride. He told me that the other man sent his apologies for the way he had talked the night before—he had been drunk, and besides, I was an honored guest from an allied country. He told me to forget the matter. He hadn't meant what he said.

But such indictments started to proliferate. Shortly afterwards, when I was at a friend's house in Teheran, someone came over, squatted next to me on the floor, took me by the arm, and started to tell me in an excited whisper how the people of Iran hated America and how they were going to throw the Americans out, the way Mosaddegh had. Then he darted away.

A while later, when I was attending classes at the University of Shiraz, a girl who heard me speaking Persian came up to me and asked if I knew Hindi, Turkish, and Arabic as well. After all, everyone in my profession did. Why else would I be learning Persian but for the sake of the profession?

About that time, one evening in a park near Shiraz, in a silence broken only by a gloomy singer and the whine of a violin, a young man with whom I had been talking took me aside and told me how miserable he was. He had nothing to live for. No one in Iran had anything to live for, he said. Everyone was waiting for the Russians. They were waiting to open their country to the Russians, to throw out the foreigners and the ruling class and escape from their misery.

When I was back in Teheran again, I visited a high school and gave a talk before a friend's class. As I was going out into the hallway after the class, one student rushed up to me and asked, "Why does America keep the Arab countries from uniting?" The teacher scared him away and hastened to apologize, claiming that the student was under the influence of Communist propaganda. Later, however, in talking with the teacher, I found that his views, though hardly Communist, were much the same as his student's.

On another evening when I was at a friend's house, an Iranian girl came to visit his wife, sat down in a corner, and directly picked up a magazine. She didn't look up when I spoke to her, and for a long time she said nothing but seemed nervous in her chair. I continued to converse with my friend. When he left, I turned once again to the girl, trying to put her at ease. When she did answer my questions, she did so evasively, never looking me in the eye and continuing to thumb through the magazine. Only when she came to some pictures of Cuban high-school girls marching with rifles on their shoulders did she speak out on her own. "They are alive," she said simply. "They are marching for freedom. They are free now." That was all she would say.

I met an intelligent young man from an old and respected Teheran family who was about to go to the United States to study. At first I thought that he was a progressive, from the way he discussed the outmoded laws of his religion; but when it came to a general discussion of religions, he defended his own, conservative though it was, against all others. In fact, he went so far as to call it "the justest and best of religions." When I asked him what he wanted to study in the United States, he replied with an ironic smile, "I want to study against America."

Even one good friend of mine, who had spent a long time in the United States, had lived well while there, and went out of his way to keep his old American friends and make new ones, used to talk the same way. "You Americans overthrew Mosaddegh," he would say. "Some day the people are going to come to power again and kill the Shah and overthrow his government. We are going to get out of our alliances with the West and have a neutralist government. We will get help from Russia, too. We won't need you any more."

In this way, I came to sense the heavy undercurrent of anti-Americanism all around me. Its presence seemed natural, since Afro-Asians nowadays appear anti-American as a matter of course, hating alliances with big powers but not giving much thought to the need for them; and certainly there is much to complain of in American foreign policy. In fairness, I must say that I had many good Iranian friends who did not share this hostility, who took me in good faith and did not try to blame me and my "imperialistic" country for the general hostility between peoples. But they were exceptional. And while many young Iranians I met would not call themselves Communists if they were old enough to remember what the Soviets had done to their country during and immediately after the war, or if they had the imagination to realize what would become of them in a Communist system, they still weighed Russia and the United States on different scales.

It was not until my second year, when I had settled down to study in one place and got to know some of the people around me better, that I came to understand the forces underlying this contradiction. Hitherto I had been misled by the amiability and ready hospitality of the Iranians, by their insistence that all men must become brothers and that the illusory walls between peoples must be broken down. I gradually realized that they had no real interest in brotherhood, and certainly not in brotherhood with Americans. When they complained about America, they were not reacting to misdeeds committed by a brother or a good friend, which once redressed, would be forgotten. They were crying out against the modern world, the very facts and circumstances of modern life.

This outcry was baffling, even to one who might sympathize with it. At times it seemed to stem from leftist thinking, at other times from nationalist thinking—which were often mutually incompatible. Many Iranians I met really were convinced Communists, Socialists, or Nationalists; yet many more who professed to be so had no concept of the ideology they were professing, no firm intellectual position.

I felt this very strongly one evening when I went out with some young poets and writers with whom I had recently made friends and whom I later discovered to have been Communists, Socialists, or Nationalists of some form or another. In the midst of drinking vodka, making small talk, and listening to various people recite their poetry, someone made a comment that instantly provoked a rain of bitterly anti-American exclamations from the others at the table. I started to argue with them—why not?—and at once the argument took fire and burst wild with insults and bitter invective. I sat shaking my head as one of them waved his fist at me and said that I had better commit suicide because the West was all washed up. Another sat back, grinning and rubbing his thumb and forefinger together, and gloated that for all the money and arms in the world America could not buy a grain of the Orient's wisdom and could not postpone her own inevitable destruction by even one day. At that moment it flashed through my mind that the people with me were not just against American foreign policy, which could never have called forth that sort of outraged, unsolicited declamation. When the confused echoes ceased, I knew that they were not even talking about the economic and political realities of the modern world, which they should have accepted as impersonal pressures, pressures outside the pay of Britain and America. What they were preaching was an anarchistic holy war, a war against all society and social intercourse and the pressures and restrictions it brought on the individual (especially that pattern of social life imposed, consciously or unconsciously, upon them by the West). They were merely clothing their declaration of war in a variegated garb of leftist and nationalist ideas—a garb that they could be persuaded to remove only nominally, and then only out of hospitality or fear for an outsider in their presence.

The most articulate of these intellectuals was a tall, slender man who had spent six years in England and spoke powerful, almost flawless English, well-emphasized by a noble, ascetic profile and a touch of gray hair around the temples. At once he made a string of withering remarks against the government. I asked him what, in his opinion, was wrong with the government. He said that it was bleeding the nation at the profit of a few degenerate millionaires (adding that he was an aristocrat himself). "Look at all those cars on the street!" he exclaimed. "Look at all the beauty shops! Look at the shops selling American television sets and cheap American records! Oh, it makes me sick. It makes me sick to watch my nation's money, the sweat of our peasants, vanish into these foreign luxuries. Ohhhh!"

He was right in saying that Iran had a weak system of currency control and that the rich were sending millions of dollars out of the country for frivolities. But the government—with strong resistance from large interests—was starting to combat this, and has continued to do so. When I told them that he could not criticize the government for making improvements, he dropped the subject. He said he really hated the government because it had come to power through American money, by overthrowing Mosaddegh. I asked him about the mobs that came out against Mosaddegh. "Oh, they were bribed. Anyway, they were made up of thieves and beggars from the south of Teheran."

"So were the mobs which supported Mosaddegh," I said.

"No!" he shouted. "Mosaddegh was beaten by American money! Not by the Iranian people! Mosaddegh was beaten by American money, and when he was tried in court, he even read out the number of the check that the Americans had paid to have him overthrown!"

"The chaos of the nation's economy defeated Mosaddegh," I said.

"That's a lie," he replied. "The Western powers were against him. What else do you expect from a blockade?" I asked him how the Western powers could have supported Mosaddegh after his stand in the oil crisis. "Bah!" he shouted. "We could have run the oil refinery ourselves! The British government wouldn't let us; that was it. She forced her technicians to leave."

I said, "They left of their own accord."

"Then Russia would have bought our oil!" he exclaimed. "Russia would have bought it! As soon as our government started trade agreements with the Russians, you overthrew it!"

"By that time," I replied, "the only people supporting Mosaddegh were the Communists."

"The Communists! The Communists!" He banged his fists in frustration. "Can't you say anything original? Must you repeat the gibberish the State Department puts out?" He shook his head. "Why do you talk that way? Why do you keep talking about the Communists? The other Americans [mostly exchange students] don't talk that way. We don't have anything against you. We like most Americans who come out here. As individuals, we like them. I'm shocked. I thought you might have some understanding. I thought, since you were interested in Persian and all that—" He shook his head.

"And they killed Fatemi," another one broke in. "They killed that genius Fatemi." Fatemi was Mosaddegh's foreign minister and quite pro-Russian. "If you could have seen what they did to him—it was a crime. The greatest crime." Fatemi had been shot. "Everywhere the Americans go, it is the same," he added. "America is guilty of the greatest crimes." I mentioned some of the crimes Communists have committed and asked him what he thought of them. He laughed and impatiently brushed my question aside. I insisted I was telling him the truth. He told me to prove what I said with photographs and articles.

"If you had not overthrown our Nationalist government," the noble and ascetic one went on, "we could have sold our oil to the Russians. We could have thrown out these foreigners. They do us no good. They take money from us and raise the cost of living. We could have built a strong economy. But you overthrew the people's government."

"How?" I asked.

"I told you! By bribery, by paying the army a million dollars to stage a coup d'état."

"What million dollars?"

"Ah, ah, ah! Mosaddegh read the number of the check in court."

"It was a check from Point Four," the first one affirmed.

"What check?" I asked. "You asked for proof—what proof is there of this?"

"Pah! Mosaddegh proved it," said the noble, ascetic one. "He read the number in court." The other one nodded.

"Here you doubt what I say," I went on, "you doubt things that were written in newspapers all over the world; and then you say something you cannot prove and demand that I believe it?"

The other one smiled. "It doesn't matter what you believe. It's what the people know that matters."

I tried another tack. "Then suppose Mosaddegh had stayed in," I continued. "The country would have gone Communist." By the end of his regime the Communist Party was the only powerful group supporting him. A friend of mine heard an Iranian Communist boast once, while drunk, that his party had planned to kill Mosaddegh when it took over.

Everyone at the table was outraged. They accused me of slandering and parroting State Department clichés. They said the Communists could never take over Iran. It couldn't be done. Every time the Russians had come into Iran, the Iranians had expelled them.

"Truman expelled the Russians from Azerbaijan in 1946," I said, "by threatening Stalin with war."

"Nonsense!" one person shouted.

"It was our prime minister!" exclaimed another. "It was our army!"

"Well," I said, "the army supports the present government."

"Ah, ah, ah," one of them retorted. "The *generals* support the government. Some officers who were sent from orphanages to military school when they were small children support the government because they have no other dignity. But most officers, the young and enlightened, don't support this government."

"Then why don't they take over the government and change it?" I asked.

"They won't let them," one said.

"The Americans won't let them," another said.

"The Americans have their guns trained on the city," a third said. "We are paralyzed."

The discussion went on. "Why can't we get aid from the Russians as well as the Americans?" the first one asked. "The Russians have done great things. Did you know that in Soviet Central Asia the literacy rate is one hundred percent?" I asked him if he could prove that. He told me that he could, by bringing me a magazine from his house—a British magazine, as no American magazine would print such statistics—but he never did. "The Americans have done nothing in this country," he continued, "that the Russians could not have done better. The Americans have done nothing but send technicians, who stay aloof from the people and raise the cost of living so that the common people can

barely stay alive. People are starving because of the Americans.
Even the so-called development programs are a farce—the dams,
the agricultural assistance, the public health improvements, are
nothing but conspiracies of big business. American aid to this
country is nothing but a bribe—a bribe to keep the wealthy and
degenerate in power so that America can continue to bleed us
dry."

"Look at Bulgaria," said one who had passed through there.
"That country has made great progress. Then look at the misery
of Turkey. Those two countries were the same once. Everywhere
the Russians have gone they have brought great progress. Look
at what they have done in Afghanistan. All the young intellectuals
in Afghanistan are Communists." I said that I knew some young
Afghan intellectuals who were not Communist. "How do you
know they aren't?" the man asked. "They wouldn't tell you if
they were. They wouldn't tell any American." I was the only one
among them who had been to Afghanistan; but again, they refused to believe what I said.

By this time it was late, so we stopped talking and went home.
But the discussion continued from then until I left Iran. From
that day on, Iranians could tell that I knew what they were thinking and they could not keep themselves from discussing it with
me. In a sense, it was as if there was bad blood between my tribe
and theirs, and I was being held accountable for it.

Other people had different things to say. Many contended—
and Western diplomats have heard the same thing—that the Communist mobs who rioted towards the end of Mosaddegh's rule
were not Communists at all. They claimed that to say so was just
propagandizing, that the "Communists" in the mobs were really
agents of the British, who wanted to scare America into overthrowing Mosaddegh. Some others—Communists—said that the
mobs really *were* Communist—in fact, that all of Teheran was
Communist and that the mobs were just the vanguard of a free
peoples' democratic movement to throw Rockefeller and the imperialists out of the country. Although the people overwhelmingly
supported these mobs, they could do nothing against American

tanks because they were weak and oppressed (of course, the Communists had also infiltrated the army very effectively). Still others, who had thought a little about the future of their country, said that it might even be for the good if Iran turned Communist. "Of course, if it did, I would be the first to get out," they swore, or, "Why doesn't America let the Russians come in and take over? Then America can become the champion of the people in their fight for liberation."

Without going into a discussion of the virtues and defects of Amini's recent premiership, or the advantages and disadvantages of laissez-faire capitalism relative to Communism in furthering the development of Iran's economy, one can easily maintain that such a discussion would be valid, and that it would not be easy to make a choice between the two approaches. Yet young Iranian intellectuals seem already to have made their choice—almost without hesitation—against any approach based on Western liberalism.

One student of my acquaintance made a revealing comment once when he told me, "All the students in Iran are leftists. Either one is a leftist, or one doesn't think." He wanted to convince me that the left was the only intellectually defensible position to hold anywhere; what he really meant was that the only political attitudes acceptable to Iranian youth as a whole were leftist ones. This is true. Many young Iranians "think" without being leftist, of course, and many have no political inclinations of any kind; but there is no active, youthful, but serious movement for them to join other than the movement of the left, and they often have to keep their disagreement to themselves in order to live at peace in the young intellectuals' world. Actually, and this is the essential point, anarchism is stronger than leftism among Iranian students. But it is the left that guides them and draws the young intellectuals away from whatever organizations might offer a program of reform within the present structure of government.

All the political goings-on, all the rallies, demonstrations, and parades that took place in the University of Teheran while I was there, all the pamphlets that went around in open gatherings or under desks—in fact, all serious student organizing—was done by leftist groups, usually by the National Front, a Socialist organization, but also by crypto-Communists sheltering themselves in the National Front.

Student Socialists rarely planned beyond the overthrow of the old order and the subsequent vendetta. They approached me from time to time, looking for argument or approval. Often they told me how they had to conceal their allegiance and pretend to be simple nationalists. They described the organization of their party to me, including the means they used to conceal themselves from the government—formation of secret meetings, clandestine sessions with Radio Moscow, smuggling of pamphlets from counterpart organizations in East Germany, and so on. With little hesitation a student would relate how Iran needed Socialism—not Communism—how so-and-so, whose word counted, had told him just that; how America could help the Iranian people by supporting this Socialism; and how I could support it by writing about it.

It may seem at first that the students were violently leftist because, after weighing all the factors, they thought anti-Western Socialism or Communism could develop their country faster than any other form of government. "Look at Russia," they said. "After all, she is beating America in the race to the moon, in armaments, in steel production, in dam construction, and so on." Yet many had heard the other side of these arguments, too. For instance, many who condemned America for not giving Iran a steel mill knew that it would be implausible to manufacture steel in Iran, that no one would invest in Iranian steel, and that the country saves money by buying steel from Germany and Japan instead of producing it herself. Many who condemned America for not "industrializing" Iran knew that America has built several factories in Iran but that the Iranian government and its employees have been unwilling to run them properly.

While I was in Iran, I read an indicative article in a popular weekly from the spring of 1958, which bitterly attacked America's foreign aid program. It claimed that Iran could do much better for herself if America, instead of sending technicians and aid, just sent a supply of drugs and medical equipment. Here we see a widespread tendency at work: the article made no mention whatever of the drugs and medical equipment America *had* already brought to Iran, or of the technicians sent with it, or of the problems they had encountered while in Iran.

Young Iranians invariably criticized American aid and found little value in it. In the last seven years America has given Iran over a billion dollars in aid. Certainly much of this money has gone to waste, through either corruption (consciously or unconsciously overlooked), inefficiency (misappropriations, experiments that did not work, American ignorance of the society they are dealing with), or misunderstandings such as one reads about in *The Ugly American*. However, American critics such as the authors of *The Ugly American* or C. Wright Mills (who in his *Causes of World War Three* expressed the opinion that American aid programs were doomed to fail in the face of Russian aid because our foreign policy was so unaltruistic and oppressive towards the Russians)—as well as the Iranian critics—tend to neglect the main difficulties. The main problem with the mission to Iran is that Iranians responsible for administering it and applying the advice it gives are often not interested in making it work for their country.

First of all, they are usually not apt to work well unless made to. But the American technical mission to Iran cannot make Iranian employees work: it cannot fire recalcitrant employees or force the government to hire enthusiastic ones. Many capable government officials, including at least one minister and several deputy ministers of the interior, have been forced to resign. One wonders whether their resignation stemmed from working well with the American mission. Others, though corrupt, have gained power through the American mission, even though it has not given them recommendations. To advise without interfering in administration is a policy on which the American government is insistent. Because this policy prevails, work often falls into the hands of the corrupt and incompetent and lags behind. Moreover, many Iranians think that America is no less imperialistic for giving Iran a free hand in administering the aid she receives.

Once I got into an argument with a couple of medical students in Mashad. They claimed that America and her fellow conspirator the British ("Always remember," they said, "that the Americans and the British are cut from the same cloth because they speak the same language") were guilty for all the misery in Iran—the poverty of the masses, the control of wealth by the few, the stagnant economy, the iron tyranny of the government. "But we will change all that," they said. "When we come into power and drive out the imperialists and the feudalists, you will see a renaissance."

"Well," I replied, "for the moment you have to live with the present government, so why not postpone your vengeance and do what you can to help your people anyway? After you get your doctor's degrees, why not go out into the poorest province, offer your services to the poor and sick (they will keep you alive), and tell your friends to do the same?"

"Ridiculous!" they replied. "Do you think we are that low, to let the clique that rules our people deceive us and bribe us to go out and live among ignorant peasants who understand nothing, not even what their own interests are? Are we so foolish as to let them disunite us and exile us from the centers of activity? Our country calls us, not those despots. We must stay here and fight."

I asked another student, who claimed that America had done nothing good for his country, why the Iranians didn't at least put what they had gotten to good use. "We will not work with America," he replied, "or with any country that has suppressed the people and thrown out its leaders and rightful representatives."

Anti-Americanism is not, however, the most important reason that draws young Iranians toward extreme leftist organizations. The Communists attract the young because they are the loudest in their denunciations of the status quo at home and the most violent in their attacks on the Shah and the present reform-minded government. They promise a great deal, especially to young people, and are impressive because of the strength of their convictions.

Iran's social structure is traditionally very paternalistic and authoritarian. The government is highly centralized and autocratic. The population of the country consists of close-knit tribes and big families, likewise governed by autocratic elders, who are too conservative and arrogant to broaden their knowledge of the world and too jealous of their own position to promote the reforms necessary for their country. As the elders stiffen in their resistance to modern ideas, they oppress their inferiors and juniors more and more, and the gap between the generations widens.

I used to hear a Western professor describe the pitilessness— often the sadism—with which many of his colleagues in the University of Teheran examined their students. The examinations were oral, and the students often passed only after the professors had established their superiority over them. They would ask the students difficult questions such as no Western professor would expect them to answer. The students, brought up to mimic their professors' pronouncements and suppress their own initiative, came in sleepless and trembling with apprehension.

I used to observe the deference students showed their teachers: they all stood when a teacher entered or left the room; they bowed their heads whenever a teacher passed by; they copied everything he said in class with diligence, never questioned him, and never visited him in his office to propose a differing opinion.* Compare this with what the students used to say in their teachers' absence: in reality they had no respect for them and accused them of all sorts of treachery and immorality. Men such as Manuchehr Eghbal, ex-prime minister and onetime president of the University of Teheran, or Doctor Ghorban, ex-chancellor of the University of Shiraz, showed a high degree of competence in their

---

* In class I once corrected a professor on a minor error, a slip of the tongue, and he spent over half an hour disputing this correction, trying, by confusing me, to force me to say in the end that he had never made the error in the first place.

university work; yet few students would admit that Eghbal was an honest man who never got rich by working for the government, or that Ghorban was a good professor of medicine and drew little profit from the twelve jobs—mostly honorary—that he held during his chancellorship.

The gap in generations is also reflected in anachronisms in the social system, which the young are entitled to oppose. There is little need any more for the intensive religious training still carried on in the schools, with its heavy memory work, studies of outmoded legal concepts, and biased historical teaching. There is little value in some of the old social restrictions either. The young people, hearing how free social life is in the West and how easy it is to find part-time work (even if it is manual) or to go out with girls, make every effort to go abroad for a superior education. Often they never come back.

Through the poets I became especially familiar with one aspect of the conflict. The young poets were attempting to find new ways of expressing themselves in their language and had come up against a very rigid tradition. To most literate Iranians, a poem must be written in the classical language, must contain a fixed number of lines in conformity to its subject, must follow one of the established metric patterns, and must rhyme consistently. It is as though no poet could gain recognition in America unless he wrote sonnets, quatrains, odes, or epics with the same strictness of meter and rhyme, and even the same vocabulary and idiom, that one finds in Shakespeare, Milton, or Keats. It is as though all respectable American literary critics or professors of English literature were to condemn the poems of Robert Frost for not adhering to the classical forms.

The free verse, or "white poetry," that young Iranians are writing now is new and inspired by modern Western poetry. In 1920 a prominent poet brought out the first work in this genre. Most of the young poets have a wide knowledge of classical Persian poetry and versification as well as of Western poetry, but it is "white poetry" that arouses their enthusiasm. Yet because the young are fighting to secure an audience for it, the elders are becoming more and more determined to fight against it, thus arousing conflict. Drawn up on one side are the old guard of the universities and their protégés, who still produce most of Iran's poetry and criticism and still control the obedience of young students of literature. On the other side are the young poets, the habitués of the coffee shops and vodka-and-shishlik hangouts in downtown Teheran, who sit around reading and discussing their own poetry as well as new poetry from abroad, gossiping about the embarrassment one of their number may have caused someone from the old guard in public, or figuring out ways to mask their radical political views so that no one else can find them in their poetry. The old guard, at their most dogmatic, ignore the young poets altogether or accuse them of opportunism and poor workmanship; at their most tolerant they shrug their shoulders and dismiss the young as immature and unconcerned with deeper human emotions. The young poets, for their part, keep striving for public approval by writing widely (even for movie magazines), staging public readings, and working on foreign scholars to translate and publish their works abroad.

What is missing is debate between the two groups. There is neither mellowing of the youthful vitality and experimentation nor revitalization of the classical rhetoric, brilliance of description, and technical skill. I heard more than one professor, well-versed in Persian literature, say that the young poets "were not poets at all." And I heard a spokesman of the young poets say, in appraising another young poet's work, "What this poet has done so far is good; now, let us hope that he breaks even further away from the traditional styles and comes to discuss more current issues." Another young poet accused one of his fellows of anachronism and insufficient enthusiasm for radical views.

Strangely enough, rebelling against their elders and their society means that the young Iranian is protesting on the one hand against the old authoritarian, paternalistic society of tribes, and on the other hand against the selfish tradition of individualism and social unconcern that is strong in Iranian society. It may seem surprising to encounter this individualism in an environment of strong class distinction and rigid social behavior, but in reality the apparent rigidities of the society are characteristics evolved to protect the individual and keep strangers out of his affairs, not to suppress him. Perhaps they mirror the Iranian's uneasiness toward society as such. Another friend of mine once claimed that the Mafia could control Iran. Because the Iranian people are dis-united and wary of their own society, any powerful organiza-tion—even a fairly small one—could paralyze and control them merely by demonstrating techniques of intimidation and extortion.

It might seem that Iranian students become extreme leftists be-cause they believe (having been told so by the enemies of the West) that their society contains ills—such as class struggles—which can be cured by imposing a variety of Marxist regimes upon it. But is a class struggle of the kind Marx diagnosed in nineteenth-century Western Europe actually taking place in present-day Iran?

For one thing, there is a very marked social mobility in the country and considerable respect for the individual as individual, no matter what his origins. An Iranian once told me that to get ahead in the country, one needed "money, connections, and gall." I met many Iranians who had acquired the two former qualities by possessing the latter—who had bettered themselves simply by pushing their own way ahead. For example, one of Iran's wealth-iest landlords started his career as an agent in a small cotton business; his boss appreciated his aggressiveness and married him off to his daughter. A young but respected professor of literature in a provincial university was the son of a washerwoman. Many of Iran's prominent people came from equally humble beginnings: several recent prime ministers, people in other high governmental positions, and certainly many in high military positions. A good many of the country's merchants started with a small shop in a bazaar, or a taxicab, or a small piece of land, or perhaps only a cartload of vegetables. The law does not force the poor to remain miserable. Any peasant can occupy and gain possession of a piece of unenclosed land by building a wall around it and squatting on it for a period of time. Even if someone else owns the land, he will have trouble evicting the squatter. I saw many poor people living on choice lots in the north of Teheran this way, and no doubt they will someday be able to sell their land and go into a small business with their profits. The only real distinction between classes in Iran comes from money and property, and this is available to one person as well as another. The Iranian people are racially homogeneous, and until the West began to give the rich real material superiority by bringing in machinery, automobiles, television, and the like, the rich lived much the same as the poor, and often still do. They ate simple meals, dined and slept on the floor, lived in homes no better-equipped (though of course bigger and more comfortable) than those of their peasants, and had no access to such secret weapons of superiority as technological power, international connections, or foreign languages. Thus there was little to prevent an Iranian who felt bitter about his humble birth from reaching the top if he was intelligent, worked hard, and had good luck.

Therefore, when the young Iranian rebels against the society of his father or grandfather, part of his rebellion is against the outmoded spirit of individualism—not just its aspects of amorality and disrespect for the law—and he often adopts a puritanical view of life. The young Iranian sees no future for a country that has no effective social security or taxation and that relies only on largesse to take care of its underprivileged; he has no patience with skepticism, debate, interest groups, and individual apathy towards society. When Cubans say that they used to be confused by their odd, corruptible electoral system and now feel that they have a more direct democracy under Fidel Castro, they are expressing what many Iranians feel about their own country.

Young Iranians are thus frustrated by the very facts of modern life. They know as well as anyone else how badly their country needs development and aid; they are as discouraged as anyone by the enormity of her needs. Yet they never really face them. Instead, they claim that the matter is out of their hands, that they are not allowed to work, that they are denied a share in running their country. The leftist and nationalist points of view help them entertain this attitude, and they exploit it as much as they can, not in order to rebuild their society but to rebel against it anarchically. Therefore, one can seriously question the sincerity of most Iranian leftism, just as one can praise the genuineness of most Iranian anarchism and the devotion of its adherents.

As I saw when talking with the poets, it is useless to question their assertions. They have one aim in mind, will use any means available to achieve it, and will not be stopped by anything. That aim is to rebel against their society, and one of the means is to reject Western liberalism (along with the rest of the modern world and its apparatus). Western liberalism has become more and more familiar to them at their own expense. It is often among those who have studied abroad, whom one would expect to be the most cosmopolitan and broad-minded of Iranians, that rejection is strongest. The young person is forced to stand up and take notice of the modern world, he comes to feel bitter for representing a poor, unhealthy country, so weak it can barely keep control over its own tribes, so poor it has to gear its economic life to the production of oil (for which it has little use and for which it has to employ foreigners), and so superstitious and fatalistic that the great majority of its population regards education as contrary to the will of God and turns to vodka and opium for refuge.

Western liberalism exposes the young Iranian to the weaknesses of his country, but it does not give him the confidence he needs to face them. It lays on his shoulders alone, and not on the shoulders of a powerful, well-organized bureaucracy in which he would have an important position, the crushing work, of confronting an opposition of ridicule, apathy, or intrigue. Nor will Western liberalism help the young Iranian gain respect from his own society. The same person who told me that all thinking people were leftists added, another time, this half-apologetic note: "We have to be—you see, it's hard to think otherwise when no one respects you." He told me that he became a Communist when he was fourteen, motivated to join the party simply by a hatred of religion.

What will come of this rebellion? Will the young, when their turn comes to manage the nation and preside over its society, bring about the radical reforms and sudden elevation of morality and public responsibility that they dream of and discuss so intensely nowadays? What will be the outcome of their veiled anarchistic rebellion against the older ruling classes?

One can expect a climate of puritanism, conformity, and self-righteousness. The society will probably be more close-knit than the old one, and probably after a number of years it will bring a higher standard of living and a fairer distribution of wealth to its people. But it will also bring a more authoritarian and obscurantist climate of opinion. Not that such tendencies are absent in any society. Isolationists, xenophobes, and puritans thrive everywhere. The alienation of the young intellectuals in Iran, not only from their fathers and grandfathers but also from the course of modernization that their country has been following for the last hundred and fifty years, is surprisingly strong, but one can find it elsewhere. The alienation of the young Iranians is significant mainly because of its all-pervasiveness.

The intellectuals carry real weight in Iran, more than intellectuals in Western countries. By being dogmatic, uncritical of their favorite theories, and confused about the forces they are rebelling against—in short, through intellectual weakness—the young intellectuals have become more united than most other elements of the population. Being better educated and more aware of their interests than most, they wield a power and are a threat to their enemies out of all proportion to their numbers, and undoubtedly they are destined to occupy positions way beyond their qualifications.

From what I have experienced and described here, I would guess that if the power of the intellectuals was increased, it would be used irresponsibly, and that the people then in power would commit excesses beyond those of the present government, obsolete, corrupt, and authoritarian as it is. There is much evidence that active intellectuals are unwilling to co-operate seriously with moderate elements in the government, or with any moderate government. Often they show themselves more interested in the acquisition of power than in sober administration. For instance, most young intellectuals of my acquaintance burst out in tune with Soviet propaganda criticizing Amini or at least expressing doubts about him. They feared that at last the old-style government of individualism, conservatism, and landed interests might provide the country with a capable administration and thus prevent the laying of groundwork for an anarchistic revolution. Many condemned Amini's reform efforts in 1961 because back in 1954 he had been the one to sign an oil agreement with Great Britain, ending Mosaddegh's nationalization decree and resuming Iran's oil exportation, at last. This action was quite irrelevant to Dr. Amini's later reform aspirations, but many intellectuals would not forgive him for putting the country back to work again in proper order.

Intellectual alienation from obvious present-day needs was probably the most disheartening thing I found in Iran, and it broke my will to stay in the country any longer. I left Iran because in the end I came to realize that the liberal Westerner has no place among his better-educated Iranian contemporaries. I had ceased to communicate with them, and I imagine that it will be a long time before they bring their country out of the society that I saw in the making during my two years there.

N.N.

You Do Your Job, I'll Do Mine

And, should the scorchèd smell
Of what we've lived through
Reach you,
Show us respect in silence
As we, in silence,
Greet you.

—FROM AN "UNDERGROUND" POEM

For one who has spent time enough in Soviet society to
have a sense of some of its human values, the eloquent stanza
quoted above has the force of a thousand similar spoken and silent
requests. For him, silence is indeed the safest policy. But it is a
negative one, and if he is an American, he has a positive obligation to pass on whichever of his impressions can cause his countrymen to ponder, in more human terms than those available ready-
frozen at the newsstands, the complex experience which is "Soviet
reality."

We need to create a broader and more balanced view of a society so often misrepresented by friend and foe. We must encourage other young Americans to undertake the serious study of

---

N.N. is the Russian equivalent of Mr. X. He continues to study Russian
affairs at an American university.

this rich and fascinating culture and to participate at some future time in the student exchange between our countries. It is surprising and distressing that, in spite of the considerable efforts of American universities to attract participants, it is only with some difficulty that we have filled our all-too-modest quota since the student exchange began in 1958.

The USSR is not yet a comfortable place to live by American standards. Life is difficult. Each day brings new demands on physical, emotional, and intellectual energies. For most American students a year in the USSR is a profound experience, often an unpleasant one. But this is a frontier, a borderland of confrontation, where the shocks, the reappraisals, the painful discoveries, and the gratifying insights are a part of the battle for understanding. It is tragic that opportunities to share in the adventure of this frontier are going begging. Nothing can be more crucial—yet not one in a million Americans has accepted the challenge.

What follows will reflect my belief that the society in which I have been a guest is a viable society, characterized by internally logical patterns of development that reflect the national past, the challenges of the present, and many traits common to other Western societies during similar stages of evolution. ("Orwell was right about man," a Russian friend used to say, "but wrong about Russia.") This is not a house of cards, nor a madhouse, nor yet a "fun-house," defying gravity and the senses by some Marxian skewness of line and plane. It is a normal society; that its norms fail to coincide with those that have been abstracted from our own limited experience is often distressing, but should be stimulating. In labeling such a society "abnormal," we but reveal our ignorance of its evolution, abdicating at the same time our responsibility prepetually to examine the validity of our own "normality."

As a full-time student in a Soviet university, I had opportunities to observe and take part in daily life to an extent uncommon for foreigners, including those resident in the "Western colony" of Moscow. My own experience was limited in the main to my relations with fellow students, members of the university community, and chance acquaintances from among the intelligentsia, chiefly Great Russians, of the capital in which I resided. I had little contact with the rural population or with the members of non-Russian groups, but since it is the most educated classes of the urban Great Russians who are the "Anglo-Saxons" of the new culture, the bearers and creators of the "Soviet" attitudes, it is upon them that the student of the society must settle as a "standard," if not an average.

The likening of the role of this group to that of the bearers of Anglo-Saxon attitudes in our own culture is but one of many such comparisons which can be helpful in acquiring an appreciation of the evolution of Soviet society. Preoccupation with political and ideological concerns has tended to distract the attention of most Americans from important processes of internal development, making unlikely the drawing of useful comparisons with phenomena that characterized an earlier stage of the development of our own society. To evoke the mood of American society in the first decades of this century is to facilitate the understanding of many aspects of present-day life in the Soviet Union.

Too often, caught up in the search for and contemplation of the real and considerable differences between the two societies, we ignore the equally significant similarities. This is especially true in dealing with the cultural and social evolution of Soviet society. We forget that the twin processes of industrialization and urbanization, which so radically transformed American society in the period before, roughly, 1920, are just nearing completion in the Soviet Union. Thus, if America moved from the farm to the factory in the half-century before 1920 (the year in which the urban-rural population balance reached the fifty-fifty level "typical" of the modern industrial society), in the USSR the same process, considerably accelerated, took place some four decades later. (In 1926, the urban population was 18% of the total; in 1959, 48%.)

There were, of course, important differences in the circumstances accompanying these similar processes, differences profoundly affecting the resolution of the social forces they unleashed.

What America accomplished at a moderate pace, without wars at home, Russia careened through in half the time, under conditions of internal upheaval and continual external pressure, at considerably greater cost to the society. While America destroyed the old only as it was displaced by the new, Russia attempted to sweep away the old and begin building from scratch. Russia destroyed much of her social, cultural, and industrial elite and is still furiously building a new one; America came to new terms with hers. While many of the millions who flooded into America's cities were the urban overflow of other advanced societies or the most adventuresome and enterprising elements of Europe's rural population, the seventy millions who came to build Russia's new cities and industries were representatives of a tradition-bound, benighted, and backward peasantry.

And yet . . . the overcrowded cities, teeming with new urbanites still bound to the farm but caught up in a whirl of new experiences, the spread of education and mass culture—all these America has known. If every American city and town had to have its opera house and public library fifty years ago, every Russian hamlet and village (for time marches on) must have its "palace of culture" and reading room today; if vaudeville and "real as life" theater knocked 'em dead in Scranton and Atlantic City then, the same jokes and "mellerdramers" are paralyzing 'em in Volgograd and Verkhoyansk this very moment; if that other and now remote age saw the first flowering of the mass culture hero, the king of sports and the matinee idol, these all flourish circa 1960 in Russia; if young America lost its head over Lindbergh, Russia has gone gaga . . . but it is not the facile enumeration of parallels that should interest us so much in choosing the comparative method as the understanding of phenomena that could otherwise be misinterpreted.

Many Americans, certainly most of those who have ever visited the USSR, are familiar with the roster of authors who represent, for the average Soviet reader, "modern American literature": Theodore Dreiser, Sinclair Lewis, Jack London. It is often pointed out that the works of these authors are selected for translation by the authorities because they are anxious to have the citizenry read of the economic injustice, social strife, and cultural stagnation that these authors took as their subject matter. This may explain why they are translated—but why are they *bought,* in millions of copies, throughout the USSR? I am inclined to think that they sell for the very same reasons that made them popular in America forty years ago; they have much the same message for the "new Soviet man" as they did for many of our grandfathers.

In a broader sense, this, the era of *kulturny* and *nekulturny,** is like our era of the spittoon joke and self-conscious gentility— the golden age of the schoolmarm. I remember the question of a Soviet student of American literature, "Do you know which American writer best describes life in the USSR today?" I didn't even guess. "H. L. Mencken. As I read his articles and editorials about the booboisie, about the influence of the schoolmarm, about the ineptitude of plumbers, I feel as though I had written them myself, only yesterday." He went on, "Do you remember the piece. in which Mencken describes the havoc created by the school- marms in the use of *him* and *me?* Before the advent of the little red schoolhouse the hayseed said, 'Me and him went to the store,' and lost no sleep about it, but when he 'got larnin,' he discovered that this was *nekulturno,* if you will, and mastered, 'He and I.' But—learning is a treacherous thing. He also left the little red schoolhouse confidently saying, 'Asa went to town with him and I.' We have this everywhere. Go to a village restaurant, and you will see the peasant, God bless him, take his salt from the salt dish in his fingers. The *kulturny* type, appalled at this ignorance of modern hygiene, and perhaps not all that confident about the

---

* *Kulturny* and *nekulturny,* and the related abstract noun *kulturnost,* orig- inally meant simply "cultured, cultivated, cultivation," etc., but in the process of the changes described above they have acquired additional meanings. Thus, *kulturny* is listed in a recent dictionary as "possessing certain social skills." (It is, for example, *kulturno* to refrain from putting one's hands in one's pockets.) Similarly, there have appeared such neologisms as *kultpokhod,* literally "culture excursion," which means a "collective visit to a museum, theater, etc." and *kulttovary,* literally "culture goods," which means in fact "stationery, playing cards, musical instruments."

cleanliness of his own fingernails, delicately takes *his* salt on the end of his knife. You and I take ours in our fingers. . . . When Russians start staying away from bad opera, *then* we shall have risen beyond *kulturnost* to culture."

It is not only in the appreciation of Soviet cultural phenomena that we may draw fresh insight and stimulation from juxtaposition with our own recent past. If we recall the whole spectrum of "illegal" activities—from the pathetic foolishness of bathtub gin to the brazen criminality of gang warfare—which were the results of an overly restrictive law, imposed by a militant minority, a law that made criminals of millions of otherwise law-abiding and sober citizens, we are better able to distinguish, as Russians do, among the "dissenters" of various stripes, and more apt to remember that the *spekulyant** and "lipstick king" are no more champions of political freedom than was Al Capone of civil rights.

Similarly, in pondering the riddles of Soviet internal politics, Americans might gain more understanding from reflection upon the conditions that produced our city boss, and upon his methods and mentality, than from searching through Marx, Orwell, or Dostoevski.

In the sections below I have attempted to re-create some of the impressions that I carried away from the Soviet Union. I am including a rather random group of my personal, impressionistic travel notes and diary entries, chosen to illuminate those aspects of my experience that seem most typical of Soviet life or most meaningful in our attempt to consider it. These are notes and observations from daily life; they reflect only the stuff, and not the forms, of government, economics, and internal politics. However, it would be untruthful arbitrarily to separate observations into categories or to disassociate questions from answers—for the spirit of his time and generation does not permit the young American to stop at observation. Even the gentle birch must pose, and answer, a question.

---

* *A spekulyant* is a speculator, or black-market operator, for whom the artificially controlled economy of the USSR provides great opportunities.

Whenever I get into the countryside, I am reminded of the lyrical associations *russkaya priroda** has for the Russian. Truly, the gentle, slender birches, rising in purest line to lay their lacy upper branches against the pearl gray of the winter sky, blending with the solid shapes of the spruce and pine, black in their greenness, create against the endless snow a classic harmony of line and shape and color—a single impression, organically one like the green, ocher, and azure of a Mediterranean coast. No one who has appreciated this landscape can fail to understand its traditional evocative power over Russian artists and poets. Even an outsider, if he has the slightest feeling for tradition, is prompted to conclude that there is, in fact, something special about the Russian countryside.

But what can it be that makes this landscape more inspiring, more evocative, more humbling, than that of Maine, Finland, or Oregon? I submit that it is the contrast between the mood created by this deli-cate beauty and other aspects of life here, in which so much is heavy, clumsy, difficult, and cruel. In order to understand the Russian's love for his *priroda,* it is not enough to see the birches, the pines, and the snow. In order to feel it, to experience it, one must see—not fleetingly but day after day, so that their monotony may penetrate his heart—the streets and yards and corridors and staircases and kitchens and lavatories, all the shapeless, gray, ugly, bleak, dulling images that fill the world of the Russian. Then he will understand the power of the light grace, of the simple, free line and strong pattern of birch, pine, and snow.

A Westerner soon discovers, on arriving in Russia, that he is somehow special in the minds of most Russians. In the almost un-translatable words of a sensitive Soviet humorist, "There's some-thing about a foreigner's puss."

Whatever it is about his "puss," a foreigner soon senses that he has stepped into a role, into a costume—American in my case—which is precreated for him in the image and likeness of his nation as viewed by the Russian. Some foreigners exploit the

---

* *Russkaya priroda,* literally "Russian nature," more generally means "the Russian countryside." Its special meaning should be evident to readers of Rus-sian literature. It is not simply "nature, Russian," just as *concierge* is not simply "janitor, French."

positive and romantic associations that their nationality elicits in the mind of the Russian; others never overcome the negative impressions created by their countrymen in other times and situations. The American inherits a costume box containing the fair-haired wig of the American of the land of Lincoln and Roosevelt, the Fordson tractor, Spam and the "Studebekker," as well as the black cape and mustache of the Pentagon and Wall Street, unemployment and the KKK, the interventions of 1918 and 1961.

Yet stock poses elicit stock reactions. To get beyond them, the American must discard some of his American clothing. He must open up and loosen up, for if the slightly superior stuffiness of the English frustrated and infuriated our fathers, our generation with its noncommittal reserve and unlimited self-assurance gives our Russian brothers, by nature more unaffected and open-hearted than the heartiest "Howdy," cause to suspect and "clam up" or to assume the well-known protective aggressiveness. If the American will, or can, open up, he finds himself caught up in personal relations more intimate, more honest, more frank and human, than those that his own relatively depersonalized society usually offers.

However, the more intimate relationship with this society brings new responsibilities and problems. The visitor has an obligation to attempt to form a balanced view, to place his several chance impressions in proper perspective, to see events and discriminate among people on the basis of the culture that they represent. This is not easily done. For instance, Americans, like other Westerners in Russia, are continually pestered by "rag merchants," young men who in open defiance of the law and with little regard for their self-respect make a living from the lucrative trade in Western clothing. Many of these people lead a Runyanesque life, one that is truly incredible against the somber background of Soviet "reality." These *Chuvaki* and *Chuvikhi** are as colorful, their life is as fascinating, as our own "guys and dolls"

---

* *Chuvak* and its feminine form *chuvikha* are among the Russian hipster equivalents of "guys," "cats," "broads," "molls," etc. Rapid changes in usage at this stylistic level in both languages make translations arbitrary.

once were—but it is neither real life nor real Russia, and most of them are hardly admirable human beings.

Many Western visitors, besieged at the doorsteps of their hotels by those types who seek out foreigners and are adept at forming acquaintances with them, are often unable to choose their friends with the same discrimination that they would exercise at home. This is also true of many journalists, who see in this "fast" crowd, familiar with Western ways and (fortunately) languages, quick with the antiregime gossip, the brilliant, martyred, idealistic, rebellious "Soviet youth." This is a sadly false impression. There are many brilliant young people in the Soviet Union, among them martyrs real and self-styled, idealists and rebels. Most of them greatly enjoy meeting foreigners. But many of the best of them are too proud, too intelligent, or too cautious to "pick up" foreigners on Gorky Street or the Nevsky Prospect. It is, of course, difficult for a stranger in any society to distinguish among types, especially when such indiscriminate use, whether in criticism or tacit praise, is made of such labels as *stilyaga*.* My own experience inclines me to agree with the words of advice given me just after my arrival by an elderly archaeologist whom I had met several years earlier in America. He had seen me on the street with some *stilyagi*. "Young man," he said, "if you've come to Russia to spend time with types like that, you're wasting somebody's money. You could have seen the same types right at home, at any race track or gambling joint. Every society has its antisocial fringes. I can't for the life of me understand why you Westerners make a political problem out of a social one. A hoodlum in Western clothes is still a hoodlum."

This is not to say, of course, that anyone who likes Western clothes or Ella Fitzgerald is a hoodlum—or that those who scorn them are admirable and wise. Many law-abiding and responsible

---

* *Stilyaga,* according to Russian dictionaries, means "pejorative appellation applied to one, usually without any higher, social interests, characterized by a penchant for exaggeratedly modish style of dress and extravagance of mannerism." The American equivalent could be the "zoot-suiter"; the English, "Teddy boy."

citizens (including, of course, Nikita Sergeyevich Khrushchev) prefer and wear Western clothing as a matter of choice. Such people wear the clothes; others brandish them.

A decisive element in distinguishing the attitudes of the "wearers" from those of the "brandishers" is patriotism—the complex, dualistic patriotism of the thinking Russian. The intellectual and emotional energies bound up in the Russian's attitude toward his homeland are startling and even frightening to Americans of my generation, by whom patriotism is often scorned as unsophisticated or even reactionary. I found it difficult at first to understand the nature of my friends' feelings about their country; but as my understanding grew, so did my respect. I found myself recalling the words of a wise and benevolent friend who once said, "To love America, Brother, means nothing; it is the love of a child for a bright toy. But to love Russia . . . that means something. It is an act of personal humility." He, and most of those whom I found I could really respect, are true patriots.

Such people are intelligent, sensitive, and genuine human beings. They are not "hurrah-patriots," who are even more ignorant and intolerant in Russia than they are elsewhere. Nor is theirs the blind and uncritical patriotism of the "organized" patriot. As people concerned with and committed to the improvement of their society, they feel that they have the right and responsibility to criticize.

And criticize they do. They criticize yahooism, narrowness, and stupidity at every level, in every phase of life. They criticize the bureaucracy, pettiness, greed, and backwardness. During one long and spirituous evening I had a discussion of such things with one who, though a patriot, is merciless in his criticism. His father's wartime assignment had taken him at an early age to America, where he remembers reading a magazine article entitled "Major So-and-so's Private War" about an American who had turned his campaigns in some remote theater into a kind of private vendetta. "I have a private war right here," my friend declared, "my own private war against [and he used the English word] crap."

Much of what such people are fighting results from the fact

that Russia, in their words, is a "heavy" country. This "heaviness," in other terms, is the weight of the past, the burden of the backwardness and conservatism of an uprooted peasant mass, made more acute by rapid changes caused by a forced rate of urbanization and industrialization.

Even the university generation is "heavy." My friends often surprised me by the conservatism, not to say backwardness, of their ways—especially in personal and rather indicative attitudes. I wrote in my diary on one occasion:

They seem terribly slow to acquire city ways, habits, attitudes. Habits of thinking. Dress. Sanitation. One thousand and one things. In the year of our Lord 1960, of the revolution the 44th, when filth and disease have been driven to their last natural strongholds, the Russian, Ivan Q. Grazhdanin, when confronted, not in rural railway stations (where it would be understandable) but in opera houses, at first-class hotels, in research libraries, wherever confronted with a spanking-new, clean, enameled toilet seat, systematically and with relentless vengeance wrenches it from its place, splits it into pieces, throws it on the floor or hangs it on the nearby clothes peg, and having removed the disconcerting obstacle, triumphantly mounts the bowl in the traditional "eagle" squat, secure in the thought that he has avoided catching a disease which, as he knows perfectly well and will tell you at great length, is no longer a problem.

This will be familiar to those who remember the move from the outhouse to the inside convenience, which accompanied the move from farm to city in our own country. In my view, few examples demonstrate so vividly the fact, crucial to an understanding of so much of Soviet life, that transporting the peasant to the city is not synonymous with making him urban in mentality. He brings his village attitudes with him, and they die very, very hard.

How hard, and the lengths to which man will go to resist changing his habits, are perhaps best demonstrated by another story from the "toilet training" cycle—for which I hardly need apologize in these sophisticated sixties.

On entering the lavatory of a modern Soviet jet, a TU-104, on a "V.I.P." flight, I was impressed by the spotless, well-lighted, roomy, and well-designed facilities. It was one of the best I had seen—at last, a washbasin large enough to hold more than a cup of water, footpedals for faucet control, a proper mirror, and good lighting. I was impressed by the hopper as well; it was situated in a separate stall, with a shining porcelain bowl and seat. I put the seat down—and discovered two shoeprints! That anyone could even balance astride the *unitaz** in the swaying and shimmying tail of a jet plane in flight is a tribute to man's physical agility; that he even tried is testimony to the persistence of the problems faced by those who are bearing the "heaviness" of the past.

There are enormous problems involved in lifting the whole nation to the levels of culture and efficiency which will permit it to perform the tasks it has chosen to set for itself. As one highly placed acquaintance was wont to remark to American friends: "If you think it's frustrating to fight against us, you should try fighting on our side for a bit. We're fighting 'Russia'—you're just competing with the Soviet Union." He was speaking not about destroying the cultural heritage of the past; he is in fact proud of his own aristrocratic background. He had in mind the struggle against the conservative, tradition-bound peasantry, which he and others like him are straining to lead, coerce, cajole, into the twentieth century. The simple, lovable carpenters, chauffeurs, concierges, even the prematurely aged women who sell so many things, are called on to perform too many tasks for which they have not been prepared and which they find very demanding, frustrating, and sometimes overwhelming. I shall never forget the many humorous and touching scenes that accompanied the currency reform in early 1961. The new ruble was introduced at one-to-ten; all prices were accordingly cut to one-tenth. Confusion reigned in many places, especially in trolleys, kiosks, and other places where most transactions involve small change and peasant women. A typical transaction:

"How much is your soda water, Granny?"

---

* *Unitaz* means "toilet bowl." The word is taken from the brand name "Unitas" on imported fixtures, influenced (the final *z*) by "folk etymology," which connected it with the Russian word *taz* ("basin, bowl").

"Well, Son, it used to be thirty kopeks, but now, since they decided to change our money, it's only three."

"Only three? What a bargain! And they're selling vodka for three rubles a bottle! Here's a new ruble."

"A ruble . . . now let's see. Thirty kopeks from a ruble . . . no . . . three kopeks from ten kopeks . . . no thirty kopeks from ten rubles . . . is that right, my boy? You know the devil himself couldn't keep these things straight."

For months stories circulated about streetcar conductors staying up half the night "cashing in" their receipts at the end of a grueling day, of salesladies being escorted from their place of work by people in white coats, etc.; but the prize was the story of the little old lady in the beer booth on New Year's Day. New Year's Eve is a major holiday for the holiday-conscious Russian, and many feel the need for a nice walk late the next morning. A mug of beer is the usual tonic for those whose "soul is on fire." One poor saleslady, confused by the complicated calculations suddenly introduced into her simple operation, was painfully slow in serving her customers, and a huge queue formed around the booth, besieging the poor vendor. Harsh words were heard. The poor woman lost her temper and closed the window of the booth, crossing her arms to indicate that no beer would be served until the thirsty citizens recovered their manners. At this point the crowd began to beg her to open up; many of them were desperate. She did, finally, but hung up a notice on the window: "We neither understand nor accept the new money."

The poor lady, like millions in similar positions, was being asked to adjust to too much, too fast, and she just gave up. That this is common is attested by the constant complaint of both foreigners and the local press about the rudeness, poor service, and inefficiency to be encountered in salesgirls, waiters, and the like. But what can you ask of a woman, for instance, who is required to perform work that is exhausting and demanding under very unfavorable conditions, often with inadequate tools, who must sprint from work in order to get a seat on an overcrowded tram in order to get to a market that doesn't sell the few things she is able to buy, in order to get home to a shabby and overcrowded room in order to get into the communal kitchen ahead of the neighbors in order to avoid the usual fights and get a tasteless and uninteresting dinner for a husband who, having spent all day under similar conditions, is exhausted and unappreciative? The whole society at all levels is under similar stresses.

As I was standing on the platform of a railway station recently, I noticed an ice-cream vendor, a little old *babushka** with the shape of a full laundry bag in repose, open a small door in her metal pushcart and, without haste but with a certain determination, take from within a cast-iron automobile crank. She seized the crank as one would a hammer or sword and began to beat the side of her cart. Were it not for the deafening sound of the trains, the whole station would have resounded with the clangor of metal on metal, for she was swinging with all of her heft, and in earnest. When she had done and replaced the crank, I approached her and asked, as diplomatically as I knew how, "Why . . . er . . . did you do that?"

She was clearly upset and answered in broken phrases, punctuated by gestures of futility and despair, "Okh, *synok,*† . . . it's the filthy . . . pigeons . . . right on my head . . . all over everything . . . all day . . ."

I followed her last gesture up into the eaves of the station, saw the pigeons, and understood. Realizing that railroad-station pigeons are particularly hardened to noises, I understood even better.

When I suggested that she move her business to another location, she answered, "When I move, they move."

I wished her a Christian blessing and walked away, happy for her that she had something to beat and something to beat with.

Not everybody does—and even for those who don't need such an outlet, those for whom hope is the largest single article of intangible consumption, there are some aspects of life that daily take their long-suffering souls to the limits of patience. The most upsetting is housing. Americans, with the possible exception of slum landlords and tenants, cannot conceive of the conditions that

---

* *Babushka* means "granny, old woman."
† *Synok* is the diminutive of *syn,* "son."

exist in housing in the Soviet Union; they simply have nothing with which to compare them. Similarly, most Americans cannot imagine the inhuman situations and oppressive tensions that they produce. It's bad enough with people living three and four to a small room, often with two, even three, generations in the same room, sometimes with two married couples thrown together by a shared inheritance—it's bad enough, in communal apartments comprised of three or four such rooms, when everybody is getting along. But when there is trouble in the common kitchen, in the shared bathroom, or as the result of someone's taking sides in a family quarrel overheard through the temporary walls, it can be simply intolerable. Oh, there's humor in it; I heard of one communal apartment where arguments as to which family was leaving the light burning in the bathroom led to a situation whereby each family had its own light bulb, which was kept in its "own" room, carried to the bathroom, screwed in, screwed out, and carried back to the room. And the lack of privacy . . .

Tonight as I returned to our room (very few can say "my" room), I met one of my roommates in the hall outside another room, having a smoke. He was a bit tipsy. He invited me into the room, which was dominated by a large table filled with the makings and remains of a banquet, and around which were seated perhaps ten students, in Sunday best. I was made to feel at home, given a *shtrafnoy* (this is a "penalty glass"* of whatever the guests are drinking, given—usually in double or triple quantity—to late arrivals; in this case it was a tumbler brimming with Azerbaijani wine), and discovered that the party was a wedding banquet in honor of two students who had been married that afternoon. It was a simple, unpretentious, and touching feast, reminiscent of rural America perhaps sixty years ago: peasant mothers in their simple homemade best, giggling friends of the bride, rambunctious friends of the groom, and at the head of the table, straight out of *Oklahoma,* the blushing bride, shushing the gigglers, soothing the *mamashi,* not knowing herself whether to smile or cry and doing both, and the groom—oh, the groom—the slicked-down

---

* *Shtrafnoy* means literally "penalty glass."

hair, the slight rash on a face still unaccustomed to the razor, the lean neck in the tight and overstarched collar, the ill-fitting new suit (I almost said, "store-bought") over powerful shoulders and arms, and the nervous, kneading, knobby hands, the broad unmanicured fingers. He was being strong and silent. The party went on—songs, a bit of dancing, the traditional cries of "bitter"*—until someone noticed the time, and people began to leave. The curfew for guests in the dormitory had arrived. The bride and groom left. Those of us who "belonged" were invited to stay a bit longer. I suppose I was the only one who was surprised when, some five minutes later, the bride reappeared. But within a few seconds I understood. She had seen her man to the door and come back to spend the night in her own bed. which she was to share with her mother, in her own room, which she shared with three classmates. And the groom took the long, cold ride to the center of town, to his own dormitory, to his own cot. For them there would be no wedding bed.

The university dormitory reflects conditions that exist throughout the society; all but the most fortunate students are crowded into drab and uncomfortable rooms, have very little privacy, and study in stuffy and poorly lighted reading rooms. But the youth, energy, and idealism of the Soviet student, the carefree camaraderie of the common adventure, and the fact that this is, for many, the best life they have ever known make the dormitory a rather happy home.

The average undergraduate is, by the standards of many American liberal arts colleges, immature, unsophisticated, and poorly prepared in fields outside the physical sciences. This is not surprising; he is among the first products of an educational system still charged with the tasks that were completed by our own a generation ago. (Sixty percent of the Soviet population had *not* completed seven grades of school in 1959.) In many ways Soviet universities can be compared with our state colleges of a generation ago, for they are charged with the same tasks: raising the

---

* The reference is to the wine, which must be "sweetened" by the groom's kissing his bride.

general cultural level of the broad base of the population and providing the basic technical training necessary to make a modern industrial state run smoothly.

The young people in them are more frank, less frugal, more impressionable, less studious, more naive, and less bored than those American undergraduates with whom I am familiar. But the most distinctive characteristic of even this young and progressive generation is the persistence of village ways, or the absence of the development of suitable replacements for them.

I have in mind not the obvious "connection with the village," as it is evident in the baskets of eggs, jars of honey, dried mushrooms, and smoked fish that the students bring with them after each vacation and receive regularly from relatives in the country. So long as student scholarships are small and the supply of food products a problem for all city dwellers, such conditions will remain of necessity and common sense.

On the other hand, although the evolution of new ways is most rapid in this group (and most meaningful for the future), the transition is far from complete. The first step has been made: the students have determined to discard the past, whether the rural tradition or that of the prerevolutionary student elite. But no new tradition, no comprehensive and distinctive code such as the one we call "collegiate," has been created to replace it.

This is most apparent in those areas of life where forms—the conventional ways of dealing with standard situations—play a primary role. Two obvious examples are recreation and the battle between the sexes. Whereas the American freshman steps into a society that requires he make Saturday's date no later than Tuesday night at the risk of getting "shut out" or of offending his prospective partner, prescribes his attire, dictates his behavior (at a cocktail party he stands and makes animated conversation, at a hayride he reclines and does not), and even orders his schedule (dinner, dance, . . . , curfew), the Russian is still very much on his own in charting a course between clumsy and frustrated shyness and bold, simple, sometimes brutal frankness. The

Russian village knows few intermediate steps; the youth of the university generation is only slowly developing the forms of the meaningful middle.

New ways *are* evolving, but slowly. There is still considerable wavering; in many situations the old ways still assert themselves. A single example can be made of the typical *vecherinka,** where the wavering is symbolized by the peregrinations of the humble table, the focal point of the traditional party. Evenings used to be spent (many still are) around a groaning board, laden with simple, tasty, and thirst-inducing hors d'oeuvres and unmeasured quantities of vodka. Heroic feats of consumption were performed, tales and gossip exchanged, songs sung, and quarrels begun and resolved. On the other hand, the focus of the "modern" party for the Russian "smart set" is, as elsewhere, the record player. Moderns dance or listen, consuming whatever refreshments are available between numbers or during an intermission. And what of the average student party? It is a struggle: the table is moved back for the dancers, forth for the sitters; the party splits in two—a table faction and a gramophone faction. More often than not the table is victorious by evening's end and regains its position of dominance in the middle of the room.

The forms of which I have been speaking are most apparent in play; at work, the Russian student is in the realm of the classical forms of lecture, essay, and exam. However, the work habits of the Russian student are characterized by fluctuations even more severe than those typical of his American brother. During much of the academic year he (I speak of the humanist) does little serious or concerted work—a bit of leisurely and peripatetic reading, perhaps some "thousands."† But with exams arrives the *shturm,*‡ the traditional Russian burst of energy:

---

* *Vecherinka* is the diminutive form of *vecher,* meaning "evening." It is a "soiree."

† To satisfy language requirements, a student must translate at home a certain quantity of text in the foreign language that he is studying, this amount being expressed in thousands of printer's units, *i.e.,* letters, spaces, commas, etc.

‡ *Shturm* means "storm" in the sense of "assault."

Exam period has arrived, in Leningrad and in Cambridge. In Leningrad as in Cambridge (and probably even Moscow and New Haven) students are scurrying from room to room, trading, borrowing, stealing, or buying lecture notes, each as his training and means permit. Here, as there, they are feverishly scanning the "required" texts, with a prayer (or a wish, for nonprayers) that the most vital information will leap from the page and lodge permanently (or at least until the exam) in their brains.

The humanists digest, refine, distill, the contents of their texts to the smallest indivisible particle, the cliché. The inhumanists—or whatever they are to be called—to the formula, the equation, which must be smuggled into the exam, used, and filed for the final. For the scientists (and a few conscientious nonscientists) this period of intense effort is but the finale—*fortissimo e prestissimo*—of the semester's work. The humanists (and a few foolish scientists) are in a different position. Their work must cover, in a grand rush, "everything" from Plato to Parkinson, or Adam "Smeef" to Stalin, 1066 to 1855, or 1613 to 1917. They do it, somehow, and some of them even learn something.

So it is in Leningrad and Cambridge, and probably even in Moscow and New Haven. But there are differences. In Cambridge (and, one assumes, New Haven) exams in the humanities are written, the essay type, and usually three hours in duration. In Leningrad (and, one can be sure, in Moscow) they are oral, consisting of answers to three or four questions drawn by lot in the instructor's presence from a pile of "tickets," which represent the forty or fifty stock questions on the subject that have been announced, outlined, and presumably memorized previous to the exam. This system, which places great stress on the ability to memorize and even greater on the facility with which the student can "snow" the examiner with prepared answers, tends as well (as a direct result of the few minutes "in private" given the student to formulate his answer) to develop the allied sciences of cribbing and overt cheating, which in Leningrad (and, alas, in Moscow) are much more common and flagrant than in Cambridge (or, one would hope, New Haven). Thus, if the student in Cambridge or New Haven emerges from the exam period with eyes weakened and red from studying someone else's handwritten lecture notes, his colleague in Leningrad or Moscow suffers from the same affliction, but caused in his case by the eyestrain involved in trying to read a chapter-by-chapter synopsis of *Das Kapital,* written by his own right hand on the palms and fingernails of his left.

As for the scientists, they always have the inside track—of their slide rules—on which to engrave the necessary information.

I feel obliged to point out that this "ticket" system is not new (it was used long before 1917) and that cheating, in my view, is neither a manifestation of the *âme slave* nor proof of some "moral bankruptcy" of Communism. It is rather "slippage" under stress, an example of the "bending" of a moral standard in a situation where obedience to the moral law is nearly impossible in view of the demanding nature of the task.

This kind of cheating is often *de facto* "acceptable" behavior in university society: students make little effort to conceal it, even from foreigners, and little opprobrium is attached to it; the professors usually "look through their fingers" at it, uncomfortably aware that in fact it "is done." They are disturbed by the moral problem, however. I once attended a *fakultet** meeting where the discussion indicated that most teachers are clearly aware of the contradiction between the requirement that the student be responsible for a mass of memorized, catechismal information and the stricture against cheating.

Moreover, cheating is most common, and permissiveness most widespread, in "required" courses, such as Marxism-Leninism, historical materialism, etc.—which some students call by the prerevolutionary name for religious instruction, *zakon bozhij.*† The amount of rote memorization is greatest, and interest least. In "real" courses, and especially in subjects closely connected with his field of concentration, cheating by a student can damage his reputation among his fellows; in the "ideological" courses, on the

---

* *Fakultet* refers to the faculty as an administrative unit, not a teaching staff (for instance, the Faculty of Arts & Sciences). It is roughly equivalent to departments in American universities.

† *Zakon bozhij,* "religious education," means literally "divine law." Required courses are called by this name in sarcastic analogy with the compulsory course on religion in the prerevolutionary school curricula.

contrary, he can lose status by refusing to help a comrade who is unprepared by whispering an answer or passing a note.

A logical result of the ideological restrictions imposed in many fields, especially in those of history, government, philosophy, and economics, is a characteristic kind of "natural selection" of students. Many of the most intelligent, sophisticated, and thoughtful students, those who would in another country go into the social sciences, go instead into esoteric and specialized fields, far removed from problems of current politics and life—into classical and oriental philology, archaeology, and the physical sciences. This "internal migration" of the intelligentsia reflects the fact that there are some fields that are discredited among the intellectuals by the fact of their ideological "contamination." As a result, many young Russians, in choosing their *fakultet* (as in our graduate schools, students are admitted not to the university but to a department), are often encouraged by their friends and parents to avoid a field such as economics, in spite of personal interest, and to choose some other *fakultet,* for example, mathematics, where mathematical methods of economic analysis might be studied, where ideological control is less strict—where it is, in the common expression, "warm and bright, and the flies don't bite."*

Since my return, I have often been asked about the beliefs of Soviet students. In what, if anything, do they believe? Are they more or less true to the faith, or ideology, of their fathers than are American students? What role does ideology play in their daily life?

My diary was of no help in this matter. I discovered that what little I had recorded on the subject would make it appear that ideology came up only in conversations with foreigners. Such is not the case. Like other official ideologies, the body of Marxist-Leninist dogma breaks down into two groups of tenets, those that

---

* There is some reason to believe that this flight from such important fields of study is ending. Economics, ethnography (in the broadest sense), and even certain areas of recent Russian history are again attracting active, original, and independent thinkers.

"fit" the life of the society that has adopted it, and those that are chiefly doctrinal and are usually used for ceremonial purposes or when dealing with schismatics and infidels.

University students generally accept the basic tenets of Marxism-Leninism. The four pillars of faith for the average student would seem to be: state ownership of the means of production and central control of the economy; the elimination of ruling classes and elites of vested interest and the introduction of social democracy (the limits of political democracy and the problem of personal freedom vis-à-vis group authority remain unclear); the methodology of scientific materialism and economic determinism; and a faith in Russian Communism as the "wave of history."

The reasons for the appeal of these principles reflect the social and cultural development of the students: Marxism-Leninism is scientific (or pseudoscientific), a fact that appeals to the newly educated, relatively unsophisticated undergraduate. It is egalitarian, an idea whose popularity in Russia hardly needs explanation. It is messianic and eschatological, promising to all the earthly paradise, the "bright future for all humanity"—full Communism —to which Russia will lead all peoples.

The uses of Marxism-Leninism, in the life of the student as elsewhere in the society, are similar to those made of similar bodies of dogma in other societies. First, it has ceremonial uses —in public meetings, in proclamations, at weddings and funerals, in the first and last paragraphs of articles in newspapers, and even in scholarly journals. Its ceremonial value is commonly made most of by those professionally involved—the *sluzhiteli kul'ta,* in the cynical reapplication of the Soviet officialese for "clergy."*

In the life of those not professionally involved, the dogmas of Marxism-Leninism are used in other ways—as vehicles for traditional ideas, egalitarian or democratic, in emotional and ethical

---

* *Sluzhiteli kul'ta* means "servitors of a cult." It is a Soviet term that arose in the twenties, during the most active years of antireligious propaganda, to denote the clergy and is applicable to all religions. Since *kul't* now has additional meaning (the "cult of personality" being the usual euphemism for the Stalin era), new uses of this phrase suggest themselves but have not yet, to my knowledge, been introduced.

arguments, to "prove" points otherwise not allowing of proof, and to clinch a good argument or conceal a bad one. This tactical use of scripture and exegesis as a weapon of political struggle, which is familiar to even the casual student of Soviet history, extends into student and dormitory politics as well. An appeal to ideological consciousness may also be used as an appeal to higher personal standards of ethics. I remember such a case: in a crowded streetcar, where there was no possibility even to move about, let alone check tickets, the exasperated ticket-taker cried out, "Comrades! How can we ever expect to achieve Communism in Russia so long as people are dishonest about streetcar fares?"

The final use of dogma is in polemics with capitalist foreigners, the infidels of the age. The command of this comprehensive and intricate body of ideas, especially of its basic propositions and of the dialectic, is very useful in dealing with foreigners and, as most Western tourists discover, provides an almost impenetrable protective shell. What these Westerners don't usually discover is that it is often they who have provoked this response, through lack of understanding of the Russian's position and by indiscriminate use of "loaded" clichés from the Western press. Fortunately, many Russians who have learned to distrust the printed word and to read between the lines understand our uncritical attitude toward our "unrestricted" press, although they are amazed at our naïveté. These more sophisticated citizens are for the most part members of a generation very different from today's students, whose impressionable years of early adulthood have been years of increasing liberalization and hope.

The experience of World War II separates the men from the boys in the Soviet Union as nowhere else. The war generation, those who came of age during the war years, stands distinct from the older, Stalinized generation, which was broken, thrust upward, or perverted by the catastrophes of the thirties, as well as from the rather naïve, idealistic, and ambitious younger generation, which has been spared so much.

This middle generation—the men who were young enough in

1940 to have avoided the purges (directly) yet old enough by 1944 to go to war—today includes those between thirty-five and fifty. The next decade is theirs; they are now waiting for the older generation, whom they rightfully consider people of another era, to pass on the roles of leadership. The impress of their wartime experience is deep within their character. They are realistic, energetic, and patriotic men, whose experiences, especially the contact that they had with other lands and nations, will doubtless influence their conduct of the nation's affairs in the years to come. The future historian will perhaps trace the events of 1965 to the bivouacs and officers' clubs of Berlin and Vienna, as Kliuchevsky discerned the influence of the Napoleonic campaigns on the generation of the Decembrists.

The Second World War was the major event in the lives of all adult Russians, even those who stayed home. This is something often forgotten by most Americans, who as a result often fail to understand that Soviet propaganda in the matters of peace, disarmament, and the German question has a very direct and emotional meaning for Russians. I remember an acquaintance, a make-up girl at one of the major theaters, who had spent the war in Leningrad and lived through the blockade, which lasted for nearly three years. She was a child of nine when it began, an adult of twelve when it was lifted; she and thousands like her (those who survived) lost their childhood and their health during those years, when they were starved, maimed, and terrorized. "While Mamma was with us, we didn't mind the cold, the hunger, the darkness everywhere; we were busy getting things to eat—bits of leather for soup, spruce-needles for a kind of jelly which was good against scurvy. But when Mamma had to be taken away to the psychiatric hospital, I became the head of the house; and I began to realize to what lengths people were being driven. . . . You would never believe the things I saw."

The complexity and strength of the feelings that have resulted from this national experience were brought home to me at a New Year's dinner in an intimate family gathering. Many toasts had been drunk. As we emptied our glasses with a toast to peace, one of the guests turned to his four-year-old son, who was playing "Russian and Nazi" in a corner, and in a flush of New Year's optimism said, "Sasha, do you know that when you are our age, say on New Year's Eve, 1995, there won't be any war?"

"Why, Papa? There'll be Germans, won't there?"

Silence. The father gripped the edge of the table with a trembling hand, "Yes, Sasha, there'll be Germans."

Mine was, above all, a personal experience, an "adventure of the spirit." In many ways I learned more about my own country than I did about the USSR, more about myself than about Russians. Not all of my discoveries were pleasant.

Many, however, were comforting. I discovered, for example, that the tales of the "sputnik" variety are largely myths arising from misunderstanding and, occasionally, willful distortion. Russia is *not* racing ahead of the United States in education, public medicine, and general technology; it *is* solving its own problems with inventiveness and vigor, as its circumstances permit. Many are problems that we solved a generation ago. If it be true that Russia must solve her problems in her own way, it is equally necessary that America solve her problems in the American way. We can perhaps learn from Russians the lesson of sacrifice and concerted effort, but we must be true to our own traditions. In the next decades, in the years that will see Russia's unrelenting drive for its place among Western nations, the decisive factor will be the struggle of each society with itself—with the burdens of its past and with the exigencies of each new situation.

A young American in Russia in the early sixties is, alas, preoccupied with the large insoluble questions of the confrontation of these two great and complex cultures. He must, yet cannot, understand, as he cannot understand himself. Each event must be interpreted, each object examined, each comment pondered and pondered. But from time to time the measured mechanics of the *what's* and *how's* and *why's* are arrested by some experience, some personal revelation, which floods the consciousness and knows no *how's* nor *why's*. These are profound and often in-

describable experiences—the first elation of a hard-won friendship, a flash of the self as seen in the other, an appreciation of
the other man's feelings about his past, his country, his homeland. . . .

Occasionally the random vignette of a promenade was noted,
enjoyed, and recorded in my diary without comment—the stuff
for some future nostalgia:

The colder weather brings with it a specifically Russian phenome-
non, that of the quilted citizen. Working folk, especially those who
work outside, undergo a metamorphosis when they get into their
winter clothes, which consist of a very bulky, quilted, gray or gray-
blue jacket, and trousers *ibidem*. The jacket, which has the properly
stolid name of *vatnik* (by contrast with its more aristocratic brothers
the *fufaika* and the *tuzhurka*), so restricts movement as to impart to
the wearer the gracelessness of an overstuffed scarecrow, and one is
hardly surprised to discover that the arms stick out at the same
grotesque angles whether the *vatnik* is on someone's back or hanging
on a peg in a workers' tearoom.

Children follow in the footsteps of their elders; the *vatnik* waddle
is clearly reflected in the penguin toddle of the very young who,
swaddled in fur from toes to nose and bound in the middle like a
sheaf of grain, look for all the world like the windup walking toys of
their American brothers.

Inevitably, however, contemplation of something even as
simple and heart-warming as the movements of the sheaf-shaped
child brings one's thoughts back to America. . . . If there is
something about the way a foreigner holds his "puss," Mr. Zosh-
chenko, it's because he is wondering, pondering, asking himself
questions he hasn't asked before. And if he wonders at the past
as he wanders through your glorious Kremlin—or stands on
Dvortsovij Most as if on the prow of a ghost ship cutting the
waves as it steams upriver through the unreal chiaroscuro of your
midnight twilight—it is what lies ahead that possesses him.

I thought of Br'er Rabbit and Br'er Fox last night as I rode home
through the warm rain in the front seat of a taxi. Chance impres-

sions reminded me of their battle of wits, which seemed to symbolize the forces that are engaged in a similar struggle today.

My driver was hurrying home to the garage (it was nearly two in the morning), but as we were in a remote part of town, he twice asked my permission to stop at the unsteady beckoning of staggering figures. Eventually his back seat was loaded with an uninhibited, childlike, lovable, and boozily loving cargo. Within a few minutes we were all *thee-thouing.* Their simple conversation, which concerned today's local elections, reminded me again of that encouraging and fundamental understanding—call it common sense or peasant cunning as you wish—that these simple people have of the forces which are at play within their society.

They will all (99.9% of them) trot off today dutifully to vote for the bloc of Communists and Independents; they were all (or most of them) more than tipsy last night—and in these facts one can see despicable weakness or childlike innocence as he wishes. I personally am comforted by the feeling that, no matter how often they get bamboozled and helplessly entangled in the Tar-Baby, somehow, someday, they'll end up in their own brier patch, sadder, wiser—but safe and sound.

That is what I thought as I rode home through the warm rain in my hired ZIS (roughly, "Stalin Automobile Factory"—now known as the Likhachov Factory) along Moscow (formerly Stalin) Prospekt.

And I wondered, at the same time, whether I would win my bet (made with a friend) that today, in accordance with some unwritten but precise code similar to our order of precedence of Saints' Days, the red banners displayed everywhere to mark election day would be draped in black to indicate that it is also the eighth anniversary of the death of Joseph Stalin. I lost—for the first time in eight years there is no crepe on display. *Sic transit,* and *sic semper . . .*

As I reconsider this, one of the last entries in my journal, I am reminded of the many times that I paused over that notebook, asking myself, "But what of Sasha, or Marat? What do *they* think? What do they think about *us?*"

To posit an average "Soviet youth" is, as I have indicated above, journalistic foolishness. Moreover, whatever "typical" attitudes about America I could reproduce would reflect my own character and experience rather than the views of my Soviet friends. Better to describe, as faithfully as memory permits, parts of a single conversation with a young man for whose sensitivity and intellect I have great respect.

I met Svetoslav shortly after he had finished a year in an American university as an exchange student. We soon discovered that we had a great deal in common. Logically enough, we could discuss many things with each other far more frankly and successfully than with most of our own countrymen.

We had coffee some days before my departure. As we took our seats in one of the few establishments where privacy in public was possible, he got to the point of our meeting: "All right, man, what's your final, total, overall impression? What kind of 'Truth' about Russia will your first book promise? *The Ugly Truth, Truth and Hope, The Great Unvarnished Truth?* You've got to have some truth, but the rest is up to you. What do you say, man?" (We were speaking Russian, but Slava had fallen in love with "man" during his American adventure, and he used it as a kind of catchall punctuation.)

I told him what he wanted to hear—that I wasn't planning any books—and then threw the question back at him. What did he, after some time to reflect, think of America and the Americans?

His first, joking answer—"America's bourgeois society is rotting, but what a way to rot!"—was followed by a reflective pause. "It's quite a shock, you know. America, I mean. Even for someone who believed the fantastic stories that people tell about your standard of living. It reminded me of my first orange. You see, I grew up in Siberia, and what with the war and so on, I never ate an orange until 1948. Oh, I knew about oranges, I read about them, even saw them from time to time. But when my mother gave me my first orange on my thirteenth birthday, when I tasted it, smelled it, squeezed its fragrant, oily skin in my fingers, that was quite a shock. And it was that orange, and that shock, which came into my mind after I spent my first whole day in New York. I had kept my orange peels for a whole year. Every once in a while I would twist one and squeeze a bit of oil from it to remind me of oranges. The fragrance would stay on my fingers for a whole day. . . . I don't need anything to remind me of America.

"But the shock does wear off. Only a fool can gape forever at the 'superness.' And the thing that makes you look beyond the supermarket, makes you pause to think what the superhighway means or doesn't mean, is the fact that, with all the super this and super that, there is no superman. When you apply the old subversive trick of *mutare mutanda,* you arrive at the conclusion that we're all pretty much alike. And I didn't have to go to America to learn that, I guess.

"But I did have to go to America to learn how few Americans are willing to accept this proposition. As a matter of fact, if I had to single out the most disturbing and disappointing discovery I made about Americans, I would mention your cockiness and inability, or unwillingness, to examine other points of view. Not all of you believe in God, but you're all confident that if He exists, He's on your side.

"I felt this in a number of ways. The most surprising and distressing demonstration of this narrowness was the snide snickers and knowing smiles that broke out even in supposedly intelligent audiences whenever I tried to present even the simplest facts about my country.

"Another example, perhaps even more indicative of the superior attitude that I so detest, was the fact that almost every time I agreed with my audience, or seemed to be talking sense, they would decide that I was either unpatriotic, disaffected, or a deceitful person. 'You must not be a very good Communist if you talk like that.' If I talked the way *they* expected a Communist to talk, I *wouldn't* be a good Communist."

I interrupted his monologue, indicated that I agreed in general, for I had encountered similar reactions in his country, and asked him my pet question: what would he, what could we, *do* about it?

"I don't know. But I do know that trying to change each other will get us nowhere. And you, or I, probably won't be much good as diplomats. The best thing for us to do is to stay home and do whatever we can to fight ignorance, hypocrisy, and Salinger's *lipa** with the extra courage, humility, and patience that we have acquired abroad. You do your job, I'll do mine."

This gave me an opportunity to ask him a question that I had been reluctant to raise. Why had he, on his return from America, taken an appointment in the very orthodox current affairs department of the institute in which he worked rather than in one of the more liberal sections?

"We're not going to get anywhere by sitting in the strongholds that we've already won, carping and giving interviews to *Time* magazine. There is too much that can only be done from within, from the flanks. We've a new constitution to write, for example, and every word will have to be taken in battle. Those battles will be fought on the inside—that's where we need the good men."

Coming into Idlewild, this time, was a bit special. "Breathes there a man . . . ?" The color, the clean, the efficiency . . . I was at home. As I walked (it was 3:00 A.M.) through the deserted lounge of the International Arrivals Building, I came up behind an old Negro who was swish-swashing the already glimmering marble floor. I heard him singing, slowly, in time with the slip-slop of his mop, "Ah went tuh see duh gypsy, tuh get mah foatune telled . . ."

I felt an impulse to speak to him, to tell him his fortune, but I did not know what to say.

---

* *Lipa* means "falsehood, sham." It was Holden's attitude about "stuff that's phony" that most struck my acquaintances when *The Catcher in the Rye* was published in excellent Russian translation in 1961.

necessity

REUEL WILSON

Some Polish Impressions

The main impression of my first weeks in Cracow was one of noise and ceaseless bustle. For days on end I spent my time looking for an apartment (I had to get away from the cacophonous dormitories), registering with the university, and negotiating with the Polish student association that was in charge of my visit, a student exchange between the National Students' Association in Philadelphia and the Polish government.

The dormitory to which I had been assigned was situated on the outskirts of the city, next to a meadow of such proportions that schoolboys playing soccer, groups of idle students, and herds of cows could all gather there comfortably on sunny afternoons. Like most Polish student houses, mine was a formless, gargantuan structure occupied by thousands of youngsters. I was amazed to see four or five students living in a room the size of a "single" in an American university dormitory. The lavatory facilities would be put to shame by a well-kept stable: the toilets were customarily

Reuel Wilson majored in Romance Languages at Harvard, from which he graduated in 1960. At present, he is getting his M.A. in Slavic from the University of California at Berkeley. He has had articles published in *Harper's Magazine* and elsewhere.

filled with lime and a residual layer of excrement; and except for a few hours in the afternoon, there was no hot water at all. The conditions were further aggravated by the primitive habits of a large percentage of students from the country. Of all the dormitories I saw, the only clean and comfortable one was the house for female pedagogical students in Warsaw.

However, what was particularly chaotic was the music and noise that resounded everywhere. Compulsive strains of American jazz records and the loud paging of students by a speaker fixed on the wall of my dormitory room (it took me a long time to find out that these ubiquitous machines, reminiscent of Orwell's *1984,* could be turned off) drove me out into the streets. But jazz also echoed from loudspeakers temporarily placed in the park that surrounds the main university building and from the official students' club in the main square. Even the *Knajpa* (Tavern) to which I went on my first evening in Cracow, a sordid bar-restaurant that was one of the most celebrated prewar eating places in Poland and, before that, just after the turn of the century, a meeting place for the "Young Poland" intellectuals, was full of raucous, drunken workers. Outside, as always in Cracow after ten, the streets were absolutely silent, almost sepulchral.

This contrast between the turmoil of the students and the city's tranquil and somber antiquity made itself felt quite early in my stay. I noticed everywhere that no group of young people stayed together very long. Personal relationships, including romantic attachments, seemed to be in a continual state of flux. Individuals wandered aimlessly from café table to café table, while within a given group the subject of conversation constantly changed. Although I heard many quips and jokes about the present regime (the Poles pride themselves on what they call "their right to grumble"), there were no outright political discussions. At first I thought that it might be my presence that impeded acquaintances from speaking freely, but after a few months I came to the conclusion that they were not really interested in politics. Their conversations were usually concerned with jazz, money, sports, and endless anecdotes called *kawaly* (literally meaning "a slice or piece of something"). Nearly all the funny stories of this genre had anti-Soviet overtones.

The students in general accept the present Gomulka regime as a *fait accompli*. Nearly all of them have been heavily influenced by Marxist dogma, at least to the extent of being suspicious of the West and of capitalism, and those who are heavily involved in party activities are quick to condemn the bourgeois decadence of America and Western Europe. Nonetheless, one notices an ill-concealed admiration for Western consumer goods, such as clothes and automobiles, and for the more modern art forms. This confusion of allegiances and admirations may partly account for the students' unwillingness to comment rationally and at length on politics, Poland, and the Cold War.

The older people, on the other hand, are often so anxious to talk about politics that they embarrass the foreign visitors. They are curious about Americans and their reaction to Poland in general, and fearful that we look down upon them scornfully. This attitude is probably a result of our government's reluctance to stand up for Poland after the war. Moreover, it is always the older generation that is ready to condemn the Soviet Union and criticize the inefficiency or totalitarian methods of their own government. Among the Polish youth the traditional hatred for Russia, "the giant of the North," has died down, or has at least been tempered with discretion. Since they see few alternatives to the present situation, the young people tend to have what they consider a more "realistic" attitude towards politics at home and abroad than their elders.

A young Pole's frame of reference consists of the terrible destruction wrought by the Nazis and the ensuing (if only superficial) classless society. The leveling that occurred in Poland as a result of the war and the introduction of a Communist state has made a university education more accessible to children from peasant families and has raised the average standard of living. The aristocracy has been dispossessed of its estates, and a noble family is fortunate today if it retains a few rooms in its former mansion. Young Poles thus have no inclination or incentive to observe the old forms and conventions. French, once widely spoken among educated Poles, has now been largely replaced by English, and the traditional loyalty towards France has become nonexistent among the younger generation. They admire instead the power and scientific achievements of the United States and Russia. But even were they interested in keeping up the old habits, they would not have the means to do it. Nearly everyone in the university receives a scholarship from the state, which seldom exceeds one thousand zloty a month—about fourteen dollars at the rate of legal exchange for Poles. How they supplement this sum remains unclear to me (the most lucrative ways are probably to work for the party or in the black market). The students must therefore dress informally, often in clothes of foreign manufacture that have been sent by their relatives abroad or obtained in private transactions.

One might expect that all these hardships would have turned the Poles into a sad and listless people. Very often the older people do describe the horrors of their imprisonment as though it was their duty to remind foreigners of the things they never experienced and could never understand. I thought at such times that my hosts' insistent demands for pity were due to derangements caused by sufferings in concentration camps. But after much experience I should say that the theme of Poland's sufferings at the hands of her hostile neighbors is common to all Poles. The young people, too, will speak constantly of war atrocities, especially to foreigners. In fact, the national feeling against the Germans often declares itself in the first moments of conversation: "You must go to see Auschwitz," the Pole says, and then goes on to enumerate Nazi atrocities, explaining that every family has lost at least one member to the Germans. Yet what impresses one almost immediately is the gaiety, patriotism, self-irony, and boastful bravery that characterize the Polish temperament. I was often taken aback by the combination of truculence and chauvinism that has been the inevitable result of hundreds of years of foreign domination, but the most articulate Poles are always able to temper their outbursts with a biting wit and a kind of romantic abandon.

The Polish students I met through the Students' Union in Cracow were in general boring, self-conscious, and anxious to please. Since Americans are popular in Poland, it was all I could do to resist my Polish contemporaries' insistences that I immediately join one or another of their groups or coteries. It was necessary to exercise the utmost discretion in choosing friends, for I discovered that unless you knew a person well, he was apt, on very short acquaintance, to besiege you with bizarre and impossible requests—such as getting him a job in America or arranging for him to receive a special type of eyeglass frame from Western Europe.

The favorite meeting place is the official Z.S.P. club café on the main square. The dingy interior of this establishment is pervaded by a stark phosphorescent light. The walls, covered with dreary modernistic designs, appear to be made of papier-mâché. The entertainment alternates between listless symposiums, at which "student leaders" mouth slogans of world Communism, and American-style record hops in which sweaty couples gyrate frenetically to the sound of rock and roll (they are probably dancing the twist today) played on a recently installed jukebox.

My feeling of discouragement because of the apparent deadness of Cracow student life was dispelled by the generosity and interest of almost everyone I met unofficially outside university circles. A Norwegian friend, sometime journalist and frequent visitor to Poland, introduced me to many artists and writers. I went often to their houses and was received with the greatest cordiality and patience (especially in view of the fact that I spoke ungrammatical and halting Polish during the first months). By virtue of being an American who was interested in the arts, I gained admittance to theatrical premières, art openings, and night clubs.

The young intellectuals and artistic people outside the university struck me by their seriousness, vivacity, and ambition. Few of them had finished their university education (which takes five years). Intelligent young people usually skip the long period of academic specialization that seems so necessary in America, and they are therefore forced out into the world and take on its responsibilities much sooner than do their American counterparts. Writers are published, painters exhibited, and actors perform in the best theaters while they are still in their very early twenties. One reason talented students so often leave the academic life is the impossibility of living on the student's meager stipend. Another is that the universities are stagnant, especially in the field of the humanities.

I found the work in history and literature very disappointing at the Jagiellonski University in Cracow. To begin with, the catalogue of courses, which was both costly and hard to obtain, contained no list of the times or places of lectures. It turned out that the overworked professors frequently cancelled their classes or simply failed to appear. Most of the lectures that I did attend were conducted in a perfunctory and lifeless manner, and it soon became evident that even the older and more respected professors thought it advisable to fill their lectures with Marxist jargon. History students sometimes ridiculed their instructors' simplified explanations of Polish history, but they had to be able to reproduce this dogma on examinations. Capitalism and feudalism became synonymous to the "activist" faculty members, and they repeated over and over that the peasants represented the most important force in all of Polish history. I noticed in literature courses that the professors tended either to approach a given subject from a purely theoretical viewpoint or to reduce it to a catalogue of dates and names. The texts themselves were seldom discussed. There seemed to be a complete lack of contact between the students and the faculty.

Perhaps the worst lecture I attended was given in a course in "Political Economics" (a euphemism for what was called Marx-Leninism in the days of Stalin). This course was abolished in 1956 but was reinstated in 1960 as a requisite for all humanities majors. I attended the first meeting out of curiosity, since foreigners, whose official status is that of auditors, are not required to take any courses in particular. In halting and feeble tones an aged professor endeavored to give a Marxist interpretation to intellectual history from Aristotle through the Middle Ages. During the lecture the students did nothing but giggle and draw caricatures of the lecturer.

Out of curiosity I also went to a few English classes and was surprised to find that, though the departments were sadly understaffed, their standards were very high. By their third year the students of English spoke quite fluently and had read a considerable amount in the original—much more, for example, than the average American undergraduate major in Russian has read in Russian. The only disquieting thing about the students of English whom I met in Cracow was that they showed an intense extracurricular interest in me. In fact, their importunity led me to suspect them of being prospective G.P.U. agents. A friend of mine, the only other American student in Cracow, was convinced that the English majors were reading his mail as a part-time job for the government. This possibility can't be entirely dismissed—our mail arrived well perused and somewhat imperfectly taped shut.

It is also interesting to note that Russian is an unpopular subject in Polish universities. It was my impression, moreover, that there were hardly any native speakers to teach it. Englishmen, Frenchmen, and Americans were, on the other hand, lecturing at Polish universities, mainly as a result of cultural exchanges and marriages.

Most of my days in Cracow were spent very much in the same way. Nearly every morning I went to the "Press Club," where it is possible to read the newspapers and periodicals of both Eastern and Western Europe. As a matter of fact, I was able to gain quicker and easier access to the New York *Herald Tribune,* the London *Times,* and *Le Monde* in Cracow than I can at this moment in California. Then I worked or attended classes until noon.

I usually lunched in one of the restaurants or *stolowki* (special dining rooms for students, teachers, etc.), near the university.

The fare was nearly always *barszcz* or another sort of vegetable soup, rye bread, and a piece of some kind of meat or fish. Pork chops, carp, or liver were always the best possibilities. These are invariably served with cabbage or potatoes, the two main staples of the Polish diet. Sometimes I ate at a large café on the main square where the décor dated from the era of Franz Josef. The gilt on the mirrors was peeling; the blue, velvet-covered chairs were caked with dust; and the glossy blue uniforms of the waitresses were full of spots. In a word, everything suggested easygoing, comfortable decadence. But my favorite eating place was the Dom Literatow (literally, "The House of Literary People"). During lunch hour this place is thronged with elderly Cracow literati, some of whom appear practically antediluvian. They mingle with young, rather haggard intellectuals and laughing school children in their blue uniforms. I once attended a party at this venerable institution at which there was dancing and a delightful homemade lemon vodka. Unlike the university, where there seemed to be a complete lack of contact between the professors and the students, the Dom Literatow was a natural and congenial meeting ground for young and old.

Afternoons I worked in my tiny room sporadically heated by a coal stove and separated by a thin partition from my landlord's apartment. The atmosphere was always clammy, since the sun's rays only reached the building during the early morning. My landlord, an aggressive and stingy petty bureaucrat of a rather harmless variety, and his wife, a motherly, nervous woman, were both absent from morning to late afternoon. My only companion during the day was their cat, a sorry-looking, aged beast who, despite the fact that she had been accidentally shut inside the stove by her master, still produced litters of kittens regularly. The hot water came from a coal heater that took skill and patience to kindle. Except for occasional visits from friends, a postman, a police spy, an electrician, or a carpenter (summoned by the landlord, who sometimes felt guilty on account of the disrepair of my room), my tranquillity was complete, and the conditions were ideal for studying.

During the evening I would often drop by the Piwnica ("cellar"), a bar patronized by the most Bohemian, though not the most pretentious, Cracovians. Every week they staged cabarets, song reviews, and dramatic recitations of some kind. This club was started in 1955, and it quickly gained a national reputation for the vitality of its clientele and the audacity of its political satires. After the political upheaval of 1956 the Piwnica, as well as the Students' Theater from Danzig, became symbols of Poland's newly gained freedom. They were publicized by the French press and quickly became known to actors and artists all over Europe.

Since that time, the Piwnica has continued to satirize Russian revolutionary songs, the regime, government work programs, Romanticism, and the twenties. One evening in 1957 a bunch of roses was thrown in through the tiny barred window opening onto the street. The donor, a total stranger, was carried downstairs into the club and regaled with vodka. (The vodka-drinking tradition is so strong among Poles that my friends often said they would rather lend someone money for vodka than for an ailing mother or other "good causes.")

Today, however, the roses of the Piwnica have faded; or perhaps they have stood too long in water. What seemed radical and new during the first few years of the political thaw has lost a great deal of its amusement value. The Piwnica impresarios have, furthermore, done little to renovate their parodies. In addition to their own loss of interest, the Piwnica has begun to suffer from government measures to curb mockeries of its institutions.* Nonetheless, I remember the audacity of a program one evening, and the confusion of a group of Russians and Czechs who were present. Glancing apprehensively at the enthusiastic, boisterous audience, the visitors, who were touring the local curiosities of Cracow, were subjected to merciless parodies of Soviet hymns

---

* While writing this in California, I learned that the authorities have closed the Piwnica. It will probably reopen, but without a cabaret.

(sung by a girl in a peignoir sitting before a mirror) and, to their horror, witnessed a transformation of bogus Russian pilots into Hungarian and Spanish dancers.

Although a spirit of satire persisted, the Piwnica became more somber. No more did the wedding parties or drunken festivities that used to *épater* the Cracow bourgeois overflow resoundingly into the antique city streets. All too often, drab student bands ground out dance tunes to groups of apathetic youths and garishly painted girls. The Friday night cabarets and song reviews attracted huge milling crowds, reminiscent of monster cocktail parties in Greenwich Village. On those occasions I met foreigners of every conceivable aspect and color: red-bearded Irishmen, consumptive French painters, East German newspapermen, left-wing Scandinavian neutralists, taciturn Africans, and even groups of Anglo-Saxon beatniks, speaking French.

Despite its somnolent atmosphere, Cracow has an enormous café life. Everyone is accustomed to meet at a café for coffee between the hours of six and eight, and the choices are unlimited. Each café, moreover, has a completely distinct character. Some are tiny, with only nine or ten tables; others can seat a hundred people. Some have a literary tradition—for example, the Literary Café, where there is an airy outdoors terrace on the second floor and a piano-player, whose repertoire consists of snatches of Chopin and sentimental songs of the twenties. Other cafés are frankly modern and their décors are far more extravagant than anything to be found on the Left Bank. The patrons are almost always elegantly dressed. In fact, it is difficult to believe that you are in a Communist country and that restaurants and cafés are owned, with a few exceptions, by the government.

Since Poles seldom entertain at home (most apartments are too small and sparsely furnished to receive many guests), their social life centers around these cafés, clubs, and other public meeting places. This does not seem to present difficulties, however, for there exists an inherent desire in the Polish temperament to meet often and publicly in large groups. An indispensable part of a Pole's social life is his *towarzystwo* ("company" or "society"). Their fondness for group activity* unfortunately poses an almost insuperable problem for Americans who wish to take out Polish girls. To ask a girl for a date almost automatically puts you in the position of the hero of a popular song during the fifties, "I Can Never Get Maggie Alone." Unlike the heroine of the song, who brings along only the members of her immediate family, Polish girls are accustomed to add to these an ex- or present boy friend, plus a horde of acquaintances. One of my American friends in Warsaw was once invited to a young lady's apartment, only to catch a glimpse of the mother hiding in the kitchen. It is a common occurrence for the woman of your dreams to invite all her friends to join her at a tête-à-tête that you have just proposed to her. Perhaps the fact that Polish girls act in this way is due to their prolonged life in the family (they live at home until marriage and frequently long afterwards), and perhaps it is a result of their natural gregariousness. In any case, despite the hindrances of the apartment shortage,† sexual activity among the young people does not seem to suffer. The Poles, however, spend little time on the long-drawn-out seduction ritual so dear to American college and high school students. They are more concerned with repeating or inventing witty anecdotes and stories that will amuse a large group of people.

The weather in Cracow is much like that of New England. In the spring it changes so quickly that rain and brilliant sunshine can alternate four times in a single day. Since the city is situated in a valley, dampness and mists are likely to prevail during the winter. The fall is monotonous and gray. The best time of year is late spring, when the streets are full of peasants' carts carrying flowers and fruits. Cherries, sour and sweet; strawberries, wild and cultivated; currants, gooseberries, radishes, and blue wild flowers are sold in the streets by old women and little children.

---

* I wonder if the Slavic fondness for orgies is not rooted in the fact that they simply have more fun in groups, and are quite bored alone.

† The movie *The Eighth Day of the Week,* taken from Marek Hlasko's novel by the same name, only slightly exaggerates the difficulties that arise from real postwar living conditions in Poland.

(Most of this is free enterprise, tolerated by the government.) Spring also brings hundreds of sunbathers, a few swimmers, and many kayak enthusiasts of all ages to the banks of the Vistula River. Little steamers, loudly broadcasting American popular songs, carry sightseers up to the ruined monastery at Tyniec.

Until the end of the sixteenth century, Cracow was the capital of Poland, and until the eighteenth, Polish kings were crowned at Wawel, the medieval-baroque castle that dominates the city. Today this castle, which consists of a large complex of connected buildings, is an awesome tomb, full of the remnants of Poland's past glories. Thousands of tourists come from all over Poland to visit Wawel, and from its parapets on a clear day you can follow the course of the Vistula until it vanishes in a blue haze. To the south you see the foothills of the Tatra Mountains, beyond which lie Czechoslovakia and Hungary. Only a few kilometers distant from the center of the city the white factories of Nowa Huta, the postwar Socialist city, are visible. One of the best theaters in Poland is located there—notable for its repertoire, direction, stage design, and competent acting. Looking to the north from Wawel, you see the "Kopiec Kosiciusko," an enormous mound covered by the ruins of Austrian fortifications. Beyond this eminence, where the legendary Polish king Krakus is supposedly buried, you can discern another mound in the far distance. Pilsudski, the anti-Bolshevik soldier and patriot who was virtual dictator from 1926 to 1935, has his heart entombed there.

Despite all its charms, Cracow is in many ways a cold, provincial town. I was delighted, therefore, to be able to visit Warsaw frequently. The tempo of life in Warsaw is fast, as in New York, and its inhabitants are lively, blasé, and sly. The capital is always full of foreigners—students, embassy personnel, tourists, etc.— who are eyed rather sourly by the local population. Recently West Coast beatniks have been making the Warsaw scene, too. An enterprising but aimless young foreigner from the West can usually talk the Ministry of Culture into giving him a scholarship. Almost any foreigner, to be sure, who manages to dramatize his typical national characteristics or eccentricities is bound to be popular in a country where everything that comes from abroad is viewed with a mixture of adulation and curiosity.

Many of our American students in Warsaw were from *Polonias* (Polish colonies in America). They arrived full of sentiments of loyalty towards their parents' and grandparents' fatherland—a Poland of folk songs, polkas, and colorful peasant costumes. Despite the American process of leveling, our democracy, and our competition, Polish Americans, even of the third or fourth generation, have preserved romantic and outdated images of an older and milder Poland. It was a considerable shock to the newly returned exiles, brought up on Kościusko, patriotic songs, and strict Catholicism, to find their speedy Warsaw contemporaries speaking a slang permeated with foreign words and dancing to the American rock-and-roll songs of two years ago. The Polish-American feels immediate sympathy for the peasants, whose manner of life has not changed significantly for hundreds of years. But the living conditions in country villages are hardly conducive to long visits: American guests are often obliged to drink straight "spiritus" (which is 96% alcohol) with their relatives, and then share a bed with several sturdy peasant women.

Like all our students in Poland, I had to adjust quickly to such aspects of Polish life as the unobtainability of consumer goods, a diet that consists mainly of fats and starches, unsanitary toilets, and the surveillance of the secret police. One of the first phrases that a foreigner hears is, "There is in general, but not at the moment." This phrase, slightly varied, also applies to official personages who are never in their offices.

Nowhere is it easy to cope with an inefficient and unfriendly government bureaucracy. Our students, furthermore, must learn the rules of discretion, *i.e.,* the art of seldom discussing politics or money as well as the rules of Polish politeness, which are more demanding than ours.

American students are wealthy by Polish standards. The monthly stipendium I received from my scholarship was four times greater than that of the average Polish undergraduate. An

American friend earned the epithet "Pan Luxus" (Mr. Luxury) from his Polish friends because he frequently patronized the three or four best restaurants in Warsaw. (The cost of a meal at the Bristol, which is the best hotel in Warsaw, seldom exceeds $1.50.) The words "American student" and "playboy" come to sound almost the same to the Polish ear, particularly since few people in the People's Democracy can afford restaurants or travel abroad. Thus the proud and sensitive Poles cannot help but feel humiliated by protracted intercourse with foreigners.

Most Poles cannot live adequately on the wages from one job; they are consequently obliged to take on a second and sometimes even a third. A lot of "combining" also goes on. The verb *kombinowac* describes the cooperation of several individuals in order to cheat the government and achieve such ends as more money, a passport, an apartment, foreign clothes, etc. *Kombinowac* is so frequently used in everyday speech that it has come, by extension, to mean simply "to borrow." Virtual prisoners of a political order that they distrust and sometimes despise, they are only sustained by their Polishness—a demonstrative, often obsessive preoccupation with the country and its historical plight.

Poles tend to accept superficial ideas about other countries because they are prevented from going abroad by lack of funds, the government, or a combination of both. America is frequently imagined as a Hollywood extravaganza of white Cadillacs, swimming pools, and pink plastic telephones. The French Fifth Republic is thought by many to be a Fascist state, perhaps on account of the wide dissemination of *Humanité,* the official organ of the French Communist Party. But the proximity of Soviet power, in conjunction with the post-1956 influx of Western consumer goods, newspapers, films, and books, has given the Poles a fairly sane and balanced political sense of their own situation. As for the students, they have a tendency to dismiss as propaganda everything they hear or read about the United States *or* the Soviet Union. At the time of the U-2 incident, for example, many were convinced that the whole thing was a ruse on the part of the Soviets, calculated to embarrass America.

Whatever his political opinions may be, the student who wants to get ahead quickly is more or less obliged to join the official Communist youth organizations. Nevertheless, although the new race of party strong men includes many students, real Communists in the all-out "we are building Socialism" sense are hard to find. Unlike their servile neighbors the Czechs, the Poles can, if they wish, openly voice their dissatisfaction with the government. Criticism of the regime is limited to conversation and to the theater; neither risks severe government reprisals. The universities, factories, and newspapers, however, are under strict government supervision. The system thus allows non-conformity in private conversation and to a large extent in the arts, but carefully curbs the possibilities for independent action; and the general reluctance on the part of students to discuss politics, even among themselves, reflects a general tendency to accept government decisions without argument. Although the students were a principal force in the upheaval of 1956, their energies have more recently been directed into demonstrations against the "War-Mongering, Capitalist-Imperialists."

Sometimes I imagine that the whole world of the future will consist of states similar to contemporary Poland. That is to say, we shall all inhabit a country where everyone will be free to denounce the government in his home, in a café, or in the theater; but because of the restrictions on freedom of choice, political ideas and events will become purely academic questions.

It is very fortunate that the Poles' charm, imagination, and loyalty to one another have saved them from a truly efficient form of dictatorship. I remember an anecdote told me shortly after my arrival in Poland, when I apprehensively inquired about the activities of the secret police. A Frenchman who was staying in a Warsaw hotel asked a Polish friend if there were any listening devices in his room. The friend replied, "Bien sûr qu'il-y-a des écouteurs partout, mais ils sont tous en panne." (Of course there are dictaphones everywhere, but they are all out of order.)

I hope that the dictaphones will never be repaired.

JANE O'REILLY JENCKS
AND CHRISTOPHER JENCKS

■ *ENGLAND*

The Lonely Queue

GRANTSMANSHIP

A new way of life, Grantsmanship, has become an established part of young American intellectuals' aspirations. Thousands of newly minted B.A.'s annually descend on the university towns (and later in the year migrate to the capitals) of Europe, armed with a passport and a grant averaging $1500–$2500 courtesy of such beneficent scholarships, foundations, and committees as Cecil Rhodes, William Fulbright, the Rotary Club, or their own college. These are most often not dedicated scholars. They do not come to Europe to further their vocation, but to escape it. They have usually won their fellowships by exhibiting some sort of diligence at their alma mater, but for this very reason they are often anxious for a brief respite. They have applied for fellowships

Christopher Jencks graduated from Harvard in 1958, where he also did graduate studies in sociology. He is currently an editor on *The New Republic* and is at work on a study of United States colleges. Jane O'Reilly Jencks graduated from Radcliffe in 1958 and has written for *Mademoiselle* and other magazines.

107

not, usually, because of driving ambition but because it is easier and less committal to get forms from the dean's office than to choose among the host of professional schools and corporation recruiters who offer pre-planned futures. Flight to Europe seems the only possible escape from parents' and friends' insistent query, "And what are you planning to do *now?*" Grant recipients have also been encouraged to take the fellowship route by their teachers and deans, who know that graduate fellowships are widely accepted by foundations and university bureaucrats as an index of their college's quality. (For a long time Reed College was known back East mainly because it had won proportionately more Rhodes Scholarships than any other American college.)

The fellowship application form usually asks for a transcript and two or three letters of recommendation. An impressive transcript helps, preferably with a liberal sprinkling of extra-curricular activities. Impressive letters help even more—either from a well-known university, or better still, from well-known faculty members. The application also asks for a short essay on what the applicant wants to do with his windfall of time and money. A great deal of time and inventive imagination go into the creation of these projects.

Successful applications have included a study of anarchists at Toulouse (a study that was promptly moved to Paris); a study of a minute point in Celtic syntax; and a grant to study the flute in Rome. Both the anarchists and the flute extracted the fealty promised them, but the Celts never won much serious attention.

We suspect the committees that approved these projects would not have been surprised, or especially disappointed, to discover this apparent dilettantism. The five-hundred word essay on the intended project usually functions only as a specimen of the applicant's ability to write prose and formulate ideas. If the various committees are more interested in plausibility than in possible contributions to human knowledge, one must wonder what their intentions are. From weary experience they know that few recent graduates will really devote their last year of freedom to Provençal poetry when there are so many other things to do in

France. They must pick their undergraduate applicants for what the grant will do for the student, not what the student will do for the grant, and hope for greater international understanding and a little education along the way.

The main criterion of selection is not a transcript of grades, or a project, but ultimately the professors' recommendations and interviews. The committees want the kind of student who has met and impressed the most influential professors at his own college, one who will not only make a good first impression but will make the most of his environment.

The majority of those cultivating the gentle art of Grantsmanship are wanderers. Usually unmarried and freed from financial worries for a year, these academic gypsies treat a fellowship as a year abroad rather than a year at the University of ———. They enroll in their chosen institution, but take up their time mainly with seeing the country they are living in, talking to the people, and either cultivating their American friends or not speaking to them at all. Having worked out an extremely favorable rate of exchange between the European principle of frequent short vacations and the American principle of occasional long ones (they take frequent long ones), they exist in a state of almost permanent travel.

Most of these wanderers learn quite a lot about Europe, even if they don't always master the subject they came to study. The very fact of living someplace for a long period of time makes learning *something* almost inevitable; even if they spend all their time in cafés reading local papers, they are likely to return to America with a heightened understanding of international differences. It takes a great deal of effort to stay abroad and make no contact whatsoever.

There are colonies of Americans, especially in Paris, who got away and never came back. They have gained enough perspective to realize that they don't want what America generally accepts as desirable, but they have not yet moved on out of the Grantsmanship class by discovering what they do want instead. They talk a great deal about what they want to do, but they very rarely do it.

They lead rather precarious lives, living on parents, on each other, or on the sale of New York *Herald Tribunes*. The windfall of a grant or an allowance sometimes supports two or three people; and in an extreme there are always other ways to live—like passport theft. The classic chronicle of this subspecies has been written: Elaine Dundy's *The Dud Avocado*.

Another category of Grantsmanship player is the Business Tripper. It includes such professional grants as the one given to an architect to tour Europe at the Guggenheim's expense in order to ripen his ideas on metropolitan planning. It also includes grants given to graduate students to complete their doctoral research. The diligent Ph.D. candidates usually feel that their visits have a well-defined purpose and are not a phase of life with a meaning they must discover. Like the professional man, the Ph.D. researcher is a "nine-to-five" visitor, who rarely finds his stay shattering, or even formative, although often pleasant and instructive. Nor do the proto-Ph.D.'s seem to win as many fellowships as might be expected. Many do not apply, for like doctors and lawyers they are worried about "wasting" precious time before they have "gotten established."

In addition to the gypsies and the business trippers, there are the Nice Young Married Couples. Whatever the theoretical purpose of their grant, they are really in Europe on a vacuum-packed, all-American holiday. Residents of an American ghetto, they live just as they would back in Forest Hills, buying pets and furniture and automobiles, signing up for housing projects, and even producing babies on the schedule they mapped out the night they got engaged. To them, a year in Europe is no different from four summers abroad, and they might just as well stay home for all the personal effect their emigration has on their habits, interests, or thoughts. The rare exceptions teach their children the local language and try to live by local standards. The worst acquire a PX card so that even their groceries will be thoroughly Americanized.

Less alarming than the Nice Young Married Couples, from the viewpoint of international good will, and more encouraging to those who support European fellowships, are the Academic Second Chancers. These are students for whom college proved the first escape from an oppressive home or neighborhood, the first opportunity to gain perspective as well as knowledge. The struggle for perspective, for maturity, or whatever, often becomes a full-time job, and formal studies suffer accordingly. With the increasing availability of fellowships even the late starter may get a chance to be a freshman all over again. We knew a Fulbright who had welcomed the chance to "get organized" but found that he repeated all the mistakes he had made his freshman year in college—a discovery that so enhanced his sympathy for freshmen that he went straight into teaching. A Rhodes Scholar from the Midwest spent all four undergraduate years making sure he would win the Rhodes. When he got to Oxford, he finally felt free to make up for time lost in extracurricular activities by doing some serious studying. In principle, these second-chancer scholars might equally well have gotten their bearings in an American graduate school, but in fact they were not sure they wanted to go to graduate school, and if the year in Europe had not been available, they would probably have been lost to scholarship forever. Furthermore, it is sometimes hard to realize on an American campus that it is possible to be both adult and scholarly.

The fact that knowledge in a specific discipline is very rarely enlarged by an undergraduate fellowship does not make those fellowships a waste of the taxpayers' or the philanthropists' money. The Grand Tour was, and still is, a broadening experience, and living abroad for a substantial period, as a permanent foreigner, has additional advantages. In some Southern states one can have the experience of being a "foreigner" simply by moving from one county to another, but this is rarely either pleasant or broadening, for to be foreign in this context is to move down the social ladder. A genuine foreigner moves off the social ladder altogether. In Europe an American starts with a clean slate—no college transcript, no family background, no crowd of friends who can't be left behind. Europe is a second chance for many who are about to plunge irrevocably into an adult world that will afford no such luxuries, a world that will indelibly record everything from the organizations joined to the tempers lost. Europe becomes a place to escape the expectations that others have slowly accumulated about you, type-casting you for a role that neither encourages nor tests your emerging talents. In Europe, no one ever asks the awful American question, "What do you *do?*" If you don't like the past, and haven't yet imagined yourself into a future, a fellowship can be a very positive way to spend the hiatus. You can try on as many masks and poses as you please. The indifference of the natives is occasionally dispiriting, but the chance to observe, and think, and grow without having continually to make an effort, is no mean reward for occasional loneliness and homesickness.

THE LONELY QUEUE ITSELF

It was a shock to discover that England had a real physical existence. Neither of us had been to Europe before we set sail in the spring of 1960, and steaming for the first time past the Scilly Isles, we could imagine how Columbus must have felt when he finally came to what he supposed were the fabled Indies.

Like Columbus, we eventually discovered that we had not arrived in the land of our imagination after all. But this took some time. Certainly the first train ride from Southhampton to London, on a miniature railroad through half-size hills greener than we had ever seen, did nothing to dispel the illusion. Stirring our bitter British Railways tea and listening to the Americans across the aisle debate whether it was safe to drink the water—and to a stentorian Southern voice demanding to know why the waiter wouldn't take "good American dollars"—we began to suspect that the whole setting had been fabricated by elves.

The popular images of England rival the once-popular images of the land of Prester John, and we had absorbed them all. The most persistent came from the advertising pages of *The New Yorker*, that purveyor of elusive images, which continuously reminded us of the England that the Anglophile thinks he knows so well: Lady Daphne, her rose-petal complexion (by Max Factor) set off nicely by a Liberty blouse (designed in North Carolina), strolls toward Picadilly in the company of Lord Wickenham, handsomely mustached and smelling faintly of lavender. Their Rolls Royce, with liveried chauffeur, follows them down Regent Street, waiting for the moment when they will be ready to whisk down country lanes to an Olde Englishe Inn for a quick shot of Olde Englishe Ginn. The picture is indeed so charming that even the English half believe it. Only occasionally do the PR men make the slip that drives away nostalgic mists—as when one of them put an ad in *The New Yorker* for an English gin that showed the bottle deep in a snowbank with the cut line, "To find out how the English have kept cool for 200 years, take a glass, a few ice cubes, and a healthy shot of ————." Anyone who has spent twenty-four hours in England remembers—how could he forget?—first, that there are no ice cubes to be had (much less snow), and second, that the reason for this is that the English drink to keep warm, not to keep cool.

Our preconceptions about England were not limited to Madison Avenue's hedgerow-and-thatch-cottage projections of England's topography. We also suffered from the more basic Anglophilic assumption that England was just like America, only slightly better. "Better," of course, has different meanings for different sorts of Anglophiles. America's seaboard upper classes still believe that England has an established social hierarchy, in which everyone knows what is what and the elite doesn't have to devote its time to remaining in power but can instead worry about running the country properly. American conservatives believe in an England that has clung to its traditions better than has America, preserving country lanes, the working-class solidarity, a sense of individualistic conscience and craftsmanship, or simply a sense of scale and propriety (no skyscrapers, no tailfins, no supermarkets). American intellectuals of both the left and right look to England as the land in which culture is given its proper setting, the country of Oxford and Cambridge (despite everything, still accepted generally as the world's leading centers of humane scholarship, dispensing knowledge according to time-tested recipes), a country of profound thinkers, far-sighted politicians, sophisticated readers, and sober voters. A country, in short, that is truly civilized, and has socialized medicine as well.

We had also fallen into the Englishman's most civilized trap: we had accepted their abundant self-explanations. They are an inquisitive people; but being misanthropic, they write books, essays, pamphlets, and plays about what they are like instead of actually mixing with one another. No other country has been so roundly delineated by its inhabitants, and an injudicious selection among the reports had confirmed almost all of our preconceptions.

Despite these preconceptions, however, neither of us had believed that the Old World really existed across the Atlantic. When Harvard offered Christopher a grant to cover a year of work at the London School of Economics, we became winners in the game of Grantsmanship and joined the throng that makes up the newest flood of transatlantic migrations. The terms of the grant made clear that we were expected to "promote international understanding" as well as learn about the development of the academic profession in England, so we felt justified in our heavy emphasis on "understanding" and—as it turned out—our very slight acquaintance with the British donnish tradition.

For the first few weeks, when people persisted in acting, looking, and speaking like the people in English movies, we were more surprised than reassured. For a while, in an effort to heighten the verisimilitude, we too acquired umbrellas and accents, but eventually we gave up and, like most Americans, retreated into the cozy belief that the whole country was operating, however obliviously, for our observation.

The greatest virtue of a grant is the chance to *live* abroad. Hitting the high spots on a conducted tour is better than nothing, but for a real rearrangement of illusions nothing beats hitting the low, medium, and high spots on a day-to-day basis. Finding a flat was the most recurrently dismal low spot we had, although the educational value was immense. We must have spent a quarter of our time prowling through London, drinking tea with prospective landladies, promising never to have children, or to have several, that we loved dogs and/or cats or hated them, that we had no friends and never entertained, that we were not at all disturbed by the presence of the owner's Ming vases and would be perfectly happy to pay a forty-pound deposit as insurance against breakage. There are three tricks to finding an apartment in London: know someone and be lucky; pay an agent an exorbitant fee and be lucky; or buy the *Evening Standard* the minute it comes out at 10:30 in the morning from a newsstand next to a phone booth, begin dialing any possibility, and take anything that answers, sight unseen.

We must have looked at forty-five different flats in a year and a half, and the four we took were no better or worse than the others—we just happened to be lucky enough to get them. They were, however, classic examples of the kind of flats young couples live in. The first was a "bed-sitter," which existed in such perfect conditions that it might be called a pure bed-sitter. Once the back maid's room in a large and elegant flat, it had been transformed, along with three other rooms, by the current owners into what were fondly believed to be autonomous living quarters. It was a fairly large room, with one window looking out over the roof tops. In it were two beds ("divans" in England, "studio couches" in America), a large table, three stuffed chairs of a shape that we never saw anywhere else in the world—sort of overstuffed Vermont rockers—an object that could only have been a kitchen dresser, a very small electric hot plate, and a very small basin. There was also a gas fire and a large meter box, which was, as everyone told us, set to eat up shillings at the landlord's whim. The bath, of astonishing chartreuse porcelain, was somewhere down an icy hall and was liberally bedecked with someone else's luffa sponges. Almost every large flat in London has at least one bed-sitter set into it. They are such popular and economical places to live that there is even a cookbook out giving recipes for delicious three-course meals cooked over an electric plate. They are also the most depressing places in the world. Ours was livened up, and made even purer, by the fact that the owners charged a huge rental because they lived more or less in Chelsea (a good address is even more valuable in London than in New York), and that the man of the house spent the entire day roaring at his wife through a gigantic mustache. There was also a hand-operated lift and the ubiquitous Indian student, but these were individual delights, not to be found in every bed-sitter.

We then moved into a two-room flat near Regent's Park that cost less and had a full kitchen (even if it was put into a closet) and a bathroom. It was on the second floor of a house and resembled nothing so much as a shambles. Not one single leg on any piece of furniture remained except on the table, which regularly fell down. The décor consisted of lavish blue corduroy home-made slip-covers and South African brasses. The smell was of the ages. But it was warm and had a balcony, which looked into a garden of roses where the alcoholic landlady was usually stalking about searching for her pet turtle, who had a habit of visiting the next door tortoise because, as the landlady explained, "Even a tortoise needs companionship."

The next flat was wildly expensive, being right in the middle of Kensington, and was a complete floor on the top of an old house. There was no attempt to cut it off from the rest of the apartments, and everyone shared everyone else's life with a maximum of distaste. The walls ran with damp, the laundry got wetter instead of dryer when it was hung up, and there was no possible way to heat it. We lived there for four months, during which time there were five total (not consecutive) days of sunshine. It was furnished in English modern, which all looks as though it comes from Woolworth's, and we spent most of our time huddled two feet from the gas fire and slowly became completely indistinguishable from the mugs of warm, sweet, soothing tea we drank all day.

Finally we took an unfurnished flat, filled it with junk-shop gleanings that would have opened a full-bred antique store in New York, rented a stove and a refrigerator, and promptly decided to come back to America. It was a marvelous flat, with a seven-foot white marble fireplace and a toilet that was approached by a flight of six stairs. As with all our London toilets, we had to put up a sign giving the proper formula for successful flushing. (Each fixture has its own combination of pulls and patient pauses, and they must be learned like friends' telephone numbers.)

Day-to-day life in London turned out to be rather what we had expected. There was the cold, and the queues (which seem at times to have become the end rather than the means of civilizing England), and the endless hours spent "doing the shopping," a daily exercise involving two or three string bags and a slow advance through the butcher, the greengrocer, the dry goods store, the dairy, and possibly the ironmonger. All of our encounters with the basic English took place while doing the shopping. There was, for example, the lady who stood in the queue ahead of us and, when she arrived at the head of the line, began to dally over her decisions. (It was difficult for us to get used to the fact that in England, once you have waited ten minutes in line, you are entitled to make everyone else wait ten minutes, too.) She finally ordered two eggs, an eighth of a pound of cheese, and half a lamb kidney. (If you think we are exaggerating, ask yourself what *you* would buy on an old-age pension that has the purchasing power of $10-$12 a week.) As she loaded these into her basket, we stepped up and asked for a pound of chicken livers. She turned and demanded to know what we were going to do with all those chicken livers. How many cats did we have?

We found English suspicion of strange foreign customs not confined to chicken livers. As Americans, we indulged in all sorts of outlandish practices. We didn't confine our winter diet to brussel sprouts and cauliflower, as the English do, but instead indulged in that strange and loathsome practice—cooking frozen food. Not only that, but we rented a refrigerator to keep it in, which showed how well off we were, since the average Englishman thinks it wasteful to keep warm any room he's not sitting in, and so uses his whole kitchen—not to mention his halls, bedrooms, and bathrooms—as an icebox. Even if we hadn't rented a "fridge," we would have been considered well off—*all* Americans are rich. And it was difficult to argue that we were really two poor students living on one grant, for by English standards we were rich even then. When, finally, we began to live by English standards, it was euphoric to relax in the splendor of being rich for nine months.

The worst foreign custom we indulged in was expecting to have some sort of social contacts occasionally. Social life in England is, as everyone knows, exceedingly slow. Englishmen live as though they had several lives to spend approaching intimacy with other human beings, and being only transient visitors, we were rarely able to enter even the present life, much less subsequent incarnations. There were people who would have liked to see us, but since they saw even dear friends only four or five times a year, there was hardly time to exchange names. All Englishmen part with the phrase, "Do come and see us sometime," and the universal American reaction is teeth-gritting, since even a neophyte can tell that they mean, "It would be frightfully nice to see you again sometime, if it could possibly be arranged, but it can't." Sometimes our transiency was an advantage. For example, we met several young couples who—unlike most of the people in London—did not have a ready-made lifetime group of friends and were afraid to see too many people for fear of getting permanently involved. There is a real terror in England of being stuck with a friend for life. We met an artist in Italy who said, "Ah, you don't know what a terrible thing it is to realize you really don't like someone after twenty years. It is far better not to get involved at all." Twenty years of friendship did not seem to make up for the hideous moment of incompatibility. However, whenever we did meet some such lonely couple, we were so put off by the regular pattern of English social life that we never saw them again; we didn't know what the proper steps were, and we were sure we would give offense by not following them.

Parties are sometimes quite gay, the kind that could easily be transplanted to New York or San Francisco, but somehow in London they take on a special character—as though they were something outside the ordinary expected range of human behavior rather than an effort to mix people up with an expectation of continuance. There is the gay young Chelsea set, chiefly remarkable for their allowances and ability to find places to go dancing. They are strongly reminiscent of the early Waugh; and, since so little else is nowadays, they are regarded with affection by the general press. Then there is the "bright young somebodies set," which we managed to crash a few times, though we felt distinctly dim. These people are the embryonic intellectual establishment, and no one ever suggested that they rose to fame entirely on the laurels of their elders. They have almost all been to Oxford or Cambridge, and those who haven't have been assimilated by grace. They know everyone and are so "in" that there is not even the possibility of another group ever forming to make them "out." Had we been "something"—preferably something who writes or is written about—we would have been accepted. However, we were in the anomalous position of being unknown students.

Theoretically, as students, we should have known some people from the London School of Economics. However, the building, which is tall and gray and drear in a tiny narrow street off Aldwych, depressed us so that we hardly ever went near it, and the only students we met were usually guests at a party somewhere—that in itself precluded ever seeing them again.

Usually, these parties are not gay at all. There are grim little dinners, where the conversation is always a rigid discussion of "things"—prices, rents, the difficulties of buying things in England, and the final admission of the exceptional quality of English weather. Then there is the ubiquitous sherry party, or rather—since one, as an American, is often segregated from the rest of the company—the ubiquitous sherry.

We were thus forced to resort to the unorganized amusements, such as theater, movies, and concerts, which were deliriously cheap, good, and abundant. But an unorganized ramble through London in search of pleasure has to end at midnight. The pubs close, the theaters close, the subway stops, and finally even Soho shuts down. One venerable gentleman told us, "I never go to town any more. It hasn't been any fun since the wars." One spring evening four of us made a work project out of finding something to do in London all night long. We had an art student along who claimed to know of all-night Jamaican jazz clubs and other exotic wonders, but they all turned out to be mythical; and she was finally forced to confess that for a real day of play she and her friends spent hours at the Leicester Square cartoon theater. We early exhausted the delights of late-night Fleet Street and the all-night Marble Arch barbecue and finally ended up at only three in the morning asking a policeman if he thought we should fly to Paris for the rest of the night. He said, "I don't know, sir, it all depends. Do you want to?"

Although the physical and social amenities of English life took a little adjusting to, we adapted very quickly to the cultural world—the paradise so long seen from afar. Piles of Penguin books began to clutter our tables and then stack up under the beds, until we finally got an apartment with a bookshelf. The literary arguments of the day held us in their grip, and we followed every quarrel in the pages of the *Observer* as if the participants were all personal friends of ours. Perhaps this was because the participants *are* all personal friends of one another, and the whole tone of literary debate is that of a big family reunion—or feud. A literary establishment is not, of course, unique to England. What is extraordinary is that, despite being inbred and self-perpetuating, despite confining its attention to the English upper-middle class and especially to its problems of communication and ennui, this literary elite draws a large part of the nation into its orbit. After a few months, when we had eagerly devoured the complete works of Kingsley Amis, Angus Wilson, Nancy Mitford, Iris Murdoch, and Doris Lessing, we began to feel that inbreeding had gone much too far and that unconscious plagiarism is a major problem of the London literary life. The final moment of disillusionment came when we read Murdoch's *Under the Net* and Waugh's *Vile Bodies* in two days, and they both seemed to be the same book.

Every morning culture came to us neatly printed in the pages of the *Manchester Guardian*. Involvement is so easy in London that we didn't even have to try to be "up"; all we had to do was breathe to be able to say knowingly, "One gets awfully tired of hearing Beethoven all the time," or to put down Ionesco as whimsical and superficial or to admit that Bergman was exciting a widening circle of yawns. It took a while to realize that the English interest in culture is livelier than the culture it is so interested in. And it was only when we heard a Fulbright, formerly the possessor of some literary discrimination, proclaim from the midst of his Penguin Library that Nancy Mitford was the greatest living novelist that we were brought up sharp and began to notice the regional flexibility of our own judgments.

It came as a great shock to us, the visiting Americans who had headed for the Isles of Culture, to discover our English counterparts who wanted to head for America. They were not, of course, like the nineteenth-century emigrants who saw in America a place to become rich and respectable. They didn't want to become Americans; they simply wanted to visit America. A recent poll by the *Observer* showed America second only to Greece as the place readers would most like to visit. A majority of those we met had gratified this impulse or were planning to do so in the immediate future. Many were hoping to study in American universities, which they imagined free from the academic rigidities and snobberies of English institutions. Others were writers, painters, journalists, or simply prospective tourists, who saw America as the wave of the future and wanted to know what it was going to be like.

There is no comparable curiosity, so far as we could discover, about any other country. A few unnationalist Englishmen would like to see England emulate Sweden, becoming an enlightened welfare state shorn of empire and outside the Cold War arena, but few are excited enough about the prospect to know or care what Sweden is really like or to visit Scandinavia. Tories are more likely to imagine that British destiny lies, as Winston Churchill has long argued, in a united Europe. Yet while every Englishman is eager to visit the Common Market countries, few really care what those countries are like socially and politically. Italy is charming and sunny, full of architectural and artistic wonders, but hardly a model for English development—at least in English eyes. Nor does France excite much admiration. Even in economic terms the English are not yet really impressed by the Common Market countries, although if present growth rates continue, their standard of living may soon surpass Britain's.

The ties with Europe seem at times mainly nostalgic. The English throng to Italy to conjure up the Romans, with whom their classical education and their imperial ambitions long taught them to identify. Pessimistic high Tories still seem to persist in identifying with the Romans, their last embattled legions facing the barbarians from both East and West. But perhaps Greece now ranks high on the list because the new realities of world power make many Britons want to identify with the Greeks, the civilizing influence in a world now dominated by the American Rome.

Because they still think in terms of classical centuries instead of modern decades, the English have had trouble coming to terms with their American future, even when they recognize it. If they look at advertisements in *The New Yorker,* as many sophisticates do, their vision of America will be as fantastic as our vision of England was before arrival. Mrs. America, an angular woman with sapphire eyebrows, is escorted through a glittering doorway by Mr. America, a graying millionaire. Both are, presumably, stifling—he in his vicuna coat, and she in her mink. To cool off, they drive down the fantastic highways along the Hudson River in his white cadillac convertible, top down and the George Washington Bridge in the background, to the nearest Anglo-Saxon country club, where they take a quick dip in the champagne-filled swimming pool.

If they actually read *The New Yorker* (they are usually the same sort of people who read the *New Statesman* here—mainly for amusement value) or countless other magazines and books, they get a slightly different picture. America emerges large, crass, and vulgar from the John O'Hara short stories and from the endlessly snippy comments of trouble-shooting New York intellectuals riding herd on their country cousins from Texas and the other hinterlands. From images gleaned from international myth-ology they believe that America has no traditions and, even worse, no standards. Chaos reigns. Nobody knows who he is or what is expected of him. The crime rate is shocking, police brutality com-mon, and political graft taken for granted. What we call "educa-tion" is a mixture of psychoanalytic hokum and academic ab-surdity, turning out half-developed minds and—much worse than the ignorance itself—disguising them as "university graduates." But first, last, and always, America is rich; although of course the poor are abominably treated in a country that has no socialized medicine and little publicly subsidized housing.

All this would be forgivable if America were Italy—merely an exotic foreign nation. But to most Englishmen America is also the residual legatee of the Anglo-Saxon tradition. If America is a botch, this is regarded not as just a failure of transplanted English institutions but as a reason to expect native English insti-tutions to fail in the same ways in the foreseeable future. Most Englishmen sense, more or less bitterly, that what they call "Americanization" is not really the result of some sinister cabal of American capitalists or cultural imperialists but rather an in-digenous outgrowth of British life, which can only be redirected, not stopped. It is, in simplest terms, the result of putting large amounts of money in the hands of what some Englishmen still call "the lower orders"; the result, that is, of unprecedented pros-perity, which not even the highest Tory has the courage to oppose.

To many of the young Englishmen we met, this egalitarian trend, this liberation of desire through wealth, is not altogether distasteful. Many aspects of American culture seem uncongenial or even immoral, just as they do to most American intellectuals, but as an abstract idea America still seems attractive. It is all very well, they think, for visiting Americans to be impressed by Britain's institutions and traditions, to extol a government that attracts the best brains in the nation and a culture that admires the most gifted writers, dramatists, poets, and so forth. "But," the young Englishmen often said, "the culture Americans admire is so dull. The politicians we elect are so timid, the scholarship we produce is so unimaginative. Americans may not know good writers from bad ones, but they turn out more good ones than England. They may not have a system calculated to reward the statesman and discourage the demagogue, but they are led by a Kennedy while Britain struggles under a Macmillan. They may not have universities properly devoted to higher learning, but the significant innovations in most academic disciplines have recently come from America more often than from England." There is, of course, the dark side of all this—commercial television, the McCarthy era, the scandal of the American high school. When he is resenting America, as he usually is, the British intellectual (like the American) will emphasize this dark side. But when the brighter side of "Americanization" occupies his mind, it is seen not as the importation of something foreign but simply as the logical extension of what he conceives to be the English tradition; then he calls it "progress" instead of "Americanization."

What is "progress" to some of the intellectuals is simply "barbarism" to a large part of the rest of the population. We had dinner one night with an Englishman who had made a tremendous fortune selling cheap, mass-produced, self-service meals to harried Londoners. His style of living was what one would expect, if one ever expected "gracious living" any more. We were greeted at the door by a butler whom we only briefly mistook for our host. We were offered twelve different kinds of cigarettes—the ultimate upper-class gesture—and what the English call "spirits" instead of the usual sherry. We naturally expected an evening of genteel culture, which, in the American inner ear at least, sounds identical with "the aristocracy."

The conversation turned quickly to our hosts' opinions on America. Standards in England were falling, the whole table agreed, and the Americans were at fault. Our hostess pointed out that girls were continually smoking; and we, noting that she was, too, worried a bit about our smoldering Silk Cut. Then there was the commercialism that currently infested English life—another American malady. We refrained from mentioning that prominent part our host had played in undermining English culinary standards by providing economy-minded office workers with cheap, foul food; but as the evening crashed on, we regretted our restraint. Roosevelt, it developed, had been a tool of Alger Hiss, which accounted for the destruction of the British Empire after the Second World War. Suez, on the other hand, was a diplomatic master stroke, which failed only because Dulles envied Eden his success. As for Nasser, he hardly counted. "Can you imagine," our host asked vehemently, "that *wog* cocking a snoot at Great Britain?" When we ventured to suggest that if Eden wanted Dulles' support, he should have consulted him in advance, the entire family demanded, "Why should he?" When we answered that Britain was no longer a great power, their response was equally unanimous: why didn't we go home if we didn't like it in England? We tried to explain that we liked Italy, too, and even Denmark, but by this time we were literally being shown the door. As it closed behind us, our hostess's final words were, "Next time you come into an English home, remember where you are."

There are, of course, less vehement forms of Tory anti-Americanism. Jane worked as secretary for an old-fashioned eccentric who must be among the last of a vanishing species. She was more mythical than real and seemed far better suited to the pages of *Mary Poppins* than to the real estate office she occupied in Knightsbridge. She *was* the agency, whose turnover seemed to be almost nil. She transacted about one piece of business a month, and after a few days in the office it was easy to see why. It was awash with Earl Gray tea, and inquiries were recorded mostly on the back of paper napkins, or on letterheads that were now serving as napkins. Filing was done by reaching into a drawer with both hands and throwing the contents in the air. She was, however, somehow connected with the Churchills (mainly, it seemed, by a medium, through whom she tried to dun her deceased cousins for favors); and evidently if you have a good name, it is possible to live in England simply by putting off creditors. Every afternoon her faithful secretary typed these off-putting letters, bought stamps two at a time to mail them, and was paid the princely sum of one pound a day. A timid complaint on the subject of wages brought the reply that all previous secretaries had worked an eight-hour day for the same sum. A further query of how anyone could live in London on five pounds a week (buying power $15-$20) was answered with a vague, "But, my dear, almost all my girls have some little allowance. And *you* have a husband."

This lady was entranced with the idea of having "one of those dreadful Americans" working for her, and she said it with the best will in the world. She was not worried about "Americanization"—she had never even heard of it. Did we have dial phones in America? Could women vote in America? Would my husband possibly allow me to drive his car? (Not as funny as it sounds, since most English cars sit in the garage while the wife goes to do the shopping on the bus.) Which of the two gentlemen running for President was the most conservative (*i.e.,* the most Whig-like?)—Nixon, or . . . what was his name . . . that Irish one? In her book we were all colonials—a bit disgraced by not having come to help Churchill until 1941 (the rest of the dominions joined in right away, after all), but redeemed by the partnership of 1942–45—when she had been a WREN captain over a lot of American women and noticed that they smelled very peculiar. The job was most pleasant, in a way; and if it hadn't been for the quarrels over whether the heaters should be turned on when the thermometer read 50° or 45° and the warning of her medium that the American woman was "the evil tiger to be avoided," all might have gone well forever, despite a certain breakdown of "international understanding."

We did, however, find one group of people that were overwhelmingly pro-American. Jane spent two weeks in a 25-bed ward in Ladbroke Grove Hospital. Not only did this experience make us firm devotees of National Health and violent enemies of the AMA, but it also provided a concentrated group of all the people we had been struggling so hard to understand for a year and a half. Most of the patients were lower-class English from the Notting Hill Gate section of London, with some West Indians, Africans, and Indians. Almost all of them were absolutely wild about Americans—but especially so were the English. They loved to hear us talk, they liked to live with Americans, and the ones who lived near American Air Force bases like Ruislip even liked to marry them. The "Americanization" that they were so eager to acquire was precisely the "barbarism" that the upper classes loathe, both in England and America. The "telly," the cars, the clothes, the jukeboxes, and the gadgets that America exports were all the things these people—with their growing buying power— had been waiting for, and they held Americans personally responsible for the brave new beautiful world.

There were no signs that increased buying power and possessions had also effected a social revolution. Everyone still knew his place and was proud to be in it. No one even imagined changing places. America is the Land of Goodies, but England is the Land of Social Position, and the only person they were suspicious of was one poor woman, an outcast from the upper classes, who had somehow been brought to the hospital in an emergency and who was absolutely ignored until we asked people to talk to her. They were surprised that she might be lonesome and pleased to help— us. Because we were Americans, people would talk to us about their homes and money problems and even their families, but we never heard anyone mention these topics (except how attractive their children were) to anyone else. Every morning the chief sister went around the ward asking how everyone was. Despite the fact that this was absolutely the only chance to let anyone know how one was (the National Health Service, while admirable, is not exactly overstaffed), every single patient—except the unruly American—replied, "Very well, thank you." It simply never occurred to them to complain to a person of authority or to question something peculiar. The universal remark was, "I am sure there is some very good reason for it," despite the fact that this attitude kept one girl in bed for an extra week because the hospital had forgotten why she was there. The only comforting remark we ever heard was, "Come along, dearie, there are those worse off than you are." Such was the stuff of the British Empire.

Anti-Americanism is not confined to dinosaurs and dodoes. A

growing rather than a vanishing source is what is called "the new left." This is primarily a youth movement, marked by the usual beards and turtle-neck sweaters. It includes some of the most energetic and agile minds of the younger generation, minds to whom the whole Cold War seems an asinine vestige of nineteenth-century imperial politics, in which England, a supposedly progressive country, has somehow gotten entangled. The Americans are not, in this view, any worse than the Russians; but since they have so many more apologists in England than the Russians and are so much more willing to listen to British criticism, they are hit by brickbats.

There was, for example, a young Oxford undergraduate so fiercely earnest that we tried to joke about America instead of defending her. But with a heavy scowl and clenched teeth he cut us off, explaining, "I'm sorry, but politics are one thing I can't joke about." Forced to accept this somber view, we settled down to the serious business at hand. He had driven through Italy on holiday with a motor scooter bearing the legend *A Basso NATO*. He wore his "Campaign for Nuclear Disarmament" badge everywhere. Naturally he felt violently about Cuba. So did we; but as so often happens to Americans abroad, we were soon drawing on unexpected reserves of patriotism, demanding to know why he should expect America to behave any differently from other countries—like Russia in Hungary, Britain in Suez, India in Kashmir, and so forth. He didn't, of course, really expect any such thing. He just wanted to make debater's points against America, which is a relatively easy task, even in America. As he talked on, it became clear that in a certain sense he was not even interested in politics, at least insofar as politics has to do with the exercise of power. Compromise and the art of the possible were, to him, not only lamentable but inconceivable. He would have echoed the sentiment of trade union leader Frank Cousins, who explained recently that "the trouble with the Labor Party in this country (England) is that it's too interested in winning Tory votes." This may be a reasonable remark about a church, but not for a political coalition that has been out of office for a decade.

Our Oxford friend was, in essence, a political bohemian, whose first premise was the repulsiveness of the middle-class world. America was, of course, a prominent symbol of what he loathed, but so too were the majority of both the Conservative and the Labor parties in England. He disliked America because it was rich, vulgar, and seemingly insensitive to the dangers to which its policy of nuclear deterrence exposed the human race. He could, of course, have vented this hatred on the Tories, but the Tories were hardly an object commensurate with the scale of the world's infection. The Tories might, after all, be wiped out at the next election, and clearly sin and danger would not. To blame them on "America" provided an explanation of sufficient magnitude for the world's maladies.

He was not very constructive, but he was typical. He knew all about economic conditions in Cuba, but it had never entered his head to study conditions somewhere else—like Pakistan. The world was going to hell, but he seemed to have few ideas on how to stop it, or even much desire to do so short of the immediate cessation of atomic tests. He was the sort of person we would have hoped to see shaking up the Establishment (the Establishment is well named: it will never be replaced and there are no alternatives; it can only be changed—slightly—from within) and presenting brave new plans for England's future. At the London School of Economics the majority of students are African and Indian, and they are so busy plotting revolutions back home that they rarely have a chance to talk to the English students. Even if they did, the effect would be slight; no one in England is particularly interested in revolution.

Instead of jumping at the chances for change and direction given by the Common Market dilemma and the current political ambiguity, the younger generation has burrowed its way deeper into the remnants of prewar established custom. Just like their American contemporaries, they grew up in the vacuum of postwar "temporary" adjustments, where nothing seemed quite real or permanent and the line was never drawn between reconstruction and progress. They are not sure who they are or what they want to be. An English novelist whom we met in Paris talked to us for three days about the appalling lack of direction in the younger generation in England, the "conscious nihilism," the shutting of the mind to the future and living simply from day to day. Yet at the end of his arguments, which were quite true, he said he was going back. When we asked why, he said, "Because I have a position in England." Since he meant a social position, and not a particularly grand one, we asked if he didn't think he could change it. He said, "No, I know my place, and that's where I belong." He, too, was choosing an old niche instead of a new identity.

What is it about this generally well-run island that creates such a widespread, albeit usually low-key, malaise among its young?

It would be an exaggeration to say that the trouble with the younger generation in England is that they live in a gerontocracy, but this is in some ways an illuminating exaggeration. Since the death of Keats and Shelley interest in the young has had little vogue in England. Even in the Victorian era, when industrialization and empire-building provided an ample arena for youthful daring and innovation, the public was more infatuated with the Gladstones than the Rhodeses. Today most Englishmen seem to accept the fact that "a nation of shopkeepers," which regards a parliamentary opposition and the spirit of compromise as its crown jewels, must habitually worship at the temple of moderate middle age. Our own impressions confirmed this. As tourists, we were continually struck by the inconspicuousness of English children. As journalists inured to hearing that every people under the sun, from Italian and Malay to German and American, are tainted with infantilism, we waited in vain for even a virulent Anglophobe to attack the English for their childishness. Senility was the common epithet. As amateur sociologists, we knew that the commonplace English virtues, from honesty and law-abidingness to courtesy and self-control, are all believed to require rigorous socialization of the young and a continuing emphasis on self-discipline. The Freudian revolution has done little to change this, and the English still regard a child as, fundamentally, "a little man." Youth, like food and sex, seems in England to be no more than a necessary preliminary to the real business of living, and few Englishmen seem to feel the nostalgia for their salad days so common among Americans.

This means that young English boys and girls are expected to grow up in a hurry. For an industrial people who have, overtly and covertly, created more leisure for themselves than almost any other people outside North America, the English keep their children extraordinarily busy. Toilet-trained at eighteen months, accomplished public speakers at three, reading in school at five, screened for middle-class or working-class careers at ten, and usually ready for full-time jobs or professional training at fifteen or sixteen, these youngsters seem, by American standards, laggard only in sex. Even parents who have enough money to keep their children on the dole more or less indefinitely seem anxious for them to put on the mantle of adulthood as soon as possible. While prosperous sixteen-year-old Americans are still dabbling in the high-school pond, their English counterparts are plunging into two years of sixth-form work that would challenge the typical American freshman or sophomore. By the time the Americans have gotten around to undergraduate life and perhaps a serious search for liberal education, the English are enrolling in university programs very nearly comparable to those of most American graduate schools.

Forced to make critical decisions that will shape their lives before they are old enough to understand the alternatives, most English children are easily pushed into whatever course their parents choose for them. In principle, of course, the middle-class child sent away to an Establishment boarding school at nine can, like George Orwell, refuse to join the ruling class when he grows up. But after ten years of immersion in Establishment culture, even an Orwell is alienated from his petit bourgeois parents and has nowhere to turn—except the world of down-and-out—if he rejects the Established life. Similarly, the working-class child who enters the grammar school at eleven may not, in the next five years, become a really middle-class sort; but unless he is quite adaptable, he will have alienated himself from the working-class neighborhood chums who went to the secondary modern schools. Many working-class parents sense the conflict that they are forcing upon their children and anticipate that if the schools succeed, their children will be alienated from them. Such parents may well be apathetic about getting their children into grammar school. But this complacency is on the wane in the working class and has long vanished among the middle classes. Some ambitious parents would rather have successful children to whom they can't talk than children who merely followed in mother and father's undistinguished footsteps. Many others do not want to lose their ties with their young. They only want to keep open as many futures for their children as possible, and they know this can only be done by sending the child to the best available schools. If the child does not attend a "prep school" at nine, his chances of getting into a "public school" at thirteen will be reduced. And if he doesn't get into a public school, his chances of a successful career in the Establishment will be slight. What middle-class parent, knowing this, has enough confidence in his own way of life and his own values, as against those built into the whole social structure, to keep his child at home and say, in effect, "What was good enough for us is good enough for you"? Those who have such assurance may be disappointed, for the child who is deliberately denied a chance to move up in the world may still be able to communicate with his family, but is likely to communicate only resentment.

One trouble with the young in England is that they haven't any real say in their own future. Moreover, their parents have to decide about their future when the children are too immature for their aptitudes and attitudes to be clear. How can you decide, looking at a nine-year-old son of a civil servant, whether he will want to become a barrister or a bank teller? No collection of teacher's reports and I.Q. scores really allows you to predict accurately whether the son of a coal miner is himself a potential coal miner (and belongs in a secondary modern school), or whether he is a potential engineer (and belongs in a grammar school). The child himself is even less fitted to make such decisions at this age than his parents. The result is inevitably a large number of wrong decisions, from the viewpoint both of a manpower-hungry society and of an ambitious or apathetic child.

English novels are full of stories about Midland boys fighting Establishment values at Cambridge but succumbing because, by the time they reached Cambridge and realized what it was all about, they had already been irrevocably cut off from their middle-class origins, friends, and family. Similarly, the working-class boys at provincial universities are often portrayed as "angry young men" enraged against the bourgeois values of the institutions they attend. But what can they do if, as is inevitably the case, they have already been de-proletarianized for seven years in grammar school before coming to a university and have only the vaguest idea what their old chums are feeling and doing—and no way to go back to them? In America these students would not start their climb up the institutional ladder (though they would start getting ready psychologically) until later—until they had some idea what it was all about. Their first decisions are in high school, when they decide whether or not to prepare for college, and the critical decision often comes when they decide at seventeen whether to attend college—and if so, what college. If they decide wrong at this age, they can still blame parents and teachers for not giving them good advice, but at least the decision is really their own.

Given their helplessness in dealing with the adult world, their commitment before reaching the age of reason to one or another social role, why isn't there more rebellion among the English young? The New Left, the Angry Young Men, the unilateral disarmers are, after all, only a tiny fraction of the English population—nothing in comparison with the fraction of American adolescents who respond to the antisocialism of beats, hipsters, and delinquents. One explanation is that the English system has so far worked so well that it doesn't occur to most youngsters to rebel. They take their fate for granted, and this is, at least in large part, because they foresee it so clearly. In a society whose ethnic, religious, and regional differentiation is inconsequential by American standards, the ability to foresee one's job is nearly sufficient to make one's whole course and way of life predictable. Since most English teen-agers realize that the great majority of jobs are, even at that age, already closed to them, they rarely experience what American psychiatrists have learned to call the "identity crisis." The prevalence of male teachers in secondary school also makes it easier for English than American boys to identify with the adult world. Whereas the American boy equates intellectuality and respectability with the effeminacy of his schoolmistress, the English boy fresh from an all-male school may go too far in the other direction, assuming that serious ideas and responsibilities are a male monopoly and treating women as mere objects of sexual exploitation—if that. Girls, in turn, having no audience for femininity, often abandon it and become career girls in the feminist rather than the feminine sense.

English schools are, then, very literal alma maters, easing the transition from the family hearth to the industrial and bureaucratic crucible. They impose a rigorously impersonal curriculum on the student, which prepares him for the equally impersonal demands of his adult employers (although the curriculum often has nothing whatever to do with the intellectual substance of his adult work, since colonial administrators study classics rather than anthropology, and budget officers similarly master philosophy rather than economics). Whether the subject matter is classics or moderns, humane or scientific, the teacher almost always assumes that the material has an objective existence and purpose beyond its effect on the student. In a very real sense, people exist to read Virgil, or Shakespeare, or physics, rather than these subjects existing to enlighten people. If the effect of the subjects on the students is considered at all—and it usually isn't—it is described as imposing "discipline." There is no "American" talk about "meeting needs," gratifying childish curiosity, or liberating adolescent imaginations. These things may happen, but it is up to the student; the teacher's only responsibility is to the subject matter. The result, as in Mandarin China, nineteenth-century

Prussia, and modern Russia, is that the impersonal curriculum develops a symbiotic relationship with bureaucracy. Men trained in this fashion seek office jobs, and then reorganize their offices so that only people who share their esoteric knowledge will sit at the conference table with them. This, of course, leads to a further depersonalization of the curriculum, whose main purpose may become passing a Civil Service examination. This is not, of course, the whole story in England, but it is an important part of the picture.

The school is a stepparent in the social sense, too, but in this realm it is far from impersonal. It is frankly paternal rather than fraternal, and as a result it may achieve closer ties between students and teachers than is possible in America. After all, a teacher cannot really be a teen-ager's "buddy," no matter how eager and accommodating he may be, but he can be an ersatz parent, even when—or perhaps especially when—he is acting as the Platonic Guardian of the Establishment (if he is in a public school) or of the middle class (if he is in a grammar school). But the major achievement—or disgrace, depending on the viewpoint—of the English schools is not the relationship between teachers and pupils but the relationship between pupil and pupil. As in America, the "peer group" is of tremendous importance. But there is a stratification within the student body, a self-sustaining hierarchy and order, which is mirrored throughout English adult society. The symbol of this order is the fagging system; and it was this system, rather than Cicero's orations, which built the British Empire. If you remember that fagging is intended mainly to benefit the fag rather than the prefect, you will not be seriously misled if you imagine the nineteenth-century empire as an attempt to turn the whole globe into a vast public-school system.

However, perhaps we are getting the matter backwards. Perhaps it would be more instructive to describe the schools as a device for "taking up the grown man's burden" and civilizing the underdeveloped republic of adolescence. It is certainly notable that English teachers are as scornful of psychology as English colonialists of anthropology (although it would be hard to say that either took their cue from the other). These "scientific" approaches to one's charges are thought to breed too much sympathy with the immature and thus reduce pressure to grow up psychologically or sociologically. An American doesn't much care about this danger because his main preoccupation is not helping people but making them like him. He wants a sympathetic bond, because his aim is affection, not admiration. (Perhaps it would be more accurate to say that he wants admiration, too, but that he values it only if it is overtly and continually expressed, which it is only if coupled with affection.) Why the English care so little for the affection of their children or their colonials is hard to say. Perhaps, being the most articulate of the world's people, they have little capacity for communication or sympathy with those who don't "speak the language" and so really don't know what children, foreigners, or "the lower orders" feel about them. But they do know whether these groups admire them, because they can see how much they are emulated. Perhaps in their mind emulation is enough. Perhaps they are still complacent enough about the English Way of Life to assume that if foreigners stop taking bribes and establish a parliamentary opposition, if children learn to speak correctly and not to cheat at rugger, then self-respect, self-satisfaction, and perhaps even happiness will automatically follow.

This sort of unempathic approach to the young may be essential to maintaining the accelerated timetable for growing up that keeps English society so stable. But it is also responsible, or so we thought, for much of the malaise of English life. The possibility that the young might want to transform the present social structure, the possibility that a well-run society ought to make this easy for them, most of all the possibility that society should adapt to the whims of its citizens instead of the other way round, all go unrecognized. In a broader sense, what is missing from English life is anything comparable to the American Dream, any New Jerusalem to build in England's Green and Pleasant Land. The Welfare State was supposed to be such an utopia, but it has never come to fruition; something in the English national character has perverted the dream of making the poor rich and comfortable into a dream of making the rich poor and miserable. The Labor Party is madder about the reduction of the "surtax" on the rich than about the scandalously low old-age pensions or the absurd lack of economic growth. The Welfare State has, in Angus Wilson's phrase, become the Opportunity State, in which most people are doomed to be poor but, at least ideally, everyone will have an equally small opportunity to become rich. There are signs that the same thing may be happening in America, but it has not happened yet; and it was pleasant to return to a country where the future is still an open book, where no dream seems altogether unrealistic, and where no life story is altogether incredible or impossible. Yet perhaps we should not treasure this restlessness too much; it is this feeling of having unfinished business, this readiness to go for broke because life is short and one can never count on leaving anything behind in America's anarchic fluidity, that may yet bring an end not only to the American experiment but to the human experiment as well. It is difficult to imagine the English ever being stampeded into a nuclear holocaust.

SMITH HEMPSTONE

■ *KENYA*

An Expatriate in Africa

I was a child of turmoil and change, born in the crash year of 1929. As the grandson of a newspaper publisher and the son of a naval officer, it was in the nature of things that I should have had few doubts, either about myself or about the world into which I was born. Nonetheless the worm of doubt was there.

It required my dispatch to a military school at the age of fourteen, where it soon became obvious that I was unpromising material for the military career for which I was intended. Despite a streak of unrepentant romanticism, I was fundamentally skeptical—quite a different thing from cynical—and this trait of character was further nurtured in a Southern Episcopalian university. What brought it to full flower was my stint with the Marine Corps in Korea, when I discovered that all those who wore the fouled anchor were neither necessarily brave nor honorable.

Like, I suspect, many young soldiers, I had not expected to

Smith Hempstone has written two books on Africa. The first, *Africa—Angry Young Giant,* was published in 1961; the second, *Katanga,* came out in 1962. He is a correspondent for the Chicago *Daily News* and a contributor to the *Saturday Evening Post.*

survive the initial test of battle, so that returning to civilian life two years later not only alive but unscarred came as rather a surprise to me, an unsuspected eventuality with which I thought I would never have to contend. After giving myself up to the animal joys of being alive, I went through a whole series of newspaper and magazine jobs, which I obtained through the kindness of friends or the intercession of my family, with an interim period in New York during which I persuaded myself that I was preparing to write the Great American Novel (an euphemism for leading the *dolce vita*).

By the age of twenty-six I had gotten married and had behind me a relatively wide (if not extensive) experience of work in the American newspaper business—in Charlotte, North Carolina; Kentucky; and Washington, D.C. I had traveled fairly extensively for one of my age through Japan, Western Europe, and Central America. My future, if only because of family connections, was secure. I belonged to the right clubs, knew the right people, and could, with reason, look forward to an interesting and remunerative career.

Yet I was strangely but violently discontented. The worm was still with me; there was no balm in Gilead. It would be easy to say that the source of this discontent was the nature of upper middle-class life in the last half of the 1950's. But I did not think this life was corrupt, fundamentally evil, or even senseless, although I suspected it was some of these. All I knew was that it bored me stiff. All around me were my friends and classmates, male and female. They were good people, and I valued their friendship; but something—young parenthood or the slow climb up the corporate ladder (with the reasonable assurance of ultimate success)—was hardening their arteries, sensual, intellectual, and moral. It was bad enough to watch this; it was even worse when the realization came to me one day that I was not only a spectator but a participant: the corruption of the dream was taking place within me as well as around me.

I was not aware of the full dimensions of my discontent. I only knew that, much as I loved my family, my friends, and my city (and I did love them), it was necessary for my wife Kitty, and myself to leave them. I had to leave not only them but the me which had been under construction for twenty-six years. To do this, I was wise enough to know, required a complete divorce from not only my city and my country but from the society that had made them and me. I wanted to test my beliefs and doubts in a new context, within an alien framework. And so (after a stroke of luck under which I was able to obtain a liberal scholarship) I came with my wife to Africa.

I had no real plans. I did not know what I wanted; I only knew what I rejected. And I suspected that in Africa—where I imagined no laws applied—I might find a clean slate upon which to write, one upon which I could work out a valid thesis not only for myself but for others like me, the discontented of a generation of plenty.

We flew into Africa at Khartoum on November 8, 1956, the Nile of the Caesars and the Ptolemys wriggling like a silver snake across the warm, midnight sands of the Sahara beneath us. Africa was to be our home until May of 1959. We were to return to this ancient and ageless continent, in response to the tug that all who once have lived here know, for the year 1960, leave it again, and finally return again in April of 1961.

None of this, of course, did we know as we stepped off the airplane into the sweltering darkness of that November night in Khartoum. We knew only that we had sufficient financial support to enable us to travel and write in and about Africa for two years. After that, the future was as dark as Africa's black heart.

The terms of the fellowship that brought us to Africa required that I write a newsletter of unspecified length two or three times a month. These newsletters, which were reproduced and distributed to the friends of the foundation and to those interested in foreign affairs, were not for publication, hence one had the freedom to write completely honestly, a freedom few writers and fewer journalists ever know. There was no editing done in the offices of the foundation; the newsletters were reproduced exactly as they were written without comment of any sort.

Anything that interested one was considered to be a fit subject for a newsletter: history, geography, politics, economics, anthropology, sociology, medicine, religion, art, sports, or archaeology. The only limits were one's own knowledge and experience. Although I wrote about most of these subjects and about others, my background as a journalist and the phase of history through which Africa happened to be passing conspired to make my principal interest political. This was doubly so since the foundation not only allowed but encouraged its fellows to write occasionally for newspapers and magazines. This was by no means as easy in 1956, however, as it is today. No nation south of the Sahara, with the exceptions of Liberia and Ethiopia who had been self-governing for many years, had then achieved independence. The chaos of the Congo had yet to come. Africa was still firmly administered by the colonial powers and, if one was to believe one's editors and colleagues, not worth writing or reading about. My former employers in Washington took a fair percentage of my articles, and a few other newspapers occasionally bought my material. But Africa was very much a buyer's market in those days.

This was fortunate in at least one respect: it gave my wife and me plenty of time to get on with the job of trying to know the land and the people of Africa. I had very little information about the continent and its people and, I think, few prejudices. The information just was not available. The flood of books about Africa had not yet begun. There was virtually nothing about the French and Portuguese territories in English and very little more dealing with the British lands, with the exception of South Africa.

Insofar as prejudice was concerned, there had, of course, been ample opportunity for me to contract this in America. I was brought up as a white Protestant with territorial ties, such as they were, to the Southern border states. But I had no real regional prejudices. As a naval officer's son, my boyhood had been spent in and around naval stations; Washington, Annapolis, Newport (Rhode Island), and Coronado (California) were almost equally my home. My class prejudices had to a consider-able extent been counterbalanced both by my rebellious nature, which led me to reject that which was accepted by those around me, and by exposure to a number of liberal professors in college.

Thus I had, I think, few prejudices against Negroes. By the same token, I had known enough of them during my boyhood and as a young police reporter to have few illusions about Negroes as a group. I felt then, as I do now, that color was no reasonable basis upon which to evaluate a man's social or economic worth. On the other hand, I was no more prepared to accept all Negroes as my equal than I was to accept all whites. Equality before God and the law I saw as each man's inherent right; beyond that I felt it was up to each man to demonstrate his worth in a personal, social, and economic sense.

I had always wanted to know more about the Negro because I was somehow intuitively aware that the stock caricature that most of us accepted was not valid. This led me, in 1956, when I was still working for a Washington paper, to devote several weeks to learning about the realities and aspirations of Wash-ington's Negro community. I wrote a long series of articles on the subject; it was never published.

I would be the last to pretend that I felt completely at ease in the company of Negroes; I did not. There was the weight of generations of mutual prejudice, of embarrassment on the one hand and resentment on the other. I was interested in black men as people, not as symbols; I knew I had a lot to learn.

The Sudan was a good place in which to begin one's educa-tion. The first lesson was one that has application outside of Africa. It is that "race" is a purely subjective matter, conditioned by such factors as religion and personal attitudes, which them-selves are the product of history and environment. In the Sudan, for instance, most of the population has some black blood. Yet the people of the northern two-thirds of the country, although they may be black as tar, are not Negroes and regard the slightly darker people of the south with immense disdain. The difference is one of religion and of history. The northerners are Muslims.

Their Arab ancestors raided the south for centuries in search of the slaves whose blood now flows in the veins of most northerners. Yet because they are Muslims and because the black people of the south have historically been regarded as belonging to a lower caste, the people of the north, no matter how black they may be, regard themselves as Arabs. Since they do genuinely regard themselves in this light, they suffer from none of the inferiority complexes that afflict the Negro. Their attitude as to what constitutes a Negro has, in fact, been codified into law in South Africa, which most of us regard as being the most racist of all nations. In South Africa, a man who regards himself as white, associates with whites, and is accepted by them as white, legally *is* white, no matter what the genetic realities may be. This, of course, refers primarily to the less sharply defined line drawn between whites and people of mixed blood, not between whites and Bantus.

We discovered in Ethiopia, to which we flew from the Sudan, that this same attitude exists among the Amhara ruling class of that country, which privately detests the Negro—although it is good politics today for Ethiopia to stress its African-ness. The Amharic prejudice has ethnic rather than religious overtones. The Amharas are a straight-nosed, long-limbed people of mixed Semitic and Hamitic extraction. Although the fact that they belong to Africa's only indigenous Christian church further sets them apart from their Muslim and animist countrymen and neighbors, their feeling of superiority seems to stem primarily from the fact that these countrymen and neighbors are of darker stock. For an Ethiopian as for a northern Sudanese, the worst insult is to be called "black."

Thus we discovered that in Africa, as elsewhere in the world, prejudice is a fact of life that exists and cannot be legislated out of existence. Some prejudices amongst the Africans seem to have a background of logic, while others are completely illogical, or at least seem to us to be so. In any event, Africa taught us to investigate prejudice, not to ridicule it in people, since it seems to be a common fault in all men. It was certainly not a thing to be encouraged; on the other hand, it sometimes had to be accepted as a part of the human condition, just as avarice, lust, and greed are a part of that condition.

From Ethiopia, traveling now in a truck, which was to serve us for two and a half years before we sold it to a Syrian merchant in the Gambia, we went to Kenya and fell in love immediately with this breath-takingly beautiful, star-crossed land where we now make our home. Again, we did not know when we first saw Mt. Kenya's polished tooth of snow, which the Kikuyu know is the home of God, that we would make our home in its shadow. But we soon came to love its parched, sun-blasted plains, its cool, well-manicured highlands, its golden beaches slumping into the incredible jade of the Indian Ocean. There was an emptiness there, and a freedom. It struck a chord in us and we responded. It was part of what we had been looking for, although we had not known it: space, silence, and solitude. As urban Americans of the mid-twentieth century, we had been denied these gifts. Although privileged members of a privileged society, we had grown up cheek-by-jowl with other human beings. Under these circumstances we had never had the time or the opportunity to hunt, to fish, to travel lonely roads, to be separated from our own kind, to look into ourselves. These things were ours in Kenya. And things that were not ours we were able to share vicariously in Kenya: the satisfaction that comes to a man who lays his hands upon a piece of virgin bush and makes it into something real and productive; the joy of creating and changing and making something better, of seeing the results of one's labors on the face of the land. This was something we had never seen or known. It seemed somehow more worthy than the scaling of a corporate ladder.

In the course of the next two years my wife and I were to visit about thirty African countries. In each our task was the same simple yet overwhelming one: to learn about the land and the people and to write about them. Consequently, the methods that we used in each country were nearly always the same. By the time we reached a country, I had read and digested almost everything that had been written about it in English. As I have mentioned earlier, this was not the task six years ago that it would be today, since the body of literature then was so much smaller than it is now. Usually we had letters of introduction from people in the preceding country to those in the new country. We always looked up such people. They were invariably kind and helpful, and they usually passed us on to other people.

First, however, before looking up anybody, I spent about a week just getting the feel of a country, the smell of it. This I did by walking the streets of the principal city, looking at things and at people, eavesdropping on their conversations, noting their attitudes, studying their expressions. Then I would read the local papers for a few days from front to back to get an idea of the topics of concern to the local people and to compile a list of people of importance in the country. My next stop was usually the local American consulate. Since this was still the colonial era, embassies were few and far between. From the consulates I received a briefing on the political and economic condition of the country. The briefings varied widely in their perceptiveness. I never accepted what these officials told me as gospel but used the briefings as a point of departure whose validity I would later be in a better position to check. With the growing importance of Africa, the American diplomatic staff here has improved immeasurably in quality and multiplied many times in quantity in recent years. Briefings nowadays tend to be more intelligent than they were six years ago, although the very size of the embassies often seems to place a gulf between our diplomats and the local people, since there are now usually enough Americans in any African capital to create a self-contained society. Consequently, few diplomats have the intimate contact that they once had with the local people.

My next stop was usually the local government press officer. These officials invariably proved helpful in providing background material and in arranging introductions to government officials. As with American diplomats, however, I never relied upon them as more than a point of departure since they obviously had a line to sell. That, after all, was their job.

I then went directly, either with the help of the government press officer or on my own hook, to the people. Africans—black, white, and brown—usually were more than willing to talk to a foreigner interested in their country. Obviously each tried to put across a point of view that taken alone was not necessarily valid. But by assembling every possible point of view, one created a mosaic that had validity, and this was what I always tried to do.

I did not, of course, talk only to politicians but to priests, policemen, tribal chiefs, farmers, doctors, game wardens, businessmen, trade unionists, teachers, agricultural officers, administrators, soldiers, miners, housewives, and fishermen. I did a lot of listening and very little talking. When I did talk, it was in an attempt to provoke a reaction, to find out what somebody really felt about something. Eventually I came to certain conclusions about each country—conclusions based only partially on my own direct knowledge of it, rooted instead in what I had learned from a cross section of the people of the country. This, of course, was a time-consuming but fascinating process. Fortunately I had plenty of time. I never wrote a word about a country until I had been there at least a month. Then I set it down quickly before I had been there long enough to get emotionally involved in the various local controversies.

That was how I worked in each of the countries we visited between November of 1956 and May of 1959 (my grant had been extended for a third year). Having a car was of immense value. Those who travel around Africa by air, visiting only the continent's capitals and major cities, can never gain a true idea of the realities of Africa. Only through traveling by car can one appreciate the immensity of the continent, the harshness of the climate, the primitive level of development that the great mass of the people have attained. Nairobi is no more Kenya than New York is America; both are an aspect of their respective nations, nothing more.

I had decided to write a book about it all, and we spent the summer and fall of 1959 working on this, first in the Canary Islands, later in England, and finally in Holland. Although the book kept us very busy (my wife typed the manuscript and helped me in the organization of the material, as well as handling all the time-consuming administrative details that accompany life anywhere in the world), both of us were anxious to get back to Africa. We felt in Europe the same constricting press of humanity that had been such an important factor in bringing us to Africa from America in the first place. We longed for the space, silence, and solitude of Africa. And when we thought about Africa, we realized that we were thinking about Kenya. We knew then that we were hooked. On a raw December day in 1959 we sailed from Genoa for Mombasa, a fourth year's extension of the fellowship clutched exultantly in the fist of our hopes.

This was our first period of real residence in an African country. Although we had spent six months in Kenya in 1957 and had rented a house set amid Limuru's green fields of coffee, Kenya was then to us only a way station in our travels around Africa, one of many countries we would be visiting. This time we were coming to Kenya with the intention of living there for a year. Out of all Africa, we had chosen it as our temporary home. It made a difference in the way in which we looked at both the land and the people: if only in a peripheral sense, we were about to become a part of Kenya.

My work, too, was different from what it had been before. Although I continued to do occasional newsletters for the foundation and to write from time to time for the newspapers (beginning at this time an association with the Chicago *Daily News* that was to end in staff status), my primary purpose was to finish the book I had begun the previous summer in Europe. Consequently, it was neither necessary nor desirable that we live in Nairobi, the capital. Nairobi is a city, not without charm, of about 25,000 whites, 100,000 Indians, and perhaps 200,000 Africans. We had a number of friends of all races there, not a great many, but too many for one who was anxious to put in seventy hours a week on his writing. Nor had two and a half years of constant travel rid either of us of our wanderlust. We still liked to get out on safari as much as possible, to hunt, to fish, to photograph game, or just to look—to savor the luxury of being alone in a vast and beautiful land. It was clear, however, that if I was to make a sustained effort on the book, long safaris would be out of the question. Consequently, the solution appeared to be to live for short periods of time in Kenya's various regions. This would isolate us from the distractions of Nairobi (we were beginning to feel about Nairobi a little the way we had about Washington), enable us to familiarize ourselves to a degree with various parts of Kenya, and provide us with convenient jumping-off spots for safaris into the bush.

The first place that we decided to settle was the Nanyuki area. Nanyuki is a one-street town set on Mount Kenya's western slope, on the fringes of the Kikuyu and Meru reserves, It was a bad spot during the Mau Mau emergency, which began in 1952 and did not officially end until 1960—although the really bad time was over by 1955. Only a few administrators, the Indian shopkeepers and a couple of thousand Africans live in Nanyuki. Its reason for existence is to serve the white farmers who live around it, and most of the townspeople themselves live on small-holdings a few miles away.

On one of these small-holdings at Timau fourteen miles north of Nanyuki we rented a three-room stone cottage from a formidable spinster who raised a little pyrethrum (a white daisy used in the manufacture of insecticides), ran a small dairy herd, and held down a full-time job in the offices of a retailer of farm machinery in Nanyuki. We paid this lady the grand sum of $28 per month for the cottage. Out back, separate from the cottage, was a kitchen with a wood-burning stove. There was no refrigerator, the flow of water stopped on occasions when the pump ceased to function, and the toilet frequently gave up the ghost.

We soon found, however, that all of the things we take for granted in America are by no means essential to one's well-being. At an altitude of nine thousand feet it was cold enough so that meat lasted two or three days without refrigeration. Milk, butter, and eggs were provided fresh daily by our landlady. Vegetables came from her garden. When we did want to preserve something for a few days or to have cold beer, we simply put it into a sack and dumped the sack into the ice-cold stream fifty yards below the cottage. Cold rather than heat was our biggest weather problem. Timau is perched on the edge of the forest, looking out over the Mugodogo Hills, and each evening the temperature drops into the forties. There was, of course, no furnace in the cottage and no electricity to provide power for heaters (there was a gasoline generator, but for reasons of economy it was turned on for only abut two hours per night). We had, however, fireplaces in both our bedroom and the other larger room. We bought from the local Indian *duka* a truckload of cedar logs, which gave off a fierce, sweet-smelling flame. With Batian and Nelion, Mount Kenya's twin peaks, glittering white in the icy moonlight and the cedar logs crackling, I worked on my book wrapped in a blanket and Kitty read by the flickering light of the kerosene lantern. Moreover, there were pink-fleshed brown trout dozing in the secret pools of the stream and buffalo snuffling in the forest clearings each morning. We were content.

It was at this time that Warutere came into our lives. We had had African servants when we were in Kenya in 1957, but they had been other people's servants whom we had taken on temporarily. We had no deep interest in them nor feeling of obligation toward them. Warutere, however, was different. He came to us on a permanent basis: we belonged to him and he to us in a feudal way, which imposed not only rights but obligations upon both parties. When he came to us, Warutere was about twenty-three and still unmarried. A Kikuyu from Karatina, he was the son of Kikuyu loyalists who had sent him to live among the Wakamba tribe during Mau Mau.

The Mau Mau emergency, in which 11,503 Kikuyu terrorists, 1,920 Kikuyu loyalists, 95 whites, and 29 Indians lost their lives, was officially declared over the month we moved to Timau. It had cost $150 million to suppress the insurrection, which was essentially an atavistic, anti-white, and anti-Christian tribal affair (only the Kikuyu tribe was involved), not a nationalist revolution. But Mau Mau was still a part of the atmosphere in Timau:

the security wire remained up around our little cottage, farmers still came to town with six-shooters on their hips, and there were oathings taking place in abandoned homesteads.

Warutere was a slight, cocoa-skinned youngster of about average height, a hard worker with a ready smile. But best of all, despite the settler assertion that Africans have no feeling for animals, he obviously was fond of our dog. Cholmondeley (pronounced "Chummly," of course) was a black ball of fuzz, half labrador, half springer spaniel, presented to us by Jackie Barrah, the game warden at Nanyuki, whom we had known since 1957. The four of us—Kitty, Warutere, Cholmondeley, and myself—were the Hempstone household.

That we had neither African nor Asian friends at Timau was a matter of circumstance and not design. It would have been possible to have such friends (although the local whites would certainly have ostracized one who did), but the question did not arise: there were, with the exception of the Sikh government doctor, no educated Africans or Asians in the area. As a general rule Asians, with the exception of small traders, confine themselves largely to Nairobi and Mombasa. The fortunes of the great Asian families such as the Pirbhais and the Ahameds are based on commerce and real estate, which demands their presence in the urban areas rather than the country. For their part educated Africans, both because they like city life and because the great political and business opportunities lie there, inevitably gravitate to Nairobi, Kisumu, Mombasa, or Nakuru.

Consequently, our friends at Timau were almost entirely white settlers or government officials: drunken old Harry, with the peacocks on his lawn and Nelian and Batian so clear in the distance that it looked as if you could reach out and touch them; "Groupie" Soden, the grounded R.A.F. eagle who flew refugees out of the Congo for eight days running, later to die of cancer; Peter Steinkamp, the stocky Afrikaner policeman who could tell by smelling an African whether or not he had eaten a stolen sheep; hulking, redheaded Ken Sutherland, a banker-turned-farmer; Sam Small, the Baltimore aristocrat ranching his scruffy cattle at the back of beyond; Piet van der Merwe, the animal trapper who had been deported from Indonesia; the Bartlett boys, each seemingly larger than the last, who farmed as a family unit like the Africans and have since left for Australia and a new life. There was nothing extraordinary about these people. What was extraordinary was the setting in which they found themselves. They were neither saints nor sinners. They worked hard, lived rough, and drank as much as the budget would stand. They were good, bluff friends. Few of them had any antipathy toward the Africans; but none of them had any illusions about what life would be like under an African government. All they wanted was a chance for themselves and their children. It was slowly beginning to dawn on them that they were not to have that chance, at least in Kenya. And the bitterness began.

From Timau we moved to Njoro, where we lived in a much larger and better four-room stone cottage next to the castle of the late Lord Egerton of Tatton. Lord Egerton, a somewhat eccentric bachelor (the castle contained a huge organ, and on the grounds was a croquet court overlooked by a small enclosed grandstand) had died in 1958 and left the heavily mortgaged estate to his manager, Hugh Coltart. Hugh was a red-faced, blue-eyed Scot with a tremendous zest for life who had come to Kenya as a boy of nineteen in 1911 with a shotgun and $140 in his pocket. I had met him in 1957 when writing a newsletter about the problems of Kenya's white yeoman farmers (Hugh owned a thousand acres of his own next to Lord Egerton's estate).

Our cottage looked across a great sweep of well-manicured lawn (although the castle was empty except for a caretaker) to rippling fields of golden wheat and corn and, beyond them, pastures studded with the bulky shapes of red poll cattle and, further on, the blue outline of Mau Summit, over which the lightning played.

Njoro was different country from Timau—fatter, richer, more intensely cultivated, more placid. And the people partook of the character of the land. They were, on the whole, skillful, hard-working, fairly prosperous, no-nonsense farmers, better read, perhaps, and more given to polo playing and country club golf than the settlers of northern Kenya. Gone was the rough, open-handed hospitality of Timau. Again we had no African or Asian friends in Njoro, because we were living on a white farm in the so-called White Highlands and one simply did not encounter Africans other than farm laborers or Asians other than storekeepers. In any case, we had come to live in rural Kenya precisely because I wanted the solitude necessary to enable me to finish my book. This we found.

From Njoro we moved to Kitale, to a house on the edge of that dull, suburban town, looking out over the Cherangani Hills, where the bongo came to the secret salt licks. At our backs was Mt. Elgon, wrapped in its mist of rain, and to the north, Lake Rudolf and its parched plains of lava rock. I finished the book there, did a six-week trip by air through Zanzibar, Tanganyika, Nyasaland, the Rhodesias, and South Africa for some American newspapers, and did a magazine piece about the threatened extinction of Africa's wild life. I knew a good deal about this subject because we hunted or simply camped out whenever we could and we had good friends among the game wardens and the white hunters. I had hunted only once in my life before coming to Africa and found that I liked it. Civilization had ground down most but not all of my hunting instincts, and it was like coming home again to do it. I had no feeling of guilt when I killed cleanly. My killing or not killing made no difference to the herd. For every one I dropped, a thousand would die of thirst and starvation when the rains failed. The hyenas would snap the half-born calves from their dams' wombs; anthrax, the lion, and the leopard would claim their share. It was all in the system of things.

We did a lot of safariing out of Kitale because we didn't like the town much. People were not creating things there, not changing the land. A lot of retired civil servants from Uganda were there, narrow people retired to a narrower existence. It wasn't our Africa at all. Rather, it *was* that aspect of Africa that is white, Protestant, middle-class, and dull—an aspect that we didn't like very much.

I had about four months left on the fourth year of my grant when we moved to Malindi to start on the second book, the one about east, central, and southern Africa, which I have never finished. Malindi is a small town on the Indian Ocean about eighty miles from Mombasa. It was one of the original Arab settlements on the East Coast and still has very much of an Arab flavor, with its white-washed mosque and its air of quiet decay. Warutere, being an upcountry African, was captivated by the "big water" (the ocean, of which he had only heard stories) and by the Arabs. For $28 a month (that seems to have been our standard figure in those days) we rented a big, three-room, native-style house with a roof of palm fronds and a huge veranda where I could work when the wind was not too bad.

In Malindi it was possible to meet Arabs such as the *liwali* ("chief") of the town. For some reason there is far less racial prejudice in coastal towns than there is in the interior, perhaps because the coastal settlements are older and the climate is too hot for prolonged controversy. Lack of electricity and the coastal heat combined to produce a modification in our daily schedule. We got up now while it was still dark and swam in the empty sea, returning to breakfast on papayas and mangoes while the sun rose pinkly over the sea. Then I worked straight through until two o'clock, either on the book or on newspaper stories. After that it became too hot. We slept for an hour, ate, had another swim, and worked until the light failed. Then before dinner we sat out on the veranda, drinking and watching the sun set. We turned in by nine o'clock, since the light was too bad to either write or read.

I had finished about four chapters of the new book when it came time to return to America. Although I had gotten a great deal out of Africa, it was not all that I wanted. Both of us wished to stay on, to get to know more Africans and Asians without being tied to a typewriter. But I had been on the fellowship for nearly four years, and it was time for someone else to have a chance. Besides, although I had written a good deal for various newspapers, I had been away from my profession for a long time and it was time to return to it.

We got Warutere a job with friends at Njoro, on the understanding that we could have him back if we returned, and left our Land-Rover with the same people. Kitty was to see about finding a home for Cholmondeley on the same terms while I started for home via West Africa, spending several weeks en route to do a series of newspaper stories. She was to meet me in December in Tangier.

My route to Tangier took me through Ruanda-Urundi, the Congo, ex-French Congo, Cameroun, Nigeria, Ghana, the Ivory Coast, Liberia, Sierra Leone, Guinea, Senegal, and Morocco. Now, after an absence of a year (with the exception of my six-week trip to the Rhodesias and South Africa), I was to be operating again as a journalist rather than a writer: my task was no longer to avoid people in the search for the solitude necessary to write, but to seek them out. The area in question was one with which I was familiar, having studied each country in detail two years before. I had friends and contacts among State Department officials, white businessmen, and African nationalists. There had, of course, been a good deal of hat-switching: a bright political officer I had known in Brazzaville might appear again in Accra, an African trade unionist I had known in the bad old colonial days might well be minister of labor. But if the roles had changed, the cast of characters was largely the same, although there were certain important additions and subtractions from the total picture. Most important of all, the problems were very little changed: while the political scenery was different, the old battle against hunger, poverty, ignorance, and disease remained. I picked up the threads again quickly, added some new ones, and wove my tapestry of words with little trouble.

This trip was important for me in several ways. In the first place, it showed me that I was still interested in Africa, its peoples and its problems. Secondly, it showed me that I could still perform as a newspaper reporter. Lastly, it showed me that, while I did not mind the solitude of writing books, I still enjoyed the business of being a newspaperman.

The knowledge of these three truths showed me what I wanted to do: to return to Africa and to do so as a foreign correspondent for an American newspaper. In Africa, and in the interpretation of that continent to the American people, I had found one of the things, perhaps the major thing, the lack of which had sent me to Africa in 1956: a job that demanded every bit of my brains, courage, and diligence—a job worth doing. We spent Christmas at home in Washington, and the month of January, 1961, was employed in re-evaluating the situation. America seemed to have changed little in our four-year absence. All of our married friends had added a child or two to their families. The men were still climbing slowly (a few, more quickly) up their respective corporate ladders; the women were intensely occupied in their battle to maintain their figures and their intelligence while still performing as mothers, chauffeurs, cooks, lovers, and accountants. There was still football in the autumn, dances at the club, martinis and TV in the evenings. There were still traffic jams and frenetic activity. Although I had no doubt that there was meaning to it all, I still found the meaning elusive. Africa, of course, was of only peripheral interest to our friends, laden as they were with the burden of their own ambitions, troubles, successes, failures, shared joys and secret sorrows. This only served to underline for us how much a part of us Africa had become. We were, in a sense, exiles in our own land. On February 1, 1961, I joined the staff of the Chicago *Daily News* as a foreign correspondent. Assignment: Africa.

And so for the third time we readied ourselves for the long journey, long in time as well as in space, back to that ancient and ageless continent, our adopted land. Once more Kenya was to be our home, although this time we were to live in Nairobi. Again it was decided that we would proceed independently and by different routes. I would first pay short visits to the colonial powers (England, France, Belgium, and Portugal), then follow a hedgehopping route through Tunisia, Algeria, Morocco, Senegal, Mali, Upper Volta, Niger, the Ivory Coast, Cameroun, Chad, the Central African Republic, ex-French Congo, and the Congo. Kitty would fly from New York to Nairobi via Rome.

This return trip took me to several new nations that I had not visited during my first four years in Africa. Among them was Mali, the former French Sudan, one of the three nations most deeply penetrated by Communism (the others being Guinea and Ghana). The Cold War had come to Africa with a vengeance in 1960. Up until that year, there had been only four independent nations in sub-Saharan Africa. In 1960 eighteen new African flags unfurled. During the colonial period—the closing years of which I had witnessed—the West had enjoyed a virtual monopoly in Africa. While they might not forbid Communism at home (both Britain and France were examples of this), the colonial powers bitterly and with considerable success opposed the spread of Marxism to their overseas territories. Africans found it difficult if not impossible to get permission to travel behind the Iron Curtain; Communist officials and businessmen were refused visas to African colonies; the Communist Party was banned in the territories; and possession of Communist literature in many cases was a felony.

All this changed drastically and dramatically when the bulk of Africa assumed responsibility for its own destiny. The nations of the Communist bloc, as was only natural, were quick to establish diplomatic and commercial footholds in the continent from which they had for so long been excluded. British and French Communists, many of whom had made contact at European universities with African students who now were nationalist leaders, found themselves welcome in Africa. From the point of view of the Africans, both of these developments were natural and good. Anti-Communism has no meaning in Africa precisely because the Africans have had no direct experience of Communism. For them, or at least for the majority of them, it represents not a threat to their newly won freedom but an alternative source of financial aid, technical assistance, and diplomatic support.

In one sense, such aid, assistance, and support is more welcome from the Communist bloc than it is from the West in that, to African eyes, the Soviet Union and its satellites are free from the taint of neocolonialism. While the leaders and people of Africa are still tightly bound to the West by links of language, culture, political institutions, trade, currency, and education, there still remains in the mind of the African a very real fear that the West poses a threat to Africa's political integrity. Despite the fact that Russia, through her actions in Central Asia and Eastern Europe, must rank as the greatest colonial power of the postwar period, this means little to the African because it has no direct effect on the policies of the Communist bloc in regard to Africa. Russia's goals in Africa are these: to gain a diplomatic foothold, to weaken Africa's commercial ties with the West, to subvert pro-Western African governments, and to embarrass the colonial powers as much as possible. These goals are quite compatible with the aspirations of many new African nations.

Because they still have responsibilities in Africa, the colonial powers are unable to comply with every whim of the independent African states. Because the United States must act responsibly in Africa out of morality, self-interest, and obligation to its NATO allies, we find ourselves in more or less the same situation. The Communist bloc suffers under no such disadvantage. It can and does give the independent African states favorably disposed toward it virtually everything they want in the way of diplomatic support because it has nothing to lose in Africa and everything to gain. If a policy espoused by the African states and supported by Russia is successful, the Russians gain great credit. If it fails, the African states can hardly blame Russia for having supported them. Russia gains, in any event, through the multiplication of the West's difficulties in the area in question.

Lastly, of course, the images of both Britain and America are tarnished in African eyes because of our domestic racial problems and policies. The Africans are not interested in the nuances of the situation. They do not see that unlimited non-white immigration into Britain poses a very serious economic and social problem for the United Kingdom; they only see that Britain's new immigration laws discriminate in effect if not in theory against non-whites. The Africans are frankly uninterested when one points out the great social, economic, and political gains made by Negroes in America over the last decade. They do not care about the fact that the American Constitution reserves to the states certain powers, thus limiting the action that the federal government can take to end segregation. What they are interested in is the fact that Negroes are still turned out of restaurants and denied educational equality in certain areas of the United States. The Communist bloc, on the other hand, suffers under no such stigma. And so it goes.

While the Communist penetration that I found in full swing through the more remote countries of West Africa's interior was new, there was much that remained unchanged and seemed unlikely to change in the future. Traveling, working, and living in Africa are not good for the blood pressure, not only of Americans but of Western man. The intolerable burden of inefficiency, slowness, and just-not-caring hangs around one's neck like Coleridge's albatross. Confirmed hotel reservations are viewed with blank astonishment by reservation clerks; appointments are not kept; airplanes fail to fly not only at the scheduled hour but on the appointed day. These observations should not be construed as a racial attitude on my part. I have received the same treatment from white Africans as from black Africans. Perhaps this has been the fundamental failure of the white man in Africa: instead of raising Africa up, he has been pulled down to its level. There are, of course, many contributory factors to the low level of performances of the continent's people in all fields: deficient diet, tribal mores, low pay, lack of competition, ignorance of modern techniques, an unfavorable climate. But the fact remains that the performance is low-level and that it causes a loss of time and energy that frequently results in misunderstandings and racial friction. He who must travel, live, and work in Africa soon learns to accept things as they are rather than as he would like to see them. Those who cannot do this soon become dour and bitter. But in accepting it, one loses some of one's own efficiency and one's nerves become frayed anyway. It is a price one has to pay for the gift of Africa.

An American friend once asked me, "If the African has not been able or willing to work and accomplish Western feats of efficiency and administration, is it because he is concentrating on something else, something we can't give him, some African way of doing things that may have a special value of its own?" I really don't think so. The African fails as a modern Western man for two reasons. The first is a technical one: he lacks the background and training, which are part of the heritage of Western society. To give a simple example, an American child knows how to do things with his hands because he sees his father working with tools, and his own toys are often miniature replicas of these tools. In contrast, a young African has to be shown which end of a hammer he must hold. He has to be convinced that the wheelbarrow is to be rolled, not carried on the head. The same applies to technicians on a higher level: everything has to be learned, nothing has been acquired. The African clerk finds himself working in a world utterly strange to him, only the dim outlines of which he comprehends.

More fundamental is the African's approach to time. The Western concept of time eludes him, perhaps understandably, since it is only in the last fifty or a hundred years, a wink in the eye of history, that he has learned to measure time in months (let alone days, hours, and minutes) rather than seasons. To the African, the Western penchant for being on time for appointments, for doing certain things at certain times, for cramming as much as possible into a brief period of time, seems an eccentric aberration. What does it matter if you see a man at 4 P.M. on Thursday rather than at 2 P.M. on Wednesday? You have seen him. What difference does it really make if you have no bed in the hotel tonight? You will find a place to sleep, and perhaps tomorrow there will be room. Will the coffee stop growing if a planter's clerk fails to get his accounts in by the end of the month, when they are due? Of course it will not. Then why all the fuss?

When Africans are criticized on this score, their tendency is to invoke "the African personality," saying that they refuse to accept slavishly Western methods and that they have their own way of doing things. This is, in the main, equivocation. When Africans take over a government or a business, inevitably there is a slowdown and occasionally a breakdown. This is fundamentally, as I have said, because the Africans lack the technical skill and the Western approach to time.

This is not to say that there is not much that is admirable in African life, particularly in social relations, a field in which we can teach them little. No man need go hungry or lack for a place to sleep in Africa: his family, his kinsmen, his fellow tribesmen owe him these things by right (which places a tremendous burden on the evolved, well-educated African wage earner and often leads to corruption, since tribal law forbids him to turn from his door any relative, no matter how distant a relative or how lazy the man may be). Africa has neither orphans nor old maids nor widows. The child has as much right in his uncle's house as he has in his father's. A woman, be she both plain and poor, finds a husband because she can work and produce children, thus bringing wealth to her husband and honor to her clan. When a woman's husband dies, she automatically becomes the wife of the dead man's brother.

From the cradle to the grave, the African has a well-defined position within his tribal society. He is never friendless, never alone, never without resources, as long as he lives by the mores of the tribe. There is little snobbery or class consciousness among Africans. All are "children of the earth," and I have seen an African prime minister at a lavish party stop to shake hands and exchange a few words with a waiter whom he recognized as a distant kinsman.

The African way of life, with its built-in "social security system," has much to recommend it. It is friendly, egalitarian, and easygoing. But it does not tend to breed rugged individualists. The kernel of its philosophy is not to change the world but to live with it, not to challenge but to conform.

Whether the good aspects of African mores can be adapted and retained in the modern society toward which Africa aspires remains to be seen. It seems likely that they will not survive. When a rural African moves to a city and takes up salaried employment, he is, to a certain extent, removed from his tribal context. The authority of his father and that of his clan chief diminish with distance. New joys, forbidden by tribal law (in most Bantu tribes, drunkenness was traditionally the right only of grandparents), are readily available. Who is to know if a man turns a kinsman from his door? What difference does it make if the young clerk speaks disrespectfully to his elders? Have not his political leaders told him that tribalism is wrong?

As a consequence, the present generation of younger Africans, men and women ranging in age from fifteen to thirty-five, are to a very great extent mental and psychological "displaced persons." They have discarded many of their tribal mores without substituting anything worthwhile in their place. Their old life is alien to them; the new is still strange and uncomforting. The man is incapable of performing his age-old role of warrior any more . . . yet he is still a very inferior typist. The woman refuses to accept docilely her traditional function as beast of burden and producer of children . . . yet she lacks the skill to become an urban worker or a nurse.

This applies even to the African cabinet minister behind his huge and highly polished desk. He is no longer at home among his people; his new environment and society are strange to him. Africa is ruled and run by shadow men, torn between two worlds. Moreover, because new vices are easily learned and old ones readily retained, the tendency has been to destroy that which was good in tribal society and to accept the worst aspects of modern Western life. In the end, a worthwhile synthesis may be produced. The grandsons of these "displaced persons" may grow up as urbanites fully at home in a modern society. But that time is far away.

The white man certainly has a responsibility for what Arthur Koestler would call the "cocacola-ization" of Africa. It was the impact of white settlement and white administration that rent the tribal fabric. Unfortunately, the white man lacked the numbers, the time, the money, and the desire (since he was only human) to build as well as to destroy. He showed the African what was wrong with African tribal society and, having smashed that society, he gave the African nothing in return, except Day-Glo neckties, Mickey Mouse wrist watches, and Cinemascope. All of us, whites and Africans, are paying for that now.

Before settling down in Nairobi, my wife and I joined forces with an old friend of ours, Chief Game Warden John Blower of Uganda, for a two-week trip by horse and camel through the desiccated wastes of northern Kenya. This is the Africa that the tourist or even the average white living in Africa has never seen (many life-long residents of Nairobi, black and white alike, have never seen an elephant outside of a zoo). It is the old Africa, unchanged and unchanging. For days on end we wandered from water hole to water hole, seeing much game and no sign of human life except a few wild and half-naked Samburu tribesmen. We hunted a little for the pot, and took a few photographs, but mostly we just rode over the eroded hills and down the dry riverbeds, looking, listening, smelling. It was good to be back.

Returning from the camel safari tired, insect-bitten, and filthy but infinitely refreshed, we began the task of reassembling our household and finding a place to live. Neither is difficult to do in Kenya these days: since the Lancaster House Constitutional Conference of 1960, which set forth that Kenya is to be an African nation with no special guarantees for its Indian and white citizens, there has been a steady economic decline coupled with an exodus of whites from the country. The recession has created much unemployment and therefore made it easy to get servants. The exodus of whites has thrown many houses on the market at bargain prices.

Servants in Africa are a necessity rather than a luxury. Unheard of are the labor-saving devices—the dispose-alls, washing machines, dryers, dishwashers, deep freezes, and supermarkets—which make a servantless society possible in America. Where such items are available, they are impractical because of their high cost, the expense of electricity, and the ability of the African to demolish almost any piece of machinery within the shortest possible time.

Most whites—perhaps as a result of the Mau Mau emergency—seem to start on the assumption that their servants cannot be trusted: the housewife carries a ring of keys as large as a medieval jailer and locks up everything from the liquor to the salt. In our early days in Africa, we found ourselves psychologically unable to do this. Our solution has been to trust Warutere completely, but to trust him alone. Nothing is locked in our house, and he has a key to the house, but he is our only inside servant. No other African, including our two *shamba* boys ("gardeners"), are allowed in the house, except in our presence or his. We have never had a dime stolen.

Warutere came from his home in Karatina to meet us at the Nairobi post office at the appointed hour. He was cheerful and glad to see us but thinner, and his clothes were in bad shape. At Njoro he had been working on the regular country rations (most servants in Kenya are fed as well as housed by their employers) of ten pounds of *posho* ("corn meal") per week plus a few extras. Most servants also depend upon gifts of secondhand garments from their employers to clothe themselves, and these have to be divided among more people o na farm than on a city block. Furthermore, financial disaster had struck Warutere in that his bicycle had been stolen by another African at Njoro. The bicycle is to the African what the motor scooter is to the Italian or the automobile to the American: a means of transportation and a status symbol. However, he told us with pride that he had bought a *bibi* ("a wife"), paying about a year's salary for her, and she had borne him a daughter.

Our attitude on rations has also been different from that of most other Kenya settlers. We give Warutere a balanced diet, which includes meat, cooking fat, sugar, tea, fresh vegetables, and *posho*. As a result, food is never stolen, sickness and absenteeism are averted, and a good humor is maintained. Paternalism? Sure. And that's only the beginning. We pay for his polio shots, provide him with soap, and give him medicine when he's ill. Kitty's old clothes go to his *bibi,* and when he goes home, we send him with a gallon of cod-liver oil for his child. We also pay Warutere $30 a month, which is close to the top scale. The fact remains that the ordinary African has too little money and that he prefers to spend what little he has on capital goods (bicycles, sewing machines, wives, sporty clothes) rather than on the food and preventive medicine he needs to keep himself healthy. Why not raise wages then? Because this can be done only if productivity can be increased, and this cannot be increased until the African learns, among other things, to eat a balanced diet. It is all a vicious circle with no easy solution.

After a good deal of looking around, we found a house, looking out over the Ngong Hills and on the edge of the Masai and Kikuyu tribal lands. It was once a part of the coffee estate of Baroness Blixen (Isak Dinesen), the Danish writer. With its tin roof and somewhat antiquated plumbing, it was nothing fancy, but it suited us. It still does.

The place had been run by the owners with a staff of eight. Under our idea of treating fewer people better, we cut the staff to three and raised wages and rations—after first seeing to it that those who would have to leave had other jobs.

Since my job is primarily one of news analysis rather than straight reporting, it was not only possible but desirable that I should work at home, where my library would be available to me twenty-four hours a day. I set myself up an office in one of the spare rooms, and my wife, who acts as my secretary, established herself with file cabinets and typewriter on the sun porch.

The two years since we have been back have produced perhaps 500,000 words of newspaper copy, my second book, and several magazine articles. Fundamentally, my work pattern has not changed in the last few years. It involves a great deal of reading (newspapers, magazines, and books), the establishment and maintenance of personal contacts, and considerable travel. At last count, I think I knew personally about thirty of the chiefs of state or important political leaders of Africa's forty-six countries. When I want clarification on a political move, I generally go directly to the man involved through his private secretary. If I don't know the man (or his private secretary), I sometimes use the country's press officer. In this respect, working as a journalist in Africa is far different and more satisfying than it is in America or Europe. Kennedy, Macmillan, and de Gaulle seldom if ever grant private interviews. Although the trend is moving a little away from this here, it is still reasonably easy to get to see Kenyatta, Nyerere, Welensky, or Tafawa Balewa. We are also fortunate in the scarcity of American journalists in Africa. To the best of my knowledge the only American publications with permanent staff correspondents stationed in Africa are the Chicago *Daily News, New York Times, Christian Science Monitor, Time, Newsweek,* and *U.S. News and World Report* (the two wire services, A.P. and U.P.I., are of course represented). Consequently, there are not enough journalists here, so we adopt a symbiotic relationship to each other. A man has to know his stuff if he is to operate effectively in Africa.

With a beat almost as large as the United States, India, and China combined, it is sometimes difficult to find the time to establish new contacts. One does his best by entertaining a good deal, attending official government functions, and getting out into the country as much as possible. Nothing is probably more important than these contacts and in obtaining and maintaining a realistic view of what is happening and is going to happen in Africa.

There is a sharp divergence of opinion, a disparateness of attitudes, between this generation of Africans and the next. On the whole, the older generation is the more favorably disposed toward the West, better educated, and more comprehensible to the Western mind. The younger generation is, in general, anti-Western, spottily educated, and less easy to understand. It should be noted here that what distinguishes one generation from the other is not so much a question of chronological age as of whether or not a certain man was trained, entered professional or political life, and matured under the colonial regime or under a nationalist regime. Thus I would classify Kenya's minister of labor, Tom Mboya, as a member of the "older" generation, although he is only thirty-one. What is more important than his age is that Mboya has been active in politics here for the past five years; he is a veteran.

There is no outstanding example of the younger generation to point to because these men are still at the junior minister cabinet rank or just approaching the top of the labor movement. They will probably begin to emerge in about five years. Their struggle —and hence their political attitudes—has been conditioned by an entirely different set of circumstances than that which faced Mboya's older generation. For the older generation, the problem has been entirely a political one: how to manipulate the democratic process at home and abroad to obtain freedom from colonial rule in the shortest possible time. That of the younger generation is far more complex. They find their countries politically independent but still plagued by economic weakness, tribal rivalries, inadequate social services, poor communications, and a shortage of trained personnel. It is impossible to blame the colonialists, because they are gone. Neocolonialism and economic imperialism, the latter used primarily in reference to the United States, are convenient targets, and so are their own African governments. The task of the new generation is to achieve a social and economic revolution to complement the political revolution won by the older generation. As always in politics everywhere, the first goal is to throw the rascals out—to obtain political power. Thus Africa is entering now into a period that promises to be equally as turbulent as was the struggle against colonialism.

It would be misleading and false to pretend to an intimacy with the Africans of the older generation, much less with those of the younger one. There are simply too many mutual barriers, perhaps the least of which is race. It is possible to achieve an intimate and perfectly natural friendship with an American Negro, because his frame of reference, his background (assuming that he is reasonably educated), is sufficiently similar to one's own. This just does not apply with Africans, as many an American Negro has discovered to his surprise on visiting this continent. The African's home life, attitudes toward sex, tribal loyalties, historical background, social habits, political interests, and psychological attitudes all serve to set him apart from Western man. It would be unnatural if this were not so, and neither he nor Western man are to blame for it. It is simply a fact.

Consequently, one knows Africans on several levels but seldom at the level of natural friendship. One knows him on the master-servant level; one knows him on the official level; one knows him as a professional colleague. Although one entertains Africans and is entertained by them, the Westerner who sees this as more than an extension of the official or professional relationship is usually fooling himself. There is just not enough common ground, even with American-educated Africans.

It may be that, as a journalist, I am faced with a special problem in reaching an honest understanding with Africans, particularly those in the political arena. They know that when they talk to me, they are talking for the record, even if they are not quoted. As an example, take the Somali situation. About eighty thousand Somalis live in northern Kenya. They differ from the Bantu majority, which runs the country, in religion (they are Muslims), race, language, and way of life. All these things they share with their fellow tribesmen across the border in the Somali Republic. Kenya Somalis at every level, from clan chiefs to their elected representative in Kenya's legislature, have repeatedly asserted that they do not want to be ruled from Nairobi, that they would like to secede and join the Somali Republic. Yet both Jomo Kenyatta, leader of the Kenya African National Union, and Ronald Ngala, leader of the rival Kenya African Democratic Union (which together form Kenya's coalition government), have told me with perfectly straight faces that there is no Somali problem, that Kenya's Somalis really want nothing more than to be ruled from Nairobi.

Secondly, many Africans have the rather disagreeable (to the Westerner) habit of refusing to admit responsibility for the consequences of their own actions. This is a practice deeply ingrained in the African way of life. In African tribal society, nothing happens outside of the influence of the supernatural: "real" life and the world of the spirit are inextricably interwoven. Consequently (to put it in modern terms), if you lose your money on the stock market, it is not because you were stupid in your choice of investments but because someone, or some evil force, willed you to lose it. If your cook drops your best Steuben glass bowl, it is *Shauri ya Mungu* ("God's fault"), not his own carelessness.

If you ask an African politician why he is making conditions intolerable for white farmers in his area when he knows that their departure will result in poverty and unemployment, you will seldom get the honest answer that it is necessary politically to distribute the white-owned lands among his tribesmen. More frequently you will get the reply that the whites' departure is an imperialist plot designed to keep the people in poverty and thus to undermine the foundations of Pan-African unity! You may invoke "the African personality" all you wish, but this is nothing more nor less than intellectual dishonesty. In mitigation, about all one can say is that many African leaders do genuinely feel themselves to be surrounded by enemies anxious to take advantage of the disunity and semichaos in which much of Africa finds itself.

There is impatience on the part of the Westerner and a lack of understanding on the part of the African. Even as polished a person as Tom Mboya of Kenya recently stated that the Western press was the worst friend the West had in Africa. When asked to explain this, he told me that Africans resented the picture of Africa drawn by the Western press. "You," he said, "would do better to identify yourselves more thoroughly with the nationalist movement." This statement indicates a profound ignorance of the function of the press in a free society. However, the "you're-either-with-us-or-against-us" philosophy exists all over Africa at the highest levels.

Thirdly, many second-level African leaders display an aggressiveness, to compensate for their own feeling of inferiority, which I personally find distasteful. At a cocktail party not long ago, a young African trade unionist asked me rather belligerently, "What are you doing for Kenya?" I replied that Kenya was his country, not mine, and that consequently it was his function, not mine, to serve Kenya. Two weeks later the individual in question was jailed for stealing from his union's funds.

Lastly—and I know this is old-fashioned of me—I find it difficult to admire politicians who can attack aggression in Suez and condone it in Katanga, Goa, or Dutch New Guinea. Insofar as international relations are concerned, I think most Africans are amoral: there is no crime except Western white colonialism. I find it difficult to form friendships with people whose moral sensibilities and intellectual horizons are that limited.

This African myopia leads many leaders, in my opinion, to construct a distorted vision of their own future. The more intelligent politicians will admit that independence leads to a decline in the efficiency of the civil service and to at least a temporary decline in their countries' economies. They state, quite honestly, that it is worth a little inefficiency and corruption to be masters in their own house. The less intelligent leaders will assert that this is "a pack of imperialist lies"—although, to give only one example, in August, 1962, the East African Common Services Organization, which is in the process of Africanizing its staff, increased the salaries but cut the qualifying typing speed of its stenographers from 40 to 35 words a minute.

All of them assert—and I think they do so genuinely—that they want a better life and standard of living for their people: more schools, better housing, higher wages. However, if there is one thing they want more than this, it is prestige. Today, Ghana has a world-wide string of diplomatic posts, its own money-losing airline, huge sports stadiums and public monuments, and an endless series of expensive and wordy conferences. But the Ghanaian cocoa farmer is getting considerably less for his crop than he did under the wicked British imperialists.

In short, the average African leader seems to me to put international prestige well ahead of the welfare of his own people. This may change in time. One can only hope so.

The Africans with whom I feel most at home are the so-called Americo-Liberians—Liberians descended from slaves repatriated from America to West Africa. The reasons are obvious: lacking any association with Britain or France, the Americo-Liberians, who are of mixed tribal ancestry, look to America in all things. The men are American-educated. They wear button-down shirts and repp ties. Their women dress in the American style. They drink bourbon, eat fried chicken, talk with soft Southern accents, call you by your first name, and know who Joe DiMaggio is. In short, an American has something in common with a Liberian that he can never hope to have with a Dahomeyan or a Kenyan.

This does not mean, of course, that America and Americans have nothing to offer Africa; they have a great deal. It does mean that it is going to take many more years of intensive contact before Africans and Americans can begin to understand one another. A common humanity is just not enough.

Having spent six years of my life working in Africa, it would be satisfying personally and professionally to see Africa as the wave of the future, a bright tomorrow dawning on history's horizon. Unfortunately, I cannot take such a sanguine view. As far as politics is concerned, I do not think that Western democracy will survive here for very long. The African has inherited from his colonial mentors all the institutions and trappings of democracy. What he lacks is the historical background, the economy, the civil service, the understanding, and the desire to make Western democracy work. This should not surprise anyone: democracy was born at a given time in history to suit the needs and aspirations of a small segment of the world's population; it died or evolved over a period of years according to the historical, economic, and political imperatives obtaining in those lands where it was tried. Such needs, aspirations, and conditions just do not exist in Africa today.

The failure of democracy in Africa does not seem to worry the Africans very much. In *Africa—Angry Young Giant* I wrote:

Africa is intoxicated with the wine of self-government and she no more cares whether her governments are democratic or autocratic than an ageing father cares whether his only child is a boy or a girl. The miracle of birth is the important thing. Africa wants not democracy but the right to rule or misrule herself, not an efficient civil service but a black one, not ballot boxes but the essential self-respect of political freedom, even at the cost of personal liberty. The slave-trade and the colonial period have left Africans with a massive group inferiority complex; what they want is to be recognized as *men,* not democrats.

I still feel that this is the case.

This is not to say, as most people assume when one speaks of the death of democracy, that either Communism or Fascism is going to triumph in Africa; they are not. Marxist-Leninism and National Socialism are concepts just as alien and unsuitable to Africa as Western democracy is. Since Communism apparently is more of a threat to the world today than Fascism, more might be said about the problems facing Africa's few professional Communists. To begin with, Marxist-Leninism in theory assumes a subordination of national interests to the class struggle; in practice, it requires a subordination of national interests to those of the Soviet Union or the Chinese People's Republic. Yet nationalism is now and promises to be for the next few years the most predominant factor of African political life. On these grounds alone, Communism is unsuitable for Africa. It is just as unsuitable on the personal level as it is on the political level. If he is anything, the African is independent, acquisitive, and un-disciplined—not qualities recommended for good party members. Lastly, Marxist-Leninism demands state control of the means of production. Peasant farmers, in every land and in every age, have proved the most difficult element to bring under state control; urban workers, on the other hand, are relatively easy. In Africa, ninety percent of the population still wrings its livelihood from the soil. While there are pockets of industry scattered across Africa's dusty face, the lives of only a comparative handful of Africa's people are touched by industrialization. Although the continent's urban population is growing, there is nothing today that could be described as an industrial proletariat.

The peasantry has been organized by Communist cadres in several underdeveloped countries, but invariably this has taken place in nations faced with a severe land shortage. While land hunger does exist in portions of Africa, such as the highlands of Kenya, it is the exception to the rule: in the entire continent there are only 230 million people. Unlike Asia, Africa does not starve. While an African peasant farmer finds it difficult to accumulate capital, he must be uncommonly unlucky or extremely lazy to go hungry.

There is always the chance, as has happened elsewhere, that a Communist system could be imposed upon the peasantry by urban leaders. Something similar to this has taken place in Guinea. However, African peasants are just as conservative when it comes to land ownership as those of any other country, and such a move, in my opinion, would encounter stiff resistance.

If neither Western democracy nor Communism is going to work, what kind of political structure can one expect to emerge in Africa? It can only be said that a new synthesis is taking place. An "Afrocratic" type of government is emerging that employs the form but not the substance of Western democracy, borrows some techniques from authoritarianism, and has more than a little to do with traditional tribal structure.

The future in the economic and social sense appears even more bleak. The facts of the matter are that Africa is faced with huge problems that her people lack the ability to solve. This is not a question of racial inferiority. Despite all the economic, social, historical, and educational problems existing in Africa, the continent has produced some really remarkable men. The problem is that they are only an unrepresentative handful. When the American television audience sees an intelligent and able man like Mboya, it may be forgiven for assuming that Kenya contains thousands of men like him. It does not. Nine out of every ten Africans still live at the level of the German tribes in the days of Tacitus. One day Africa may produce the equivalent of modern Germany; but that day is hundreds of years ahead.

The introduction of Western medicine, the elimination of famine, and the end of tribal warfare has made for a population explosion in Africa, which finds the continent's population doubling about every thirty-five years. Consequently Africa, which starts so far behind the rest of the world, must register considerable economic gains just to stand still in terms of the provision of social services for its people. For the moment, Africa enjoys a vogue: foreign technical and financial assistance is expected and will be given. But for how long and at what rate can such assistance continue? No one knows the answer. The brutal fact is that Africa must soon learn to stand on her own feet or face the prospect not of an immediate and dramatic collapse but of a slow but certain decline into mediocrity.

Is there any way in which the latter doleful eventuality can be avoided? I think not: things are going to get considerably worse in Africa before they begin to get better. With a very few exceptions (such as the Ivory Coast), the new African nations have done little to encourage private foreign investment and a good deal to discourage it by loose talk on the part of political leaders. They have immeasurably weakened their own economies (in countries such as Kenya) by encouraging the departure of white settlers, and they have damaged the efficiency of their civil services by giving Africans preference for appointment and promotion over better trained *local* whites and Indians. There are political imperatives for such moves, of course: a politician who encouraged whites to stay and promoted nonblack residents over Africans in the civil service might well lose the next election. But this does not alter the harm that such moves do to Africa.

The slide into mediocrity can be delayed and softened by government-to-government assistance on both the financial and technical levels. Private institutions and organizations can help by providing scholarships for African students. Voluntary groups can assist Africa by working in the African countries and by passing their members' skills on to the Africans. Yet the fact remains that to be lasting, a solution for Africa's problems of poverty, ignorance, disease, and immaturity must be an African solution, one devised and implemented by Africans for Africa. In my view, it will be at least two generations before Africa has the trained man-power to attempt its own regeneration. Even then, the funds will be lacking and the efforts demanded of all members of the population will be great.

Taking all this into account, has it been a mistake to give Africa its freedom so early? In my view, it has not been a mistake. Had it been possible to maintain colonial control (which, for a variety of reasons, it was not), the slump that Africa is headed for in the next few years would have been averted. On the other hand, the possibility of the continent's regeneration in twenty or forty or one hundred years would not exist. The colonial system as a whole provided a just rule. It failed to command the total loyalty and energies of the governed. Consequently, the possibility of great things did not exist. Africa may never succeed, but at least the opportunity for men to work out their own destinies now exists. This is something that could not and should not have been denied the African people.

In the creation of a new Africa, the United States and its citizens can offer at this stage only a little technical and financial aid, and a good deal of personal sympathy. When one considers the barriers that still exist between ourselves and the nationals of the countries from which most Americans have sprung— England, Ireland, Germany, Italy, France, Poland, and Scandinavia—I think it is false romanticism to believe that close bonds can exist between Americans and Africans for generations to come. This should not, of course, discourage us from making the effort. But to build too many hopes on false foundations is to prepare the way for psychological defeats of immense importance. This, I think, should be remembered.

My wife and I have had six years in Africa now, and we will probably have several more. How many more will be determined by the unfolding of events. I would not pretend that the Africa of the future is the place where I want to live. There was too much in the colonial era that appealed to me to make that possible. I think, however, that Africa will always be my second home, the land to which my thoughts will return no matter where the course of events may take me. For the African people, with their warmth and good humor, I will always retain a great affection. And for Africa's vast, brooding, lonely plains, tawny in the afternoon sun like a lioness' pelt, I already feel the ache of their absence while I am still here. Twice I have left Africa; twice I have returned. One cannot say what will happen a third time. There is something about Africa that gets you, and I am well aware of the fact that I am hooked.

The one great lesson Africa has taught me stems from a great failure—the failure to become of Africa while being in it, the inability completely to understand the African. As I have said before, I do not think it possible for an American to identify himself completely with an African, to reach a full level of friendship. This is the result not of race but of differences in background, language, and national personality. The discovery of this fact led me to the realization, which I had sensed before I came to Africa, that no such differences exist among Americans of different races—or, if they do exist, they are inconsequential. One comes away from Africa with a deep knowledge of what a marvelous synthesis has taken place in America in the brief span of less than two hundred years. This has been Africa's gift to me, and it is a great one.

JULIAN MAYFIELD

Ghanaian Sketches

I have lived in Accra nearly eighteen months. I am, there-fore—according to usual practice—an expert, not only on Ghana but on all of Africa. By now I should have written at least two books and several lengthy articles purporting to explain to Western readers the strange creature called the African giant. Even if I had not met or even laid eyes on Dr. Kwame Nkrumah, at least three of my articles should have been an analysis of his personality, explaining why he is such a bad guy for refusing to line his country up with what we like to call the Free World.

But the fact is that few Westerners, black or white, can say truthfully that they *know* Ghana or Africa. This is especially true of anyone who has not lived here for many years and does not speak any of the major languages. As a child of the West, he cannot help but assign Western interpretations and values to everything he sees—which is to say that he understands very little.

Julian Mayfield attended Lincoln University in Pennsylvania. He is the author of three novels—*The Hit* (1957), *The Long Night* (1958), and *The Grand Parade* (1960). His articles have appeared in *The Nation, Commentary, Dissent,* and *Freedomways*.

Each day I spend in Africa is still a day of discovery. What I thought I knew last Monday turns out to be completely erroneous on Friday. The man I was prepared to dismiss as of no consequence is revealed to be the most valuable person I could know. The man I took to be my friend has been working overtime cutting my throat. Moreover, it develops that most of the books my wife and I devoured in preparation for our trip were entirely useless. I don't mean the the books were without facts, but that few succeeded in conveying a full image of the people, their land and their culture.

Therefore, it is a timid authority who now sets out to describe what he has found in a small part of Africa. Ghana is about twice the size of Pennsylvania and has only about six million people. But, as anyone who reads the newspapers could guess, she is the most important sub-Saharan nation in the African revolution, the unchallenged leader of the movement for independence and strong African unity.

On the first leg of my journey to Africa I sat beside a Scot who boarded the jet airliner at Nova Scotia. He was a heavy-set, gruff, friendly fellow, old enough to be my grandfather and well supplied with Canadian whiskey, which we drank as we soared across the dark Atlantic. He had probably seldom conversed with a black man in his life, and he took a particular interest in me. I liked him because of his straightforward manner and his readiness to take as well as give in conversation.

When I told him I was going to Africa, he assumed—perhaps because of the British cut of my suit, which I had purchased in Montreal—that I was a diplomat returning home from the United Nations. He wondered if he had seen me on television, and I told him that he definitely had not, that I was going to Africa for the first time.

"But," he said accusingly, "you told me you were *from* Africa."

"I told you nothing of the sort," I replied firmly. "You assumed I was from Africa because I said I was on my way to Africa."

He fixed me with angry blue eyes."Well, if you're not from Africa, where are you from? And what the hell are you anyway?"

"Surely you know," I said with elaborate patience, "that people of my complexion have been scattered throughout the Western hemisphere for hundreds of years. I am from the United States. I am an American Negro, or an African-American, or an Afro-American, or—if you prefer—I am an American of African descent."

The old goat hooted with laughter. "Lad," he said, "I don't give a damn what you are. I just wish *you* would make up your mind and let me know."

I had to laugh with him, although I was sure we were laughing at different things. I was thinking about all of the furious arguments raging at that very moment in the States over the question of the Negro's identity. And, all jokes aside, it was about time we did make up our minds.

After a few minutes the old man said, "Well, I wouldn't worry about it too much, my boy. In a sense, you're going home also, just like me." He spilled more drink into our plastic cups. "Come on, man, have a wee bit more of the spirits."

Just like me. I had no way of telling him that my going to Africa was in every way different from his returning to his native Scotland for a holiday. He and his sons ran a small business in Nova Scotia, where he had lived for nearly half a century, but he had not, as far as I could tell, lost a trace of his accent. When he left the airplane at Prestwick, he would know exactly what his place was in society. Throughout his long years in his adopted country he had probably let no one near him forget that he was a Scot, damn proud of it, and he had almost certainly instilled the same pride in his children.

On the other hand, when I landed in Accra, I would be in almost every sense a stranger. The mode of life and the attitudes of the people among whom I intended to live for several years would be just as alien to me as their languages. And if there was pride in the knowledge of my African ancestry and comfort in the fact that nearly everyone in my new home would be of my color and look more or less like me, they were a newly discovered pride and comfort, which it would never have occurred to me to cherish before I was twenty years old. Unlike my Scottish companion, who had imbibed his sense of identity with his mother's milk, every imaginable pressure had been brought to bear upon me as a child to make me ashamed of any connection I had with Africa. In boyhood my face was constantly being bathed in Nadinola bleaching cream and my hair plastered with Tuxedo dressing in the futile hope that the skin would somehow grow lighter and the hair straighter. An uncle used to grip my nose between his forefinger and thumb, then crease it up and down painfully over and over again, with the declared objective of making the nose less flat and therefore more attractive. Furthermore, rushing out to school with my hair uncombed or my shirt out of my knickers, I would be brought up short with the terrible admonition that I looked "just like an African." As ridiculous as this may seem, it was understandable in the American context. I doubt if anyone in the neighborhood where I grew up in Washington, D.C., had ever actually seen an African.

There was no influence to correct the African image presented to us, for few cultural remnants had survived the Atlantic crossing. Slavery was always and everywhere a brutal business, but in North America it was cruelest, for the black soul was stripped of every shred of dignity and cultural clothing. Family ties were deliberately slashed, and languages and customs were lost in a generation. If he were to live at all, the black slave had first and foremost to adjust to his new environment. The miracle of the American Negro is not that he has accomplished so much—which he has not—but that as a people he has survived at all.

It is this total erasure of a past, of a sense of having ever belonged to anybody, that perhaps accounts for the bitterness, the frustration, and the pain of my generation, which now seeks, often too uncritically, an identification with the spirit of black nationalism sweeping the African continent. Racist brutality, discrimination, segregation—all of this we have borne; and, as the American nation matured, we might have forgotten. But what cannot be forgotten, and perhaps never forgiven, is that until recently the white world, because of its power, succeeded in persuading *us* to accept their image of us. Thus we leapt into adulthood crippled, with no real knowledge of our worth or our potentiality.

In my neighborhood our view of Africa was derived almost solely from the comic strips and what we picked up on Saturday at the Rosalia movie theater, where pathetic Africans (who were really pathetic Negroes from Los Angeles) beat tom-toms and threatened Jungle Jim, Tarzan, or other intrepid white adventurers. We recoiled from these cruel portrayals or howled with embarrassed, defensive laughter—not because we knew the portrayal was cruel and distorted, but because we saw the Africans in the comic strips and the movies as a white man would see them, and we American Negroes, who wanted nothing so much as to be accepted by the whites, were afraid that the white man would identify *them* with *us*.

This point requires some elucidation, for I have found it the most difficult of all for American whites to comprehend. They never understand why young Negroes object to *Porgy and Bess,* with all its beautiful music, or the lovable Amos 'n' Andy, or the Lone Ranger and his faithful Indian companion Tonto. It has never occurred to most whites that until recently there was seldom a non-white hero in their movies, books, or other communications media; it has never occurred to them to wonder why the few non-white heroes are all patient, noble, 150-percent Christians who labor in the vineyards of tolerance and charity.

Because we accepted the image, many of us rejected whatever was good and our own. Today Negroes have to fight their way through a crowd of whites to hear Mahalia Jackson, whereas twenty-five years ago "educated" Negroes would have avoided her like the plague. My parents, for example, always loved gospel music. They were from the South and had listened to it all of their lives. But we first-generation slum children hated it and begged our parents not to play it when our friends were near. Jazz was all right because the whites danced to that, too, but in those days only Negroes listened to the rocking, swinging gospel songs. And just as we rejected what we had created in America, so we shied away from any identification with Africa.

"Well, I'm glad you're going out," said the Scot later on, after he had dozed for about an hour. "It will do you a lot of good, and it will do *them* a lot of good. It will let them see the kind of chap the West is turning out." He meant this as a compliment. He meant that I was not unpresentable, that I was a writer who seemed fairly intelligent, and that this was a score in the West's favor. Like many of my own countrymen, he saw Africa only as another great battleground where the West and Russia contended.

He dozed off again, and when he awoke a few minutes later, he told me—this likable old Scot, who had never set foot in the United States, who had never in his life been turned away from a job, a house, a school, a beach, or anything else because of his color—told *me* that in ten years' time there would be no racial problem in America.

"I certainly wish I had your optimism," I said, "but I don't."

"Figure it out for yourself, Lad. This new President of yours, this young fellow Kennedy, obviously means business."

I said that after the recent attempt to invade Cuba I was positive the President meant business and, frankly, it scared me to death. "He will certainly," I predicted gloomily, "stand up to the Russians."

The Scot agreed enthusiastically. "But don't you see? He's going to have to clean up his own house first, and that means getting rid of all that stupid discrimination you have in the States." He nodded his head in firm conviction. "You're too close to the problem to see it objectively. Ten years. You'll see."

I knew better than to argue with him. His optimistic view was fashionable in the States, and woe unto him who went against the trend. I had recently left a race war in Monroe, North Carolina, where I had seen white men and black men taking pot shots at each other every evening as if they were shooting at rabbits. I had walked through the streets of Harlem and Chicago's south side and felt the dangerous hatred festering there, like a cancer on the prosperous American body. I had watched the astonishing growth of the Black Muslim separatist movement as to it flocked the depressed, frustrated, and downtrodden Negroes, the people whom God, the N.A.A.C.P., and everyone else had long since forgotten. And I had wondered what the Muslims— and those millions of others who were so bitter, so bereft of hope, that not even the Muslims could reclaim them for any sort of social utility—portended for a society that seemed unable to face ugly facts until disaster stared it in the face. I confess that as the Scot and I streaked through that dark Atlantic night, I was aware of a great sense of relief because it would probably be many years before I would again have to grapple directly with the pressures of American reality.

When we left the plane at Prestwick, I walked with my traveling companion to the barrier that separates the transients from those who are entering Scotland. He wrung my hand warmly and I wished him a merry holiday, promising to send him a postcard from Accra. "Keep up the fight, Lad," he said. "Don't let them get you down." He was talking about the Russians again, for he had read that out there we—the West—were losing. I was sorry to see the old fellow go, but perhaps it was for the best, for if he had been going on to London, I might have tried to explain to him that as a soldier in the Cold War I was a total bust, my country's weakest link, its Achilles heel. I would have told him I didn't need Russians to put the fear of God in me or make me fighting mad. All I had to do was think about home.

In London the next afternoon I met my wife and five-year-old son, who had flown out from New York. Her field is public health medicine, and it was her contract with the Ghanaian government that was taking us to Africa. As our propeller-driven plane pushed its way down the baked Sahara, we speculated on what we would find in Ghana, which at that time, as usual, was very much in the news because of the visit of Her Majesty Queen Elizabeth. A couple of weeks before, some of President

Nkrumah's political opponents had set off a bomb in an attempt to blow up his statue in front of Parliament House. London newspapers had raised a hue and cry that the Queen's projected visit should be canceled in view of "unsettled conditions" in Ghana. These newspapers hinted at a popular uprising, presumably due to explode at any moment, which would overthrow what they called Dr. Nkrumah's dictatorial regime. After a visit by one of Mr. Macmillan's ministers to reassure the world that civil war was not imminent, it was announced that the Queen would keep to her schedule.

We arrived at the Accra airport just two days after the Queen and her husband had arrived from England. All private and public business seemed to have come to a complete standstill. The entire populace seemed to be in a state of intoxicated jubilation. There was much singing and dancing every night, and for these affairs many of the women wore ankle-length dresses emblazoned with photographs of Dr. Nkrumah and Queen Elizabeth. (I have never been able to determine what merchant —probably a Syrian or a Lebanese—had the foresight to order this printed cloth. He must have spent many an anxious moment when it seemed that the Queen's visit would be canceled.)

If the Queen's life was in danger, no one in Ghana seemed to know anything about it, and certainly not the people who were in charge of the preparations. There seemed to be no more than the normal number of guards and police escorts, which seemed totally inadequate to me, and the police were not even armed! In a country whose government was supposed to be in a virtual state of siege I saw neither rifle, pistol, nor any other lethal weapon until a friend took me to his farm to hunt bush fowl two months later.*

---

* This does not mean that the government could not show its muscle when necessary. Some months later when an attempt was made to assassinate Dr. Nkrumah and fifteen people were killed and more than two hundred wounded, weapons did appear in the hands of soldiers, who knew how to use them. A state of emergency was declared in Accra and a curfew imposed. The point of the story related above is that large sections of the Western press dislike the Ghana government enough to distort news about it deliberately.

That was a busy first week. Not only did we have to get settled in a new house, but my wife was expecting our new baby at any moment. There were all sorts of errands to be run and purchases to be made. However, with business at a standstill, we were considerably hampered. Several times I was stopped at road crossings by a lone policeman. Usually a small crowd would have gathered. Soon the Queen would be driven slowly by the crossing in the largest, most brilliantly polished automobile I have ever seen. She would be accompanied by either the President or her husband the Duke. Madam Fathia, Ghana's handsome first lady, would follow in a car a few yards behind, accompanied by whichever man was not beside the Queen. None of them showed the least sign of strain, despite the fact that riding in open cars on these public occasions was an open invitation to any provocation from the violent opposition.

I last saw the Queen at an intersection near the airport on the day she and the Duke were leaving the country. There was nothing to do but get out of our car and join the crowd along Independence Avenue, for no one was being allowed to drive across the intersection. Everyone looked expectantly in the direction of the President's office, from which the Queen would come. After a long while a Convention People's Party (C.P.P.) car with a loud-speaker mounted on top appeared. The spokesman within the slowly moving car addressed the crowd in a low, hushed voice: "Her Majesty the Queen of England is leaving Ghana, perhaps never to return again. Look happy for the Queen so that she will remember you. Kwame has done his job. Kwame is well."

In a few moments the Queen and the Duke passed, looking cool and unperturbed. Everyone waved and cheered, and the royal couple waved back. Then President Nkrumah's car passed, with him waving and smiling brightly as C.P.P. women along the way raised their voices in songs of praise. The royal visit had been a great personal triumph for him. Now that it was over, Ghana could settle down to normal again.

In the spring of 1961 Mr. Harold Isaacs published an article in *The New Yorker* under the title "Back to Africa." The article purported to be a serious study of American Negroes living in Africa. Its style was considered and its documentation impressive. It concluded that most American Negroes in Africa were unhappy and unwelcome. The reaction from Negro intellectuals was swift and angry. Those who had visited Africa denounced the article as a series of inaccuracies and distortions. Those of us planning to go to Africa for the first time were concerned, for we suspected there was a good deal of truth in it. However, we did note that the publication of the article coincided nicely with the assassination of Patrice Lumumba and the subsequent riotous demonstration by Negro intellectuals and nationalists in the United Nations building—a demonstration that shocked many whites, who had not realized how closely young Negroes identified with the African revolution. The Isaacs article, and a less impressive one by Russell Howe that appeared in *The Reporter*, were regarded as shots in a campaign to dampen such identification.

Although I shared this general view, no one unfamiliar with Africa could lightly dismiss Mr. Isaacs' closely reasoned article, and his gloomy conclusion was very fresh in my mind a few months later when our airplane set down at Accra. If what Mr. Isaacs said was true for most American Negroes, I was in for an especially difficult time, for I am not gregarious by nature and I value privacy above all else. I doubt if I have ever initiated a conversation with a perfect stranger, and the idea of establishing a friendship with anyone who lives within walking distance seems to me fraught with the terrible danger that at any moment the friend may interrupt my reading. Books are better friends than people; you may shut them or open them at your will without running the risk of injuring their feelings.

Despite this antisocial tendency I did wish to make a few friends in the country to which I was moving with my family, but I was quite prepared to find the rejection that Mr. Isaacs predicted and to carry myself in such a way that the rejection would not seem to hurt. My fears were groundless. I had been in Ghana hardly two weeks before it was clear that, at least where I was concerned, Mr. Isaacs was slightly off base, and I wondered that in New York we had paid him so much attention. For the common sense of the matter is that in every country in the world people make friends with those they like and avoid those whom they do not like. A person's strangeness or his nationality may be an initial barrier to intimacy, but in the end his attitude and behavior will determine whether he makes friends or enemies.

The first house we lived in was a large old frame bungalow on the grounds of Achimota College. As I have said, we were expecting a new baby, and there were a thousand and one details of adjustment that would have been impossible to overcome without the help and advice of the Ghanaians we met soon after arrival. Henry, who drove a lorry for the institute where my wife would work, was an especially good and welcome friend. He was the kind of person who knows how to do everything, where to borrow or buy anything, and exactly how much to pay for it. Because of a rather irregular childhood, he had lived in every section of the country and was fluent in all of the important languages. He was naturally biased in favor of his own group, the Ewe, but he had traveled broadly and had an intelligent and sympathetic appreciation of the other ethnic groups. Of an evening he would relate their histories, customs, and myths in rich detail, some of which, I later learned, he supplied from his own imagination. I forgive him his few excesses because it is almost impossible to hold an audience and stick to the naked truth, and Henry was a born storyteller. Anyway, I think I told him a few lies myself.

On the eighth day after the birth of our child—a son who is called Kwasi because he arrived kicking and screaming on a Sunday—Henry and a number of his coworkers gave an "outdooring" ceremony for him, a rite that is roughly similar to a christening except that it occurs long before dawn and involves a good deal of drinking. This particular ceremony was conducted by a tall man, very old, with fierce eyes and a bald head that looked as if it might have been carved from ebony. In his head he carried several generations of Ewe history and custom. He scolded the younger men who seemed to have forgotten the rites, correcting them when they chanted the wrong words and laughing at them when they appeared ridiculous to him. A lot of good palm wine and gin was poured on the ground as libations, and each of the men present gave a speech as the representative of his family. These speeches, with the exception of the elder's, were always heckled by the onlookers and invariably ended with the wish that the new baby would have a long, happy, and prosperous life. Then a shilling or two—"not because you are poor," as Henry, who had been interpreting into English, hastily assured us, "but only as an expression of the joy we feel that this blessed babe has been born on the soil of Ghana." We were much moved by the ceremony, not least because we knew that the people present earned only a few shillings a day, and that several of those who had arisen at three o'clock in the morning and dressed themselves in their finest had never seen or heard of us before!

Most of our early friendships were based on that "out-dooring" ceremony. The people present visited us again and again, and we visited their homes. I wondered if Mr. Isaacs had spent very much time in Ghana, and I thought of him weeks later when it became evident that we were going to have to sacrifice some of our friends if we were to get any work done in the evenings. It was January and February, when the heat during the day made concentrated work impossible. Even reading was difficult; I wanted only to sleep in the shade. Night seemed the only sensible time to work.

Yet there was seldom an evening when we did not have one or two visitors. They were the drivers, teachers, and clerks whom we had met in one capacity or another, and I remember a particularly adhesive college student who had the idea that I was a rich and important American who could secure him a scholarship to study in the United States. Many of our friends seemed to think we would be offended if they passed our house without coming in to greet us. It was therefore with wicked relief that I received the news that the college was reclaiming the house we lived in for a member of its faculty. We were forced to move into another neighborhood, somewhat less busy, several miles away.

None of this is to say that there are not American Negroes in Ghana who are very unhappy. One fellow I know came out with a few thousand dollars' capital with the intention of converting it into a million. He tried to swindle a Ghanaian who was a descendant of fifteen generations of traders. Now the Ghanaian has the few thousand dollars, and the businessman from America is, to say the least, very put out. There must also be a few Negro women who married Ghanaians abroad and came to Ghana totally unprepared to fit into a family system very different from the American pattern.

I believe that if Mr. Isaacs in his travels had looked more closely at his interviewees, he would have discovered that they felt unhappy and displaced not because they were *Negroes* but *Americans*. They are products, whether they like it or not, of the most highly technological society in the world, and their reactions to much that they see and experience are exactly the same as their white compatriots' or many Europeans'. They just cannot adjust to a society where things do not work with the same snap and efficiency as they are expected to in a highly industrialized nation. They see not what this nation has accomplished in less than ten years of independence, but only what has not been done.

Thus many a visitor, white or black, American, European, or even Russian, is very easily upset by superficialities. Delays in simple business transactions, often bungled by poorly trained and underpaid clerks, will have him pulling his hair. The mere act of making a telephone call can drive him mad, for if his own phone is not out of order, the one he is calling is likely to be, and if he is finally connected, he will either have a wrong number or have to talk over another conversation that is somehow being carried on the same line. In all probability neither the business transaction nor the telephone conversation will be of supreme importance, but if the visitor reacts to them as if the fate of a nation hung in the balance, he cannot survive many years in West Africa.

Very soon he is a walking hymn of complaints: It is not only the telephones and the transportation system that are atrocious; the people with whom he does business are trying to defraud him, and his house servants are stealing him blind. All of his complaints are composed in the same key and sung to the same tune. If he has a political background, let's say conservative, Ghana is a Red dictatorship that is rapidly going to the dogs; if he is a radical without a cause, Ghana is not having a revolution at all but merely undergoing a few bourgeois reforms. No matter what his political complexion, nothing in Ghana works well enough for him. And finally, what infuriates him most is the Ghanaian's stubborn and peculiar belief that he knows his country better than most outsiders.

Such people are members of a club called the Bitchers. When traveling in France and Italy, they pursue Coca-Cola because they cannot trust the local wine or water. In Cuba in 1960 at a celebration in the Sierra Maestra, I saw a group of American radicals threaten a counter-revolt because certain plans had gone awry and our contingent was without food and water for several hours. But I do not wish these examples to give the impression that the Bitchers are only Americans. They come from both sides of the Atlantic, and from both sides of the Curtain, and Africans find it difficult to distinguish between them. Whether from the East or the West, they wear the assumption that their technological superiority—which no one can question—is synonymous with cultural superiority—which is ridiculous.

The University of Ghana is set on the gentle green hills of Legon near Accra. Its white buildings with their rust-colored shingled roofs are a happy blend of oriental and colonial architecture. The lecture halls are spacious and airy, and I have been told that the laboratories are well equipped. The library is excellent, and there is an efficiently managed bookshop that would put to shame most of those in the United States outside of New York City. The university is one of the most attractive institutions of learning I have ever seen.

I soon felt, however—I think it was after my third or fourth visit—that something was very wrong at the university. Every place I had visited in Ghana thus far had seemed to bustle with life and color. In the principal marketplace my ears and eyes had been assailed by a prolonged explosion of languages and color, as around me swirled, it seemed, thousands of people selling and buying and haggling, arguing and laughing and hawking goods. The streets of Accra swarmed with people all engaged in some furious activity or other, while the children who were not themselves involved in some form of commerce ran laughing and playing, jumping over gutters, darting in and out of the crowds of passers-by. Even the offices of the ministries hummed with life as boys, in the style of the British Army, jumped to attention, responding to the cry of "messenger" with "Sah!" At the time I had little idea what Ghana was doing or where it was going, but it certainly seemed to be crashing along.

In comparison there was an almost deathly stillness about the university campus. One searched in vain for that atmosphere of youthful intensity (mixed with horseplay) that usually characterizes institutions where boys are girding intellectual loins for their leap into manhood and responsibility. One looked long and hard for the group of youths who assert that they have discovered the answers to all of the problems that have plagued mankind for thousands of years; or for the vocal minority of dissidents who insist that they have uncovered unmistakable evidence that God does not exist; or for the equally vocal minority who assert that He does indeed exist. All of the sound and the fury one associates with university life seemed to be missing.

I used to pick up student hitchhikers on my way to and from the university, which I visited frequently because my wife's office was there. From the students I expected to learn something of campus life, of Ghana, and of their attitude toward the world. With one or two exceptions they seemed to regard the university as a vocational school where one prepared for a job; all whom I met wanted to go to England or the United States to study, and I had the idea that if they got their wish, most of them had no intention of returning. They seemed to have little knowledge of the world outside Ghana and, worse, little curiosity (except about the wealth of the United States). I knew that most of them were attending the university on government grants, yet I never met a single student who expressed any commitment to, or interest in, the government's vast program to improve the lives of the common people of Ghana.

Now, this is a serious comment to make about an institution of such importance to the development of a small nation, and I certainly would not make it if I had not the observations of many others to support my own. In order to understand this unfortunate situation, I have asked questions of many different people. Their replies indicate that it is due in part to the intense, often irrational, bitterness of the faculty toward the government; in part, to their philosophy of education. I remember the political science lecturer whom I sought out because he had advertised certain household items for sale. A middle-aged Englishman, he was busy packing when I arrived. My accent told him I was American (and, therefore, a friend), so he set off on a tirade. Did I know, he asked, that Ghana had more embassies and high commissions abroad than New Zealand? Did I have any idea how much it cost to keep an embassy or a high commission? Countless thousands of pounds a year, he said. He shook his head bitterly. The country had once been a decent place to live (for whom? I wondered) but not any more. Well, he had had enough. He was bound for Australia, and that was why he was selling everything he could not carry with him.

I know now that many of the lecturers share his almost hysterical attitude toward the government. In their view everything the government does is wrong, and its mistakes are a constant source of mirth and sarcasm at their parties and dinners. Politically shy and incompetent themselves, they are distressed and frustrated by Dr. Nkrumah's ability to retain the support of the Ghanaian masses, despite the blistering his government takes weekly in the Western press.

Whereas the lecturers cannot and will not take to the political platform, they are not without power, and they know it, for they have within their hands the minds of the best educated youths of Ghana, and with this material they are putting up a stubborn resistance to government policies. At the heart of the matter is the fact that the government is Socialist and most of the lecturers are not. The government wants a university that will produce a man who not only is educated but is dedicated to perpetuating the ideals of the nation. Many of the lecturers, Ghanaian and European, to whom I have spoken seem to regard the university as a factory for the production of "gentlemen," in the English sense of the term. They speak angrily of the need for academic freedom, which, in my view, is merely another way of saying they want the right to continue turning out graduates who are either opposed or indifferent to the fundamental concepts of the government that provided them with their education. Dr. Nkrumah has made clear the position of the government on this question. Addressing students at a university dinner in February, 1963, he said:

"Not only as Chancellor of the University, but also as President of Ghana, I would like to assure you of my readiness to defend at all times this right [academic freedom] of the university, and to encourage all those who work within it—students, research scholars, and professors—to work with honesty and objectivity.

"There is, however, sometimes a tendency to use the words 'academic freedom' in another sense, and to assert the claim that a university is more or less an institution of learning having no respect or allegiance to the community or to the country in which it exists and purports to serve. This assertion is unsound in principle and objectionable in practice. The university has a clear duty to the community which maintains it and which has the right to expect concern for its pressing needs.

"We know that academic freedom can be perverted and even abused. It can also become a dangerous cloak for activities outside the academic interests and preoccupations of the community or of the university. Where this has happened, a grave disservice is done to everything for which knowledge and truth really stand. True academic freedom—the intellectual freedom of the university—is everywhere fully compatible with service to the community; for the university is, and must always remain, a living, thinking, and serving part of the community to which it belongs."

In a nation as dynamic as Ghana the problem of the university cannot long remain unresolved. Even as this paper was in preparation, Dr. Conor Cruise O'Brien accepted the vice-chancellorship of the university. It was Dr. O'Brien who, as the late Dag Hammarskjöld's representative in the Congo, authorized the use of force against Moise Tshombe.* As an intellectual rather than as a "gentleman," he resigned from the Irish Foreign Service to recover his freedom of expression—then accused the British government of bad faith in its Congo policy. A man whose courage and integrity one takes for granted, Dr. O'Brien still has his work cut out for him at the University of Ghana, but already one senses a change. The students seem livelier, and some of the more horse-and-buggy lecturers, who wanted to make the university a little Oxford or Cambridge, are cursing Dr. O'Brien over breakfast, lunch, and tea while they seek appointments elsewhere.

The Hausa Man found us soon after we moved into our bungalow at Achimota College. Actually he was only one of many Hausa men who passed our way bearing a large variety of trinkets, rugs, and household decorations for sale; but when we say Hausa Man, we always mean this particular fellow because he called himself that as if it were his name—and also because we knew and liked him better than any of the others and he seemed to like us. He came late one afternoon just before sunset, a tall bone-thin fellow, ebony black, with narrow features and a wisp of a white beard, garbed in a splendid white robe with golden stitching. Behind him walked his bearer, a muscular, poorly dressed Hausa

---

* See Dr. O'Brien's *To Katanga and Back* (New York: Simon and Schuster, 1962).

boy* from Northern Nigeria who bore on his head the load of masks, jewelry, and ornamental bows and arrows the Hausa Man wanted to sell.

I went to the porch to greet him and attempted to dissuade him from displaying his merchandise, explaining that we had everything we needed, and that if there was something we did not have, we no longer had the money to buy it. I was still in the stage where I translated every price quoted to me from Ghanaian pounds into dollars, and I was shaken by what seemed to me the high cost of living. I bought only what was absolutely and immediately necessary. (I maintained this resistance until a friend warned me that I must stop thinking in terms of dollars. "You earn pounds; spend pounds. If you think in dollars, you'll never spend a cent in Ghana.")

The twinkle in the Hausa Man's eyes told me that he did not believe I was without money, and he ordered his bearer to display the goods. I warned him that he was wasting his time, but he replied that time was a thing of no importance. His voice was rich; its vibrancy and the flowing manner in which he spoke reminded me of Sir John Gielgud in the quieter moments of *Richard of Bordeaux*. His goods were superb: the flat little Ashanti dolls with their white earrings and golden waist and neck pieces were the best we had seen; the bows and arrows looked almost authentic; and the quaint little figures wrought in iron, supposedly two centuries ago, caught my wife's fancy immediately. But, alas, when I cautiously inquired the price of these objects and then translated into dollars, I shook my head angrily, outraged at what seemed to be an attempt to plunge me into bankruptcy. I knew that by careful bargaining I could buy the objects I wanted for half the price he was asking, but even that seemed too much.

---

* I first described him as an Accra boy. Albert Kumah, who was typing the final draft, discovered my error. Mr. Kumah, who had never met this particular Hausa man or his bearer, said, "No Ghanaian would work for a Hausa man." "Why not," I asked, "if the Hausa man was paying?" Mr. Kumah shook his head. "None of us would work for him." Little matters like this are likely to trip the "expert."

He sighed and ordered his bearer to wrap up his merchandise. He did not seem greatly disappointed, but instead settled down for a chat. He was a Moslem who neither drank nor smoked, but he would take a glass of cold water. I must forgive him for asking, he said, but he guessed from my speech that I was an American. The great dream of his life, he said, was to see New York City. "My goodness," I said, astonished. "Why?" He said that during the war he had known many American soldiers stationed in Ghana, then the Gold Coast, and they had told him all about New York.

"Wonderful people," he said of the Americans, his dark eyes misty with reminiscence. "I liked them very much, and I was very sorry to see them go."

Now I was genuinely puzzled. People are usually not very sorry to see *any* army leave, so I pressed the Hausa Man to explain. "Well," he said, "they were always laughing and they always had very much money. Hausa Man would show them a watch or a doll or a rug, and they would buy it, just like that, the first price you asked." He shook his head in wonder. "I had never met people like that before. Oh, I was very sorry to see them go."

The Hausa Man came to see us several times, usually in the late afternoon when the heat had begun to lift and before the mosquitoes had rendezvoused in sufficient force to drive us off the front porch. He, at least, had some vague notion of the nation from which I came, garnered from the fanciful tales of American GI's and the motion pictures. I knew practically nothing of his people and culture, who traced their history back into antiquity. We used to entertain one another with tales of our different customs. I was conscious sometimes of exaggerating a point to achieve a certain effect, and I suspect that he did the same, for, like Henry, he was a born storyteller. Sometimes there existed between us a total lack of comprehension, like a great river that neither could cross. Once, for example, I tried to explain to him about the fate of illegitimate children in the United States. I had been making another point and had mentioned the illegitimate children as a side issue, but he bristled, unable to grasp the concept that any child could be illegitimate. For my part, his emotional and cultural attachment to his family was completely beyond me. It was not only his four wives and sixteen children back in the northern region of Nigeria for whom he worked, but a vast network of sisters, brothers, aunts, uncles, and cousins. He once told me that he spent so much time away from home because his relatives borrowed money from him, and I found it difficult to understand why he did not tell his relatives to go jump in the lake.

The Hausa Man went away for several weeks, and I realized for the first time how much I had come to count on our afternoon talks. Then, one day I looked up and saw him strolling across our front lawn like some biblical prince, his flowing robe caught in the breeze, his high pointed cheeks shining, and his eyes bright. He said he had been away to his home in Nigeria, and I expressed the hope that he had found his wives and children happy and well. He said that he had, but that the cost of living had risen so sharply that he was thinking of going into a new line of work, perhaps in his own country. He complained that it was becoming increasingly difficult for him to cross the borders of Togoland and Dahomey to get to Nigeria, borders he had been crossing for forty years without any difficulty. Now, because each was a sovereign nation, every border guard wanted papers, passes, and visas. It was either a question of his moving his family to Ghana, which he would have preferred, or returning to Nigeria to live permanently. The latter was the only course he could afford, and eventually that is what he did.

We never bought anything from the Hausa Man because we could not afford it; but before he left, he made my wife a present of the two funny little men wrought in iron that were supposed to be several centuries old. Now they sit with their mocking smiles on my wife's night table to remind us of the Hausa Man.

Soon one becomes aware of several coexisting communities that are superimposed on the ordinary society of Accra. The diplomatic community, for example, has a life all its own. The international importance of Ghana may be seen in the fact that more than forty nations are represented here by either an ambassador or a high commissioner. Each mission has at least one cocktail party or dinner a year, and most have several in honor of their respective national holidays. Usually these affairs are given at the swank Ambassador Hotel to the accompaniment of music from a fireman's-brigade type of band. None of the hosts is very strict about the invitation list; anyone who can scrape up a jacket and tie can saunter into a reception at the Ambassador without being noticed.

A few months after coming to Ghana, I began to write a thrice-weekly column for *The Evening News,* the ruling Convention People's Party newspaper. Consequently, the invitations to receptions and cocktail parties poured in, and because I had never attended diplomatic functions before, I tried to go to as many of them as I could. Before I tired of them—which was very soon —I learned that the idea was to stroll in wearing your black suit and shake hands with the miserable ambassador and his wife, who usually stand with their first and second secretaries at the entrance, smiling, bowing, and shaking hands. After that, unless you particularly like the ambassador, you need no longer pay any attention to him. When you have worked your way to the bar, grabbed a couple of sandwiches and a drink, you look for one of your closest friends in one of the islets of people standing nearby. Nothing of the slightest importance is ever said on these occasions. If you are a working journalist, the problem is to avoid the people whose countries you have written against the previous week. This is not as difficult as it may seem because they have usually seen you first and contrive to remain on the opposite side of the room. If perchance you should meet at the bar or the sandwich table, you smile and pretend you do not hate one another.

Naturally the hardest-working diplomatic staffs are the Russian and the American, with the Chinese and British running a close second. Probably because they were once the masters here and have had more experience in Africa, the British seem more at ease. They have left their substantial imprint on Ghanaian life and institutions, so they do not spend much energy attempting to sell Ghanaians the glories of the British way of life. They are knocked regularly in the local papers, but they are used to it and do not scream so loudly in protest. By their attitude they seem to say: "We may no longer rule here, but it will be many generations before you can forget us."

Here on neutral ground the Russians and the Americans are startling not so much for their differences as for their similarities. On an airplane some months ago I sat beside a young British engineer who was returning home after spending several months in the Soviet Union and the United States. He had left England with a natural bias in favor of his American cousins, but now he was very much bewildered. He told me that the Cold War now seemed to him a horrible mistake, a great misunderstanding between the two major parties. "I know you won't believe me," he said, "but the Russians and the Americans, they are so much alike it is incredible. They want the same things—material progress and all that it implies. It is just this stupid question of ideologies that divides them."

Perhaps the engineer was overstating his case, but in many ways the Russian and American diplomats in Ghana are alike. I think the basic similarity is in their attitude. They *know;* they have the message; they have come to instruct and to lead the way to the promised land. They show motion pictures, hold trade and book fairs, and wring your hand as if you were a long-lost friend suddenly risen from the dead.

In any popularity contest the United States would win hands down. There are probably Ghanaian youths who wish to study in Russia, but I have never met any of them. It is the image of the United States, as transmitted in motion pictures, magazines, and books, that has aroused their curiosity. The Americans have never cracked the whip in West Africa, and they still have a reservoir of good will here, despite the African's concern at reports of American racial discrimination. Moreover, since English is spoken by most Ghanaians of any education, their language gives Americans a decided advantage over the Russians.

Yet American embassy people here seem always to be on the defensive. Their standard reply to a question about racial violence in Little Rock, New Orleans, or the University of Mississippi is that things are getting better all the time. Look at the record, the Ghanaian is told: there are more American Negro college graduates than there are English graduates, etc. Look at what the Russians are doing to the Jews. The young Ghanaian goes away confused. He had asked his question in innocence and without rancor for, unless he was educated abroad, he simply does not know what racial discrimination is. Unlike the African who has lived in such white settler areas as Kenya, the Rhodesias, and South Africa, the West African has never experienced day-to-day naked white oppression. Therefore, he does not expect to be thrust into the middle of the Cold War—which is no concern of his—merely because he asked a question about something he had read in the newspaper.

I can think of one distinct advantage that the Soviet diplomat has over his American opposite. The Russian is used to dealing with the terms "colonialism" and "imperialism" as realities. The American always puts them within quotation marks, as if he did not quite believe in their existence, as if they were loaded Communist terms. A casual remark about United States imperialism in Latin America is liable to plunge him into a spasm of anger. "Where," he demands to know, "do we have troops in Latin America?" But "colonialism," "imperialism" and "neocolonialism" are all words that convey certain definite images to people in West Africa.

The Chinese are the most impressive and interesting people I have met among the diplomatic corps. Except that they tend to be a few years older, they remind me of the present Cuban leaders. Like the Cubans, the Chinese are disarmingly candid about their mistakes and difficulties. They do not ascribe all reports unfavorable to China as slanders of the lying capitalist press. The food shortage, for example—though never as severe as reported in the West—did exist. ("Poor weather and bad policies.") Differences with their Soviet ally? ("Of course, what can one expect between two sovereign nations? But don't expect us to make war on one another just to please the Americans.") There is a quiet confidence about Chinese embassy people. Their job is to win friends for their country, but they are less obvious about it than the other Cold War embassies. They seem to say for China: "Nonrecognition by the United States . . . exclusion from the United Nations . . . yes, those are major worries, not only for us, but for the world. But we know that no major problem can be solved without us. So we wait and work."

Another distinct community is composed of African refugees from the white settler territories of the Rhodesias (which will be renamed Gambia and Zimbabwe when they are free), Nyasaland, South Africa, and the British High Commission territories of Basutoland, Bechuanaland, and Swaziland. Many are not strictly refugees but students and professional men and women. The political activists among them are called Freedom Fighters. They are imbued with the single-minded purpose of freeing their countries, which are lumped together on the rich southern toe of the continent. Theirs is a lonely existence, for most have left their wives and children behind, and despite the generous support the Ghana government gives them, they are poor. Some have endured frightful hardships, a few have spent many years in prison, and it is safe to assume that the best of them—those who represent the greatest threat to the white settler regimes—will be imprisoned or killed before they are very much older.

The Freedom Fighters are always anxious to tell you about their countries, and there is a depressing sameness about the realities they describe. They are convinced that in nearly every territory only physical force, warfare of one type or another, will compel the white rulers to yield to the demand for "one man, one vote," which is another way of saying black self-government. Some of the leaders are extremely able men, widely traveled and possessed of great political wisdom. There are, unfortunately— as anyone who has lived in Harlem can see—a few very obvious frauds among them, who remind me of two or three of the more objectionable black nationalist leaders in New York. They are opportunistic men, who have found a good thing and are playing it for all it is worth. One knows almost instinctively that these particular fellows will never seriously threaten the rulers of their countries and that in a crisis they could not be trusted to face up to the terrible responsibilities (prison, deprivation, death) of being a leader in a revolution. They have merely managed to escape from their countries and now represent themselves as heroic figures they never were at home.

Fortunately the frauds are very few; most are genuine men who regard the future as a life-and-death struggle between them and their oppressors. They never sound foolhardy or walk about like outsized heroes; they are simply people who intend to solve the problems in their respective countries and, beyond that, to work toward the accomplishment of African unity. Talking to them, I sometimes think: If Africa's future rests in their hands, then surely Africa has a future.

The representative of a large news agency once told me, "I'm responsible for all of West Africa, but the truth is that to do my job I hardly ever have to leave Accra."

This was only a slight exaggeration. Ghana does set the political pace for most of Africa outside the Moslem world. It was Ghana's initiative in the United Nations, and her announced readiness to intervene unilaterally with other African nations if the U.N. could not, or would not, do the job, which saved the Congo situation from complete disintegration. It was Ghana's President who quarreled with Mr. Harold Macmillan about the haste with which the British Prime Minister had decided who was in the right or wrong in the Sino-Indian border dispute. And it was Ghana again who led the Afro-Asian bloc in the vital role it played in the 1962 Cuban crisis. One could cite many other international situations in which Ghana has played a leading and constructive role. In the movement to free Africa, Ghana has, until now,* held undisputed leadership as the first black African state to achieve its independence in the new era, and as the symbol to which the nonfree peoples of the continent looked for example and inspiration. The next generation of Africans—who do not read the harsh criticisms of Ghana in the Western press but who do listen to the powerful voice of Radio Ghana—look to her as an example of the kind of progress their own countries can make under strong Socialist leadership.

Such eminence is bound to arouse envy and jealousy in educated Africans not inclined toward Socialism. No one likes to be outdistanced, and there is no denying that Ghana is far ahead on nearly every count. I remember the startling reaction of a normally calm and shy, and apparently rational, Nigerian girl I met in Canada. She flew into a sudden rage when I happened to mention Dr. Nkrumah's name. "That man!" she cried. "I can't stand him!"

"But why?" I asked. "What has he done that's so bad?"

"Nothing. But why is it that every time I pick up the newspapers, there's his name?"

"Perhaps because he makes news."

"But why must he make the news all the time? Why not give someone else a chance? Just because they got their independence first!" Then she added, in an outraged wail, "And they're such a little country!"

This brings us to Dr. Nkrumah himself, who in a very real sense is the axle on which the Ghanaian wheel turns. It is not only that he is the founder of the nation and his Convention People's Party the only party backed by the masses. His personality, his spirit, his resourcefulness, are doing much to shape the destiny of an entire continent. This is difficult to comprehend for those of us who come from large, stable nations where presi-

---

* The independence of Tanganyika, and soon of Kenya, should relieve Ghana of the responsibility of having to bear the burden practically alone. The views of Mr. Nyerere and Mr. Kenyatta on Pan-Africanism are similar to Dr. Nkrumah's. Another factor is that their countries are geographically closer to South Africa, the liberation of which all African leaders place at the top of the agenda.

dents and prime ministers come and go regularly. Americans would react with shocked indignation to an attempt on President Kennedy's life, but there would be no fear that the Republic would not survive his death. Last August when President Nkrumah narrowly escaped assassination at a place called Kulungugu, not only Ghanaians but politically alert Africans everywhere felt they had almost been set back twenty years.

It is Dr. Nkrumah's vision of African unity—and his constructive activities in that direction—that raise him above the level of politician to statesman. A lesser man than Dr. Nkrumah might rest on his laurels, of which there are many. Or, since Ghana has tough internal problems—unemployment, inadequate education and housing, and a lack of highly trained civil servants who are both honest and loyal—he might devote his full energies to these problems. Certainly under his dynamic leadership Ghana would remain viable and prosperous for a few more years to come. But, when all is said and done, of what importance is Ghana by herself? Or Guinea, Mali, Dahomey, or even Nigeria with her autonomous regions? Political independence, a seat in the United Nations General Assembly, diplomatic representations—these are merely trappings as long as those states are so poor and underindustrialized that they cannot acquire the economic strength that is the only foundation for true independence. Dr. Nkrumah believes that Africa is at the crossroads now. If she allows herself to be Balkanized, as Latin America was, she will continue for perhaps another fifty years to produce raw materials, cash crops, and minerals for European and American factories, and to consume the finished products from those factories. She will continue to have the lowest standard of living in the world, although she is the world's richest continent.

These are a set of facts almost never reflected in American newspapers and textbooks, but most African leaders—especially President Nkrumah—know them by heart. They believe that the great wealth of Europe was built on the exploitation of Africa and Asia, and they are determined that in the new Africa such exploitation shall cease. However, this will only become possible when all of Africa is free and united politically and economically. It is known now that Africa has nearly everything it needs to produce adequate food, clothing, housing, and transportation for its 200-odd million people. This includes producing every hard piece of machinery that must at present be manufactured in the United States or the Soviet Union. When would it be possible to attain such economic independence if all of Africa were free and united tomorrow? Not for ten or twenty years—but certainly within the lifetime of a baby born as this is written.

Heady stuff? Of course. But so was the dream of a United States of America in 1775—what would have happened if each of the original thirteen states had decided to go it alone?—and so was the dream of a Soviet Union in, say, 1916. In all of Dr. Nkrumah's speeches, and in his person, one senses an urgency on the question of unity that cries out to all Africans, "We must start now before it is too late." He knows that the road toward unity is long and difficult, and that too many leaders are prone to take handouts, such as associate membership in the European Common Market. Therefore Ghana and Kwame Nkrumah must keep the pressure on by setting the pace. And no one can doubt his sincerity, for he has repeatedly offered to sacrifice Ghanaian sovereignty in the interest of the dream of all Pan-Africanists: a United States of Africa.

SHEPARD L. FORMAN

■ *BRAZIL*

Up from the Parrot's Perch

The youth of Brazil inherit a nation obviously on the road to political, economic, and social maturity. It is an anxiety-producing legacy that now weighs heavily on a new middle class. Formerly, the exclusive heirs were a traditional elite, concerned only with their own potential and with the nation only as it served their personal needs. The technological and social revolution that has come to Brazil amidst the cacophony of the twentieth century has redirected the will to new inheritors.

Brazilian society is undergoing a radical transformation. This fact never leaves you throughout your short or extended stay in the country. The amazing population explosion promises to make Brazil one of the world's leading nations, at least in number of people and land area. While the country is predominantly rural, the centers of power are shifting to the cities, where rapid growth has been accompanied by changing class structures. Industrialization is creating a large urban proletariat; bureaucracy and com-

Shepard L. Forman graduated from Brandeis in 1959 and went on to get his M.A. at New York University. He is currently doing graduate work at the Institute of Latin American Studies of Columbia University.

mercialism have swelled the number in the new middle and upper classes. Even in isolated rural areas where traditional patterns are still strong, the great processes of change have begun. Plantations are being mechanized, and the old system of paternalism is giving way to more "businesslike" approaches to labor relations. Peasants are migrating to the cities or are following the harvests throughout the countryside, and they are banding together to seek solutions—legal or otherwise—to the problems that have beset them for centuries.

The migratory flow from rural areas into the cities has added to the existing problems of the natural increase in urban population and the large-scale immigration from abroad. Overcrowding has created very serious difficulties in housing, health and sanitation, water supply, transportation, and education. Neither production nor means of supply has improved enough to meet growing demands. Food shortages are common in both the cities and the rural areas. Eventually Brazil's enormous frontiers will be used to redistribute the population and stave off their hunger.

The rapidity of change in all spheres has led to a crisis of leadership, which is probably the most alarming of all the acute problems that confront Brazil today. Each successive government wanders ineffectually through the muddle of political and economic emergency. There has been a tendency of late to "lean to the left" and pay at least lip service to necessary reform. It is difficult, however, to distinguish between honest conviction and political demagoguery. A clear political ideology and a decisive program are yet to be elaborated. To be sure, there has been a general awakening to the Brazilian revolution; the urban and rural lower classes cry out in desperation, and the upper class is far from indifferent. It has a definite stake in the affairs of the nation. Nevertheless, its energies are expended in consolidating its own position. Meanwhile, the middle classes, the most heedful segment of Brazilian society, are enmeshed in their own needs and frustrations. They are suspended somewhere between the traditional values of the "old aristocracy" and new patterns of behavior that are yet to be defined. The youths of this class, however, have conceived of themselves as the "new leaders" of the future and as the spokesmen of their people. They are thoroughly aware of the enormous potential that is Brazil and are determined to realize it.

For two years I followed the transformation of Brazilian society from afar. At New York University's Brazilian Institute I was able to study Brazilian history, economics, literature, music, sociology, and anthropology. I drank *cafezinho* and *cachaca*, an alcoholic beverage made from sugar cane; tasted black beans (*feijao*) and manioc flour (*farinha*); watched Bangu win the international soccer games at the Polo Grounds; and even danced the samba at an authentic carnival ball in New York. Many Brazilians in the United States—students, businessmen, foreign servicemen, and tourists—became my friends. The impressions that I gathered were overwhelmingly satisfactory, and I had an insatiable thirst to study *in loco*. I wanted to live among the Brazilian people, the approximately seventy million people who are the "stuff" of the great nation, and to see for myself the full vitality of change. Fellowships under the National Defense Education Act and the Fulbright program gave me my opportunity to travel throughout Brazil from June, 1961, to July, 1962.

From the air, Rio is unquestionably the world's most beautiful city. It stretches out from the green and black chain of mountains and hills to the excellent harbor and blue waters of the Bay of Guanabara. But the overwhelming beauty that was Rio at first sight was tempered on the ground. I left the airport and drove through the industrial zone with its huge smokestacks, smoldering dumps, and squalid slums. The tall, modern skyscrapers and bustling traffic cleared my vision as I passed through the busy downtown section of the city. Once the sea was again in view, Rio reclaimed her aspect of fantasy.

From my hotel on the beachfront in Copacabana, the playground of visitors to Rio and the most sought-after residential area of the city, one can walk along Avenida Atlantica and look out at the sea and the carefree bathers on the beach; admire the comfortable hotels, well-stocked shops, sidewalk cafes, and imposing apartment houses that line the streets; and marvel at the few remaining private homes—opulent keepsakes of not too long ago. Only in this past half-century have they bowed to the enormous demand for space in the "marvelous city."

Living conditions in Rio de Janeiro exemplify a national urban pattern. Upper- and middle-class demands for housing have created a building boom, accompanied by excessive land speculation and extremely high rents. Young people and the lower middle classes, operating on limited budgets in Brazil's runaway inflation, are forced out to the distant suburbs, from where they must commute many hours a day. The very poor live anywhere and nowhere. They take any piece of available land to build their miserable slums, called *favelas*. In Manaus, the old Amazon rubber capital, they cloister on the riverbank. In Salvador they balance on stilts above the Bay of All Saints, now sometimes called the "Bay of All Saints and of all devils." They surround Brasilia. Laborers often sleep on the construction sites where they work. A carnival song describing the plight of urchins in Salvador explains the derivation of their nickname, Sand Captains. It goes, "I have nowhere to live. Therefore I live in the sand!"

In Rio de Janeiro, the slums are in glaring contrast to an otherwise wholesome atmosphere. Wooden shacks, most of them electrified but without water or sanitation facilities, climb the hills throughout the city. They defy the elements in their precarious stance. How long can they withstand wind and rain before they are pushed or washed down from the hills? Sitting on the roof of one of the buildings along the beach, I once watched an entire tenement hill catch fire. The dangers are always imminent.

The overcrowded conditions in Rio have not been alleviated by the building of Brasilia. The urban problems caused by overpopulation go unsolved. Once-beautiful mosaic sidewalks are cracked and broken and littered with rubble; walking down dark streets at night, you can easily fall into a gaping hole or step into a pile of rubbish. Pipelines built many years ago cannot possibly conduct water for over three million inhabitants, and therefore many of the finest apartment buildings are forced to ration water.

Women and children can be seen in their daily descent from the slums with empty water cans on their heads. The same condition applies to telephones. The lines cannot be stretched to service demands. A family without "pull" may wait as long as ten years, or forever, for a telephone installation. Existing telephones are often sold along with apartments. They bring a much higher rental.

Traffic congestion seems to be an impossible dilemma. The beautiful Bay of Guanabara has been partly filled in to widen Rio's existing roads, and there is talk of building a tunnel under it. Tunnels already have been cut through the mountains. Many of the transportation difficulties stem from bad planning, of course. Until recently, for instance, a streetcar line ran the wrong way on the important one-way avenue that leads from the beach suburbs into the city. The basic reason, however, is the huge influx of cars.

Despite constant talk of improvements, with each successive government promising additional trains, buses, and streetcars to service disgruntled commuters, transportation companies continue to run at a deficit. The financial condition of the streetcar line in Rio was so bad that company officials offered to abolish fares if they could cut crews to one man per car, and only pressure from influential labor groups forced government officials to refuse the request. Each administration also promises to supply water and telephones, to clean up the city, and to demolish the slums. Candidates' platforms stress the same necessities in every election year. The *cariocas,* as the inhabitants of Rio are called, have gradually become immune to disappointment. Their reactions are usually the same: "It must be done, but let's not expect any miracles!"

The patience of the *carioca* is, in all certainty, a virtue. An American in Rio delights in the aesthetic comforts of the city, but is short-tempered with the lack of public service. The family of a bank officer with whom I lived for a time in Rio has a lovely apartment in a high-priced co-operative building in Copacabana. Three elevators service the seven-floor, twenty-eight family building. Invariably, two are shut off due to lack of power, and waiting for the third becomes tedious. The building rations water to one half-hour each morning and another half-hour in the evening. The bathtub, sinks, pots, and pans hoard the water supply for the day. Mineral water was bought for drinking purposes. The family waited for over three years for a telephone to be moved from their previous residence. Each morning, while the water was running, the lady of the house would plug in her new washing machine, only to blow a fuse. She never complained, but walked gaily through the house singing, "In the morning we have no water . . . at night we have no light!"

The *laissez-allez* attitude, which is necessary to stave off madness, is used to rationalize the worst blight of the city, the slums. Most *cariocas* insist that the *favelado,* or slum dweller, is happy in his wretched state. They explain that he lives as he does to avoid paying rent so that he can squander his money on *cachaca,* soccer games, and carnival costumes. Fortunately, this is untrue. Fellow students introduced me to many *favelados,* among them Alberto, who manifests the basic dissatisfaction of his contemporaries. As a boy, Alberto migrated to Rio with his family. They moved into a small shack on one of the hills, with his father working as a laborer and his mother as a domestic. Alberto and his brother, forced to contribute to the family income, had to pass up school and take jobs on a construction crew. At twenty-two, his one desire is now to learn to read and write so that he can get his driver's license, increase his earnings at much more pleasant work as a chauffeur, and move down from the hill. Alberto is a typical case.

Though I spent extended periods in Rio de Janeiro and Porto Alegre, I traveled as much as I could throughout the countryside of North and South Brazil. The unending flow of traffic into the cities goes on here as elsewhere. The most attractive destinations are São Paulo, Rio de Janeiro, and Brasilia. However, migrants come from the interior in steady streams to all of the state capitals and to the other cities that are sprouting along the heavily traveled new highways. Many travel with their families, but most come alone. The majority are young. Once exposed to the promises of the city, few return to their homes. All of these migrants have been collectively designated *pau de arara,* "parrot's perch"—an apt description of the passengers who travel down the hot, bumpy highways standing in open trucks and clutching the railings for balance. They also make the trip daily on buses and trains, or even on foot, sometimes leading a mule heavily laden with their meager possessions.

Wherever you go in Brazil, you are accompanied by *pau de arara.* I took a trip on one of the four paddle-wheel steamers that journey along the São Francisco River from Joazeiro, Bahia, in the hard-pressed Northeast, to Pirapora, Minas Gerais, from where there are bus connections to São Paulo. The passengers suffered devastating heat and dryness. They slept on top of cargo on the lower deck or in hammocks strung one above the other on flatboats. First-class cabins, consisting of two bunk beds, normally accommodated as many as six or even eight people. The trip upstream to the South takes up to twenty days when the river is low, and it is known to be dangerous. I caught malaria on the ten-day trip downstream; and the week before, a young man had died of food poisoning. Yet this never seems to stop anyone.

In addition to limited occupational opportunities, rural towns and villages do not offer sufficient educational facilities. Many towns are entirely without schools. In some rural communities, facilities are limited to the first few years of primary school, and even those wealthier communities that offer both primary and secondary education suffer the enormous gap between the increased number of students and available teachers. There is a huge and growing demand for teachers in the large urban centers, where primary and secondary schools have been forced to adopt double and even triple sessions. Most teachers prefer to remain where entertainment and companionship are readily available. Entertainment in even the large interior towns is limited to the local movie house, Sunday soccer matches, or an occasional dance at the local club. Many rural towns and villages cannot even boast these diversions, so there is a compelling attraction in the city's promise of excitement in addition to work or school.

Even the residents of Bom Jesus dos Passos, truly a "tropical paradise," cannot be satisfied. This is an island community of about two thousand inhabitants, located in the Bay of All Saints about one hour by motor launch from Salvador. It is an island of fishermen and lacemakers; but nearby oil riggings have largely destroyed the fishing economy, and handmade lace products, despite their beauty, are no longer in demand. Thus the island's chief product is people, a large majority of them very young. Though there is a primary school on the island, the teacher is rarely there. She feigns illness in order to remain on the mainland. The only outlet for these people is to leave the island—and the young are doing just that in increasing numbers.

It is a rare case, however, when the city fulfills its promise completely. The great demand is for skilled labor in Brazil, but the bulk of rural migrants are equipped to do little more than manual or domestic labor. Their slum shacks are possibly worse than their previous homes in the interior, and although the federal government subsidizes secondary education, many cannot afford the time for schooling. Time is money to those who must work to eat. In many ways, the poverty that they try to leave behind accompanies them to the cities. Nonetheless, their lot is vastly improved. Their pitifully low salaries are still considerably higher than their previous earnings, even when their rising pay scales have to compete with skyrocketing prices. But whatever improvement they achieve never lives up to their expectation. These newcomers to the city are therefore frequently economically and socially frustrated. They are an uprooted people, unprepared for the challenges of a sophisticated urban life. They try to forget their dissatisfaction in play—*cachaca*, soccer, and carnival. Still they are desperate. They seek bonds with their fellows and join clubs and unions, looking for leadership and becoming likely prey to the appeal of a charismatic leader or even a demagogue.

Occasionally, of course, there is a success story in the city.

There is a certain amount of social mobility that is based on educational or economic attainments, and race is not a factor. A racial consciousness does exist in Brazil, but there is no racial problem as we know it. To be sure, color lines darken as you descend the rungs of the social ladder. However, color is not a barrier to assuming new class status. I know of a young Negro student who left his lower-class family in the interior and moved to the state capital on a government subsidy to attend secondary school. He entered the university and received free room and board and a small monthly allowance. He led his class academically and was elected president of his school council. He is now a highly respected member of the university community and recently took a part-time "white-collar" job in a government office. He was thus able to rise above his lower-class position. His new status was clearly reflected in the form of address used by a lower-class mulatto, who called him *meu branco,* "my white man."

The largest exodus in this country of continually shifting populations is from the heavily populated Northeast, the most economically depressed area in Brazil. The region offers little to speak of in the way of industry and is, by and large, given to an agricultural economy. A narrow belt of coastal lowlands devotes its rich, black soil almost exclusively to the cultivation of sugar cane. Although sugar cane has now become a drag on the national economy, landowners have done well on federal price supports and subsidies and are unwilling to redirect their attentions to the production of necessary food products. Moving inland, a higher and drier land area is primarily exploited for the production of cotton, henequin, fruits, and relatively few foodstuffs. This is a transitional zone between the coastal lowlands and the periodically drought-ridden interior of the region. There is some arable land in the *sertao,* or backlands, but most of this massive unproductive area is covered with scrub brush called *catinga.*

Most all of the land throughout the Northeast is held in large landholdings called *latifundio,* which are, at times, corporate ventures. The great majority of peasants seek their livelihood on them. Traditionally they received the protection of the landowner, but in the competitive markets of today there is little room for the paternalistic patterns of the past. Landowners are more concerned with the profits from a commercial crop than with feeding the local peasantry, so that sharecroppers and tenant farmers, whose families may have been on the land for generations, are frequently dispossessed. Labor is hired on a work-a-day basis at an average daily wage of 150 cruzeiros (at the 1962 exchange, this equals 40 cents). The inflated prices of even the most basic foodstuffs—beans, rice, manioc flour—often make these minimal necessities inaccessible to the rural workers. Supplies of wheat, powdered milk, and other products from the United States under the Food for Peace Program prove inadequate, in both quantity and method of distribution. All too frequently they are the object of commercial speculation and find their way to the shelves of supermarkets in the coastal cities; as a result, there has been an increasing number of raids on markets in interior towns and villages by hunger-driven peasants.

Missing the protection of the traditional *patrao,* or "boss," Brazil's exploited peasantry is banding together and turning to new leaders. National Congressman Francisco Juliao (of the Brazilian Socialist Party from the state of Pernambuco) has been the recognized leader of Brazil's downtrodden rural masses since he undertook their defense in a legal battle in 1955, which established a communal, state-owned farm at Galilee in the county of Vitoria de São Antonio, Pernambuco. There the first Peasant League was created and given the high-sounding title of the Agricultural and Breeding Society of the Planters of Pernambuco. Juliao has met with limited success in building up his charisma, but he has been relatively unsuccessful in his attempts to make the Peasant Leagues an effective national organization. The leagues are rather loosely organized around local and state leaders who concentrate on making the peasant "aware of social justice and his rights." They provide legal aid, often defend squatter's rights in court, and have instigated many land invasions.

Since their beginning, the Peasant Leagues have been highly criticized in some circles and greatly overrated by the Brazilian and American press. They have been labeled Communist by conservatives, are generally misunderstood or ignored by moderates and "cringing" liberals, and have recently come under fire from the Communists and extreme left-wing elements in Pernambuco. With the leagues' expansion and increased activity, including the recent land invasions associated with them, a rather diverse opposition has grown up. Rival leagues have been started by federal and local organizations and by certain elements of the clergy. Local landowner leagues, often accompanied by their personal armies of hired guns and such terror groups as the dreaded Syndicate of Death, have sprung up in opposition. As the undeclared war is waged at a grass-roots and an ideological level, the landowners and the middle class of interior cities are reacting with fear. At a Peasant League meeting in an interior town of Pernambuco, guns aimed at the meeting's youthful organizers wounded a peasant and killed a twelve-year-old boy. In João Pessoa, capital of the Northeast state of Parahiba, over five thousand peasants gathered in a march to protest against the assassination of their state leader. Such determined resistance on the part of the landowners could well force the hand of the humble, but desperate, peasantry.

Conditions in the Northeast have awakened both the Brazilian and the United States governments. The Superintendency for the Development of the Northeast, SUDENE, is receiving massive support from the Alliance for Progress. Celso Furtado, the Brazilian economist who directs SUDENE, has received pledges of $131,000,000 from the United States for public works projects in the region over the next year. The Brazilian government promises to contribute even more. The Northeast is also receiving technical aid from Israel, Holland, Germany, and France, and industrial development projects from behind the Iron Curtain, principally from Czechoslovakia, are underway. Still, even under the most favorable conditions, the land area of the Northeast cannot support its twenty-three million inhabitants. Only mass migration can stave off wholesale starvation.

An American agronomist, a specialist in the area, told me, "Brazil still has time, because it has a frontier." Many of the large, uncultivated land areas are, however, already the object of commercial speculation that could lead to another monoculture cycle. Preferably, these lands could be used for a responsible agrarian reform program, but the legislation providing for government purchase of unproductive lands is currently bogged down in a conservative Congress. Even if they were to act, which is unlikely at present, the Brazilian government could not possibly afford to conduct a large-scale operation of this type. There are, however, scattered instances of land reform. The governor of the state of Rio Grande do Norte, Aluisio Alves, recently expropriated land in his state and is dividing it among peasants in the area. The land in question was a privately owned plantation forfeited to the federally owned Bank of Brazil, and the usurpation of this land was a bold move on the part of a state governor to by-pass federal immobility. Such action brought direct aid from the Alliance for Progress to Rio Grande do Norte. The United States ambassador to Brazil, Lincoln Gordon, promised to help finance similar projects in the state of Pernambuco. SUDENE has planned colonization to the northern state of Maranhão and to reconstitutable land along the São Francisco River. But these projects are far too limited. Even SUDENE's modest program has already been exceeded by voluntary migration to these areas and to the South.

The South of Brazil will probably pattern the future of the nation. It is highly developed, in contrast to the more backward North and Northeast, and one can already see that it is leading to the emergence of a new Brazilian society. At the turn of the century this area of Brazil pioneered in large-scale immigration from abroad, particularly from Germany, Italy, Poland, and Japan. The colonization projects were planned to counterbalance the large commercial crops to the North and have contributed to the predominance of smaller, more productive farms engaged in a diversity of agricultural pursuits. Thus the South suffers far less from the traditional patterns that dictate the way of life in many other regions of Brazil, where the large plantations necessitated a slave-holding economy. Many of the interior communities are able to furnish sufficient occupational outlets and schools for their inhabitants, and some of the large interior cities can support rural universities. One need only travel through the state of São Paulo to see a totally different Brazil from the one I have described so far. The city of São Paulo, with well over four million inhabitants, belongs very much to the twentieth century. Its growing industry, its active commerce, and its energetic people set the pace for the entire nation.

Rio Grande do Sul, the southernmost state in Brazil, offers no comparison to the industrial importance of São Paulo. Yet it stands as a fine example of development in contrast to the backward North and Northeast. The industriousness of the European has combined with the strong individualism of the gaucho, weaned on the great ranches and on continuous border wars, and has produced an energetic and progressive people. To be sure, poverty and illiteracy still exist, but in much smaller proportions than elsewhere in the country. There are hungry people, but less starvation; small properties, but fewer displaced peasants; more industry and less unemployment. The great processes of change are readily apparent. One farmer rides across a field on a tractor, while his neighbor bends over a hoe. Next to a modern shoe factory, women stitch sandals by hand. Skilled craftsmen work in their homes across the street from a large silver factory. A cathedral tower is silhouetted against the sky, but it shares the panorama with the small steeple of a Protestant church.

When I moved from Rio de Janeiro to Porto Alegre, the capital of Rio Grande do Sul province, I noticed more than the sudden change from the warm sea breezes and sunny beaches to the cold winter rains of June in the South. There was also a change from the cosmopolitan indifference of Rio to the warm hospitality of the gaucho. The apartment-house complex and the comparatively high rents of Rio de Janeiro made living conditions difficult. Space is at a premium in Rio, and few families have room for visitors or even paying guests, so that I spent most of my time moving between boarding houses and hotels. There was little opportunity really to acquaint myself with the life of a Brazilian family. Social and academic contacts were those of a "temporary observer," and my outlook was largely transient. In Porto Alegre I was given the opportunity to participate fully in the daily lives of Brazilians. I went there with seventeen other American students to take part in a special summer seminar at the University of Rio Grande do Sul. The program, sponsored by the Luso-Brazilian Center at the University of Wisconsin, consisted of four courses conducted by visiting Brazilian lecturers in regional studies of linguistics, literature, and anthropology. Although it was winter recess at the university, many Brazilian students attended our classes and we were thoroughly integrated into their social activities. Immediate and intense contact with Brazilians was also provided through the living arrangements made by our host university. Brazilian families showed us a maximum of hospitality in opening up their hearts and homes.

My Brazilian family lived in a comfortable one-level home in one of the middle-class residential zones of the city. At the top of a hill, above the house, stands one of the city's many private primary and secondary schools. Directly behind the house, on sunken land unsuitable for construction, are three slum shacks, each housing sizable families, the inevitable chickens, dogs, and some goats that wandered freely on the streets nudging passers-by. Porto Alegre was at once inviting and comfortable. The city, consistent with national patterns of growth, boasts some 600,000 inhabitants. It is bounded on one side by the Rio Guaiba, where five tributaries come together to form a river port. Behind the city, suburbs stretch for miles across gently rising hills. Modern skyscrapers and multiple-unit apartment houses rise continually in the downtown area and sharply contrast with the old imperial

architecture of the government buildings, the older intown resi-
dences, commercial dwellings, and the slums that surround them.
Buses, streetcars, and automobiles crowd the city's narrow, hilly
streets. Like all of the major cities in Brazil, Porto Alegre has a
main street of commerce that is closed to motor traffic by the
movement of shoppers and the congestion of idlers who gather to
talk. Rua da Praia, or Beach Street, houses hundreds of well-
stocked shops to fill the wants and needs of the growing middle
class and boasts several fashionable movie houses, restaurants,
and bars, which along with the abundant private clubs in the city,
quench the gaucho's thirst for entertainment.

My Brazilian "family" had their place in the life of the city. The
father represented a building supply firm and distributed *erva
mate,* a tealike herb used to make a hot drink favored by the
gauchos. His work required constant travel in his home state, and
he was away as many as fifteen days at a time. On these occasions
his wife substituted as the head of the household. She was kept
busy constantly, working along with the maid in the daily household chores, supervising the education and social life of her two
sons, and doing the marketing and cooking. The two boys attended secondary school. The elder one, twenty-one years old,
was preparing to take the entrance examination to the university.
He held a part-time job in one of the commercial establishments
in the city. The son of seventeen, who was about to enter senior
high school, occasionally helped his father in the office. Both boys
attended classes in the evening.

My Brazilian family was comfortable by any standards. Their
house was equipped with every type of appliance, from toaster to
washing machine, and though they did not as yet have a television
set, each member of the family had his own radio. They drove a
twelve-year-old European car, still a sign of status in Brazil.
Summer vacations were spent in travel or at a nearby beach resort. They lived according to middle-class values as we know
them in the United States, but still adhered to many of the traditional patterns of behavior. The father of the family was truly the
head of the household. Discussions were held on most subjects,

but his word was always final. He was also considered the patriarch of the extended family, as its oldest and most successful member. In traditional paternalistic fashion they took care of the maid and her six-year-old son, making themselves responsible for the child's housing, clothing, food, and education.

I soon entered into a daily routine. Each morning I walked down the hill and caught a streetcar or a bus to the university, either returning home for the big midday meal with the family or having lunch in one of the two low-cost restaurants provided on campus for students and professors. Entertainment was centered around family visits, dances and parties at the private clubs that are the focal points of Brazilian social life, or an occasional movie. The theaters showed a majority of Hollywood films, which unfortunately furnish Brazilians with most of their misconceptions about American life; but they also presented many of the European film vogues and, from time to time, a festival of films from behind the Iron Curtain. The young Brazilian film industry, trying to appeal mainly to the lower classes, was the object of considerable joking; though several Brazilian movies have won international awards, they are usually of an extremely low caliber. Occasionally, a play or concert provided some variety. Dating was rare due to a strict Brazilian code. Most social activity was conducted in groups, although even this tradition is fast breaking down among the middle classes in the large coastal cities. Thus my contact was mainly with students. They were quite politically oriented and adored discussions, principally about the state of Brazil.

I arrived in Porto Alegre in the last few months before the resignation of Janio Quadros from the presidency of the republic. The climate of public opinion at that time was generally favorable to the chief of state. He was the "champion of the downtrodden," pledged to major efforts on behalf of the Northeast and Brazil's other chronic problems. The middle classes admired his apparent honesty and dedication. His administrative experience as governor of the state of São Paulo seemed to be paying off in Brasilia, the national capital. The nation was moving ahead. In general there was overwhelming confidence in the dynamic young leader. Brazilians were working hard and eagerly, answering their president's call to sacrifice for their own futures and for the good of the nation.

However, not everything went well for Quadros. Although he was elected with the largest mandate in Brazilian history, a conservative opposition Congress refused to support his domestic program. His foreign policy was also causing consternation among conservative elements. He pressed for re-establishment of diplomatic relations with the Soviet Union and for the development of economic relations with the Communist bloc nations. Brazil undertook the diplomatic defense of Cuba; and the highest national honor, the Order of the Southern Cross, was conferred on Che Guevara. Quadros thus came under pressure, both military and civilian, and he knew that he could not carry out his plans for Brazil without sweeping executive powers.

After being denounced by an opponent on a nationwide hookup for an alleged coup d'état, Janio Quadros announced his resignation to a perplexed nation. It is obvious that Quadros never expected his resignation to be accepted. He counted on the fact that Vice President Jango Goulart would be completely unacceptable to congressional and military leaders and to the bulk of the Brazilian people because of his extreme leftist tendencies.

Quadros was surprised. Congress accepted his resignation, and the military, acting in a swift power play, sent him scuttling out of the country. Mounting public support was quickly turned away from Quadros when the military, in violation of the constitution, refused to allow Goulart to take office. The whole country cried out for constitutional legality. Federal administrative machinery came to a complete halt. The banks were shut down, and there was a general work stoppage. Although strict censorship was imposed on all newspapers and radio and television stations, the "voice of legality" was broadcast throughout Brazil on shortwave frequencies. The idea of legality caught on, and the clamor went up throughout the nation. The middle classes raised their voice against the threat of military dictatorship and in support of crumbling democratic institutions. Students effected a general strike and manifested their solidarity with organized labor. Congress and the military were forced to compromise. They quickly arranged a makeshift parliamentary system that would transfer many of the presidential powers to Congress. Goulart was welcomed back into the country and ushered into the "limited presidency" as the personification of constitutional legality.

The stability that Janio Quadros promised the Brazilian nation has been replaced by immobility. Despite the prestige that Goulart gained after official visits to the United States and Mexico, he is still unable to govern. He is trying desperately to win back complete presidential powers from a lameduck, do-nothing Congress. At the same time, Congress is unwilling to relinquish its new-found authority. In the hope that a national plebiscite will destroy the relatively unpopular parliamentary system, Goulart is busily creating an image of national ineffectiveness, using Congress as a scapegoat. Upon the resignation of the military man designated prime minister, Goulart nominated a man whom he knew Congress would reject. His second choice resigned after a squabble with the president over cabinet appointments. On his third and final chance, he came up with a compromise candidate.

While the power struggle continues, the nation waits. The industries, mainly in the South, produce in sufficient quantity, but inflation continues its upward course. The price of the dollar per cruzeiro increased from approximately 200 to almost 500 between June, 1961, and August, 1962, and has gone up since. The great commercial crops—sugar cane, coffee, cacao, cotton henequin—exhaust enormous amounts of land and labor that could be redirected to the production of fruits, vegetables, and dairy products. Instead, the commercial exploitation of land, inadequate means of supply, and price speculation all contribute to the shortage of foodstuffs in Brazil. Even the major cities near the centers of production are at times without food supplies. There are always long lines for milk in every Brazilian city. Rio de Janeiro went for a time without sugar, and Salvador spent several weeks without bread because of wheat shortages. These are only isolated examples. While buying power has increased generally throughout Brazil, it is of no avail when foodstuffs are not in the markets. Important headway is being made in transportation, steel and oil production, hydroelectric power, and automobile manufacture, yet none of these are exercising their full potential for growth.

As a result of the constitutional crisis, the atmosphere in Brazil has changed from one of national confidence to one of discouraged hope, but continued ambition. Brazilians have by no means lost sight of the future. Yet they anticipate elections with increased anxiety and tension. What Brazil needs—and everyone is well aware of this—is honest and imaginative leadership.

The future leadership in Brazil will undoubtedly come from the articulate youth of the middle class. These young people have become extremely conscious of the needs of their nation because they are unquestionably affected by them. They cannot conceive of a personal future apart from a national one. Since they believe that they have the power to set things right, they are totally immersed in politics and ideological discussion. A group of young men in Manaus, anguished by the stagnancy that has accompanied the death of the rubber boom, bands together on a street corner at night. Once they were content to express themselves in the weekly literary supplement that they contributed to a city newspaper. Now they openly support political candidates and even consider launching a candidate of their own for public office.

The training ground for such youth is obviously the university, but the university in Brazil—indeed the entire educational system—is also in dire need of reform. Under the terms of the Fulbright program, I attended classes in the faculties of philosophy at both the University of Brazil and the Pontifical Catholic University in Rio de Janeiro, as well as at the University of Bahia in Salvador. During four months of summer travel as the guest of both commercial and government airlines, I visited many more Brazilian universities and came into contact with many student leaders and their organizations. My course work was naturally directed toward material dealing with Brazil in particular. In the absence of postgraduate courses, I attended sophomore and junior classes (the fourth year is reserved for methods of teaching). On several occasions my professors apologized to me for the level of the work, blaming it on the students' unpreparedness to cope with university studies. In turn, the students constantly pointed up professorial inability. In most cases, they complained that the nature and content of the material presented was not in keeping with the realities and needs of present-day Brazil.

While I did meet excellent and dedicated professors in Brazil, there is a definite problem in the recruitment of people for the profession. The faculty of philosophy trains teachers for secondary schools, but there is no advanced program for university professors. There are no graduate schools; and while there are some specialized research institutes, they are relatively new. In effect, once graduated from college, a student is on his own to master his field. He can actually enter the university as an assistant upon completing his college course. Doctoral degrees are given, but there is no program to approximate the intensive advanced training in the United States. Similarly, a university professor qualifies for a chair on the basis of an examination in front of a university board. A full professor, or *catedratico,* receives life tenure. Low pay, however, often forces him to seek outside work. This, of course, limits time for research in one's field and for availability to students. Some professors never appear in classes after receiving their appointment; instead, they send young assistants to take their places.

The problem is cyclical. The university student is basically unprepared to meet his academic responsibilities. The secondary schools, despite a theoretically high level, do not train the student sufficiently. The great number of subjects covered—as many as fifteen at a time—cannot but be treated superficially. As a result, students are often unable to pass the entrance examinations to the various university faculties, who in turn seldom fill their quotas. The fact that a student applies for admission to a specialized field also limits him. There is no liberal arts college as we know it to prepare students for advanced studies. Instead, students enter directly into professional schools, such as law, medicine, architecture, engineering, and, with considerably less frequency, the faculty of philosophy.

The classroom approach to subject matter also leaves much to be desired. Professors pedantically spoon-feed material to their students; there is little or no incentive to individual research. Students go to the library only when an assignment is given, and these are usually mere repeats of lectures to ensure that the students are "swallowing" the material. In an experiment in a classroom in Bahia, a professor asked his five students to locate a particular topic in a book. They all began by thumbing through the pages and were baffled by the professor's helpful suggestion to use the index. It is rare that a paper is assigned in a Brazilian classroom. Grades and promotions to the next year depend largely on a series of final examinations. The student's main concern is to pass these examinations, receive his degree, and get out—usually into one of the professions in which he can earn a decent living.

The School of Geology at the University of Bahia is an example of another malady. As geology is a fairly new discipline in Brazil, professors are either very young or are imported from abroad. Because of a lack of textbooks in Portuguese, English was adopted as the official language of the school. This forced the student to master an already difficult subject in a foreign tongue. One young student summed it up: "Why bother to go to school? I can't understand anything anyway!"

This pessimistic attitude toward education is an incentive for frequent student strikes. The academic year is often so thoroughly interrupted that it makes learning relatively impossible. I was ushered out of classes on three different occasions, each for a considerable length of time. I started classes at the beginning of the second semester, which runs from August to mid-November, but most of September was spent on strike because of the constitutional crisis. Then students refused to attend classes from the first to the fifteenth of November in order to cram for exams. Classes

resumed around the middle of March, after the summer recess—
but the faculty of philosophy at the University of Bahia went out
on strike early in April to protest the appointment of a full professor. In June, another national student strike was called in an
attempt to force one-third student voting participation on the
governing boards of the universities. This last strike was unpopular with many students, who suffered because of minimum class
hour requirements in certain faculties. However, the opinion that
student participation on the governing boards was necessary to
university reform, along with the general fear of chastisement
from fellow classmates, brought about complete student solidarity. The strike lasted throughout the semester, and examinations
were postponed until after the winter recess.

The student in Brazil is somewhat of a special elite, and his
identification card is a passport to privilege. He attends the university free of charge and receives medical attention, food at
low-cost restaurants, and whatever limited housing the university
can provide. He enters the movies at half-price, has special rates
for performances at municipal theaters, and is allowed reduced
tariffs on transportation facilities in many cities. In Salvador students pass in front of endless lines of people waiting for elevators
between the upper and lower cities. Group excursions within
Brazil and abroad are often subsidized. Still, there are serious
difficulties other than the academic shortcomings already mentioned. Library facilities, while not in great demand, are inadequate. Books are comparatively expensive. Students from the
interior live under extremely hard conditions; and though much
better off than the lower-class migrants to the cities, they have
comparable attitudes. They, too, are frustrated and restless. They
turn to their fellow classmates and to the student councils, which
have become the sounding boards for Brazilian youth.

Brazilian students seek direction through the *Uniao Nacional
de Estudantes* (UNE), "the National Student Union," a representative organization comprised of delegates from autonomous
student councils. UNE, a highly centralized authority in Rio de

Janeiro, is often criticized as a haven for Communist thought and activity. It is generally conceded that some individual members are connected with the outlawed Brazilian Communist Party, but the entire organization cannot be guilty "by association." UNE is merely controversial by its very nature, as it calls and directs national student strikes, promotes demonstrations, effects political and nonpolitical alliances, maintains a literacy program, and presents plays throughout Brazil that point up national problems and keep the students "on their toes." It is common to read student declarations in the newspapers throughout Brazil, often made in conjunction with a labor union or other organization. At one student council meeting in Belem, the gateway to the Amazon River, students gathered to protest the machine-gunning of the UNE headquarters in Rio. They were joined by representatives from several labor unions. By the meeting's end they had not only condemned the attack on UNE but also issued statements concerning the National Council of Petroleum, the governor of the state of Guanabera, and a host of other subjects.

It is interesting to note that these young Brazilians do not preach the Cuban Revolution. On one occasion I interviewed a peasant who had been in contact with the organizers of the Peasant Leagues. He had never heard of Fidel Castro, and no one had told him about Cuba. The peasant did say he had heard they were "fighting a war over there" and then asked me, "Who won that war anyway?" Although they strongly sympathize with the Cuban people, Brazilian youths realize that there could be no Cuban-type revolution in Brazil. They take into consideration the size and diversity of the country, her possession of an active and growing native industry, and the profound religiosity of the Brazilian people. Actually, the student organizers of the Peasant Leagues rely, in large part, on teachings of the Bible to reach their audience. They are most concerned with concepts of self-determination, nonintervention in the affairs of another nation, and neutrality. For instance, they rush to the defense of Cuba when the United States attempts censure through the Organization of American States or as we did at Punta del Este, and they tend to regard news articles concerning worsening conditions in Cuba as American propaganda, resenting what they consider to be a campaign to influence sister republics in the hemisphere.

As is true of most Latin Americans, Brazilian youths are generally suspicious of the United States. While these suspicions are often unjustified, they are nevertheless deep-rooted. They fear American economic aid as a weapon that threatens their nation's sovereignty, being convinced that it comes "with strings attached" and is used to bring undue pressure on their government. While accepting the philosophy behind the Alliance for Progress, they are skeptical of the program itself, doubting that financial and technical aid through the alliance will filter down to the people. In this case, however, they are quick to blame interested parties in their own government; they are generally critical of their own officials and alleged economic alliances with foreign big business. Foreign investment is considered to be a necessary but temporary ill. They insist that Brazil can, and will, run her own utilities, and they welcome any move in this direction. They demand that private capital from abroad be directed into basic industries that will contribute to national growth, and they want strict control over remittance of profits. To their way of thinking, many American companies in Brazil are superfluous industries (soap, soft drinks, and the like) that merely serve to drain capital. They often use foreign investors as scapegoats—for instance, if anything goes wrong in the nationalized Brazilian oil industry, they point a challenging finger at American oil interests. They also believe that big business exercises too much influence in the United States and claim that self-interested parties corrupt the nation and dictate American policy.

This, in general, is the basis of the distrust. It does not, however, affect their attitude toward individual Americans. I never had difficulty in approaching young Brazilians; in fact, I was warmly welcomed by Brazilians in all walks of life. The usual stereotypes of the American—the aloof tourist, the self-indulgent businessman, the misunderstanding diplomat—were not applied. I was always considered a student first and an American second.

Brazilian youths seemed flattered that I had come to study in their country. They showed curiosity about the United States, particularly with regard to our university system, student life, and technological achievements, but were particularly critical of American race relations, atomic testing, and "imperialism."

The extreme nationalism at play in Brazil does not allow young people to admit of international Communism as a system in their country. They are adamant that they would never submit to any sort of satellite relationship. Nevertheless, the lack of any active moderate group in which they can truly express themselves often forces them to react with the extreme left and even within the Communist complex. Still, they are not particularly seduced by Communist propaganda. As one Brazilian student leader wrote, "It is necessary for us to fight against the misery and poverty of our people, lest the country fall into the hands of the Communists. Our people do not want Communism or any other ideology. They want to eat . . . only to eat. They need schools for their children, land to cultivate—the basic necessities of life. I have to go along with UNE, knowing it is directed in large part by Communists, because it is the only national entity which defends the common people. In the Northeast, children die every 42 seconds. We have an illiteracy rate of over 50%. Who will defend these people if their representatives in Congress won't?"

Most Brazilian youths believe in a paternalistic form of government with a strong central authority in Brasilia—indeed, a government of all the people and not only of a small elite. In the words of a young Brazilian, "I want an economic, political, and social system in which the state takes the greatest initiative for the development of the country and for the well-being of the people." Most see Brazil on the road to Socialism, but a Socialism based on Brazilian tradition and need and with a place for responsible opposition—for the spirit of debate is high among young Brazilians.

The reactions of these young people have inevitably brought criticism from the older middle classes. To many Brazilians these students appear completely irresponsible: they go on strike "when they should be in classes and involve themselves in national affairs at the expense of their studies." Irresponsibility, however, is not an apt description of Brazilian youths, whose motivations are honest and stem from idealism. They are far too serious to be called mere agitators or rabble-rousers, for they supplement their protests with a good deal of social work of all kinds. Many young doctors devote their talents to the sick in the isolated interior; young lawyers volunteer their time to dispossessed tenant farmers and sharecroppers, who are no longer forgotten men. The collective voice of the engineering students at the University of Bahia cries out an Easter message on a poetic leaflet:

I ate,
I ate too much,
I ate to do as everyone does,
Because they have invited me,
Because they were society and it was difficult
     to act otherwise.
And each plate,
Each mouthful,
     And each spoonful was hard to swallow.
I ate too much, Lord,
While at the same moment, in my city,
More than 1500 people lined up outside the
     soup kitchen with an empty can.
While that woman, in the hovel in which she lives,
     ate what she picked that morning
     from the garbage can.
While these children, in their huts, shared the
     cold leftovers of a scanty meal from
     the old folks' home.
While ten, fifty, a hundred, a thousand wretched,
     in the same second, throughout the outside
     world, twisted in pain, starved to death
     among themselves, in desperation.

These are the best of the "new heirs" to Brazil. The new consciousness that has grown up among them is not only to personal needs but to national ones, and their call word has become reform. They are possessed by the great pending need to actualize this reform. In their zealousness to see Brazil move ahead, they have entered into a series of intricate alliances and deep involvements with labor unions and Peasant Leagues, with local and national politicians. There is great prestige in these alliances, since through them the voice of the student is magnified, but they also present certain dangers. Since Brazilian youths lack direction, they will crowd the lectures of any man, idealist or demagogue, who offers a platform for change.

Moreover, they have no real program of their own. In the Northeast I came into extremely close contact with the youthful organizers of the Peasant Leagues, who were concerned only with the plight of a desperate peasantry. They did not offer any "party line" propaganda. Instead, their ideas were strikingly individual and diverse. While telling me of the movement's origin and aims and projected plans, their own personal differences became apparent. The only common denominator was their eagerness for change.

The youthful clamor for reform—economic, political, and social—is, in a sense, almost too eager. Young people fail to see the political ramifications that could result from over-anxiety. If Brazil were plunged into a state of chaos, they would undoubtedly lose control to the organized elements on the extreme left, most probably to the Communist Party. They are themselves currently unprepared to give direction to their revolution. Hopefully, the coming years will allow them the time they need to formulate coherent and humane programs.

JAMES W. ROWE

■ *ARGENTINA*

What Ever Happened to the Happy Lands?

Far out over the muddy vastness of the Plata River, even before the flat littoral and sprawling profile of Buenos Aires came into view, I knew that this time Argentina would be different. I had been in Buenos Aires before, but on one of those brief, highly planned visits where tightly squeezed official interviews, museum-peering, and an evening's experimentation with the tango come in ordered sequence and the compass of one's activity is confined to the few cosmopolitan blocks that stretch from the Plaza Hotel to Argentina's pink "White House." In late 1961 I returned for a year's stay, armed with a research fellowship and a determination to know the other Argentina—something of the lives that are led far from the Plaza's faded elegance, in the dingy industrial suburbs of the capital and the broad Pampa beyond. This time there were no welcoming faces at the airport. Argentina was to be my home for many months, and I purposely chose to

James W. Rowe got his B.A. from Vanderbilt University and did graduate work in political science at George Washington and Georgetown Universities. He has served in the State Department, worked as legislative assistant to a United States Senator, and been a member of the Governmental Affairs Institute. He has contributed articles to *The New Republic*.

232

begin my new life in the anonymity of Buenos Aires, unguided and uncommitted. In an effort to understand Argentine politics, it seemed best to shake off preconceived notions, live like a *porteño* (inhabitant of Buenos Aires), and move in the widest ambit possible.

Bargaining for a *pensione,* learning the intricacies of subway and *colectivo* bus routes, and tuning my ear to the soft deformities of Argentine Spanish, I began to realize in those first few days how different Buenos Aires seemed from my earlier impression. At first the great metropolis appears to have a life more akin to that of Western Europe or the eastern United States than to that of the older and more exotic cities of Latin America. Leafy parks, broad avenues, and statues in the heroic style combine with the mansard roofs and gray sobriety of town houses built in the 1890's to give a Parisian quality to much of the city, while the theaters and discount record shops of Avenida Corrientes make a district that resembles Broadway. Similarly, the spirit of urban Argentina seems close to that of North America: businessmen clad in tweeds and flannels scurry briskly through the financial district of Calle San Martin; women are as free as in New York to follow commercial and professional careers, go out alone, or smoke on the street; fewer and fewer families can afford a domestic servant; supermarkets and underground parking have arrived. It doesn't take long, however, to recognize that despite superficial similarities Argentina is profoundly different from the United States—thoroughly Latin in many respects, *sui generis* in others. I had sensed that 1962 would be a critical year, but was as unprepared as anyone to see the patched-up social truce of the last few years shattered so quickly and Argentina in an institutional shambles, once again on the brink of dictatorship and civil war.

Now, after a year crammed with events that have always been absorbing, frequently perplexing, and sometimes deeply discouraging, I find it interesting to look back at the reasons that brought me here. For several years—like many North Americans—I had experienced an awakening interest in the people and problems south of the Rio Grande. The world's highest rate of population growth, mounting pressures for social reform, occasional spurts of phenomenal industrial progress, as in the São Paulo area of Brazil, intermittent waves of "anti-yanquismo," the jolt of Cuba —all suggested a froth of change filled with important consequences for the United States in the years ahead. In the United States a certain amount of attention was gradually directed toward the economic and demographic problems of its southern neighbors. Yet political studies of the Latin American area have remained in their infancy. While United States scholars have probed into the Congress Party of India, the structure of local government in the Soviet Union, and tribal politics in West Africa, serious political investigation of even the larger Latin American countries has scarcely begun. Add to the problem the fact that there are twenty nations in the region, and it becomes ever more apparent that the concept of Latin America as an entity contains more fiction than fact—some characteristics are shared, but each of the countries is unique. This is especially true of Argentina, with its traditional aloofness from its neighbors, its largely European population, and its wealth. I chose Argentina not because it is typical but because among the nations of the hemisphere it is easily one of the most important and the most puzzling.

As large as the United States east of the Mississippi, containing a tenth of Latin America's population, Argentina boasts the highest degree of industrial development in the region and leads it in all indices of wealth except per capita income (Venezuela's elite petroleum labor force gives that hot country the highest average). It has a literacy rate approaching ninety percent, more physicians per capita than the United States, and a real middle class—not to mention a largely temperate climate and physical resources that range from the fabled soils of the Pampa to impressive petroleum deposits now being tapped throughout much of the country. Yet the very attributes that put Argentina in a different class from its less endowed, less developed neighbors make its national behavior over the last thirty years extremely difficult to understand. From

Jefferson's day to the New Frontier, Americans have assumed that stable democratic government depends on certain social prerequisites—above all, education and a degree of economic well-being. Political scientists laboriously attempt to demonstrate the correlation between political behavior and socio-economic development; Alliance for Progress planners must accept it as a working assumption. Argentina's recent history leaves both groups scratching their heads. Since 1930 the country has been the scene of continuous political crisis, social fragmentation, and virulent nationalism, passing a decade under South America's closest approximation of a full-blown modern dictatorship, spending much of the remainder on the verge of military adventures and incipient coups d'état. Somewhere there must be an explanation.

Specifically I had hoped to explore this puzzle by studying the national legislature. The Argentine Constitution is modeled closely after that of the United States and assigns, at least on paper, a structure and role to its Congress which resembles that of its North American prototype. But like other Latin American legislatures, the Argentine Congress has been subordinate to the executive, frequently chosen in rigged elections; under the dictatorship of Juan D. Peron it degenerated into a rubber-stamp body. Even so, in the half-century of relative tranquillity and prosperity that Argentina had enjoyed after 1880, the Congress had attracted some of the nation's ablest leaders, bred a high level of debate, and provided a forum from which meaningful criticism of the executive power could be launched. After the overthrow of Peron in 1955 and the return to constitutional government, much attention was focused on the Congress elected in February, 1958, to see whether, after thirty years of atrophy, it could regain some of its old prestige, serve as a genuinely representative body, and effectively fulfill the separation-of-powers mission assigned it by the constitution.

From a distance, it was extremely difficult to tell if it was succeeding. The scanty evidence available suggested that it was having difficulty finding its role; and despite some able members and interesting talk about legislative independence, the center of

the political stage was far removed from the musty old congressional chambers with their interminable dawdling, broken quo-
rums, and procedural nitpicking. By determining the accuracy of
this impression—with the same kind of methodical observation
and interviewing by which we have recently come to know more
about the United States Congress—I hoped to shed some light on
the Argentine enigma. At the very least, the legislature is generally a convenient focal point to learn something about a country's pressure groups, electoral system, and political parties. Since
half of the Chamber of Deputies was up for re-election in 1962, I
arrived in time to observe the campaign and balloting and
planned to spend the following months watching the Argentine
Congress at work.

The first part of the plan worked beautifully. Accompanying
various candidates on the campaign trail provided not only a
wealth of information about the issues and techniques of Argentine politics but also an opportunity to meet and talk to a great
number of persons in small towns and the countryside. Chatting
in a casual, impromptu way with party rank-and-filers, volunteers,
country lawyers, and schoolteachers—always eager to recount
their lives and aspirations as well as political views—I obtained
a clearer understanding of the mingled frustrations, memories,
and hopes that make up post-Peron Argentina. However, as the
campaign ended, my plans, like those of so many Argentines, were
changed abruptly. On March 18 the Argentine voters in a free
and fair contest elected Peronist candidates to 11 out of 14
provincial governorships and to 45 seats in the 192-man Chamber
of Deputies. The middle-of-the-road government of President
Arturo Frondizi and his *Union Civica Radical Intransigente*
(UCRI), which had had to play a kind of hide-and-seek with
Peronist-controlled labor unions on one side and the anti-
Peronist armed forces on the other in order to stay in office after
1958, had permitted the Peronist parties to run their own candidates for the first time since Peron was ousted. It was a daring
move, designed to reap electoral benefits from all sides and perhaps to lead the strayed, those who had supported Peron, back

into the fold of democracy; but it didn't work. The polls had hardly closed when it became apparent how wildly the scheme had backfired; and after Frondizi refused to accede to widespread demands for his resignation, the military commanders in chief arrested him on March 29 and sent him off to Argentina's St. Helena, the Plata River island of Martin Garcia.

This was Argentina's fourth military coup since 1930. The armed forces, rather than assuming power directly, permitted Senate leader Jose Maria Guido to take the presidential oath and form a civilian cabinet. His government maintained a semblance of legality, even though its every move was circumscribed by the military—whose basic position is that Peronists shall not be allowed to return to power, even if democratically elected. In a series of measures designed to undo the damage of March 18 and prepare for eventual return to constitutional government, Guido annulled the 1962 elections, sent federal "interventors" to administer the provinces, called for new elections in 1963, and sent Congress into enforced recess.

With the legislative chambers dark and empty, my project had to be shelved, but I used the following months to have a look at various sectors of the Argentine public that help mold opinion and shape policy: political parties, university and church groups, trade unions, business organizations, and—to the extent possible —the armed forces. In each area I had especially interesting contacts with youth. In a country like Argentina, one can hardly escape the conclusion that many of the nation's difficulties stem from unfortunate social and civic habits. I was interested in finding out whether these habits were shared by young Argentines, and whether they were changing. What was the reaction of youth to the chaotic situation of mid-1962; what are the hopes for tomorrow?

At the outset a caveat is necessary. The problems raised—finding the key to the Argentine dilemma and discovering whether the younger generation is changing in a way conducive to its solution—are large and complex. Final answers are elusive, but there are some benchmarks along the way. My experience in the country suggests, at least as a working hypothesis, that two factors have had a critical influence on the thought and habits of older Argentines. The first is the gap between words and facts—the essential failure of the "scientific attitude" to become the guiding spirit of Argentine inquiry. The second is the curious mixture of aggressiveness and apathy in the Argentine character, perhaps related to the ambiguous blend of permissiveness and authoritarianism children encounter at home as they are growing up. The one is an intellectual problem; the other, sociological. Yet they would seem to go far in explaining certain economic and political phenomena of the day.

For example, until recently most of those in charge of economic planning, whether in the private or public sector, have preferred theoretical abstractions over empirical studies, making decisions on the basis of doctrine rather than data. The politician of 1962 is working in the same tradition as his predecessor of 1900, who, complained the writer Augustin Alvarez, "manufactures manifestoes, programs, theories; lives in a world of words, of pure fancy, cut off from reality by the impenetrable cloud of his own ideas." The aggressiveness of the Argentine, so frequently noted by the visitor, is manifested in his noisy public behavior, keen sense of competition in sports, the world's worst driving habits, and other forms of individual activity. Apathy, on the other hand, is a little less obvious, for it appears as the typical reaction to community or national affairs. Shadow and substance, aggression and apathy—examples are scattered through the following pages; but a recent set of events deserves special attention as an instance of both. In March, 1962, after surprise Peronist victories at the polls set in motion institutional turmoil, there were several days during which the armed forces would have settled for less than the ouster of President Frondizi, provided all democratic parties could collaborate in forming a union cabinet. These parties, in turn, were each opposed to military intervention and in favor of "the constitution" and "legality." With every opportunity to avoid a constitutional fracture the parties issued loud calls for "consensus," "compromise," and "sacrifice for the common good"—and refused to collaborate. Since Frondizi's overthrow, the tanks of rival generals have several times rumbled into Buenos Aires for traumatic midtown confrontations. With the nation at the very door of civil war, the parties continued calling for unity and sacrifice on the verbal level while in practice they grew ever more divided and unwilling to make the slightest concession—despite the fact that with almost seventy percent of the electorate behind them their combined strength could keep both Peronism and military adventures within bounds. Meanwhile, whether it was the fate of the constitution hanging in the balance in March of 1962 or the streets clanking with armor in April and August, the Argentine public displayed a profound indifference.

"What?" said a friend soon after my arrival. "You mean you're not going to take in the elections in Santa Fé next week? It will be very interesting, and besides, the countryside is pretty up there—and the *chicas* too." I had known that Santa Fé and two other provinces would hold their elections earlier than the rest of the country, on December 17—but had thought it wiser to get settled in Buenos Aires before venturing into the interior. An invitation from Dr. Angel Prece, a UCRI Deputy up for reelection, to accompany him to his district for the final stages of the campaign proved too much to resist, especially after my friend's prodding. It was a fortunate temptation. Those few days in the country impressed on me from the beginning that there are two Argentinas—Buenos Aires and the rest. They are still worlds apart, even a century after the *caudillos* ("strong men") of the provinces fought the Buenos Aires unitarians (supporters of centralized government) in the time of "Bloody" Rosas.

The road from Buenos Aires to Sunchales, about five hundred miles away in upper Santa Fé, hugs the Paraná River up through industrial Rosario and old Santa Fé City, then traverses the wide Pampa. There is a splendor in the landscape offered up by the vast Argentine grasslands, not so dramatic as the rugged Andean spine to the west or the wooded lake district of the far south, but a panorama of green and fecund beauty in the late spring. The luxuriant fields of alfalfa and clover that stretch to the horizon are black-dotted with cattle and broken by clumps of tall thistles and an occasional grove of eucalyptus or lombardy poplar. Sunset on the Pampa is a lengthy and theatrical affair, which decorates the sky with dozens of multicolored cirrus folds and fragments. After hours of the gaudy pageant the last slivers of crimson fade suddenly and night is complete, bringing an overwhelming sense of solitude and distance.

Land tenure in much of the Pampa is characterized by huge *estancias* ("cattle ranches") and absentee ownership, but in upper Santa Fé holdings are smaller and family farms are numerous. Italians from the Piedmont with their special flair for agriculture formed a major part of the immigration in this area, which produces barley, flax, corn, and dairy cows as well as the traditional wheat and beef cattle. The rich black soil and land tenure pattern make for a modest rural prosperity and an atmosphere not unlike parts of the American Middle West. Sunchales is a pleasant community of nine thousand, founded seventy or eighty years ago, now distinguished by the presence of the largest creamery in South America. A few paved streets, a large Catholic church, and the inevitable plaza mark the center of town; traffic is about evenly divided between carts drawn by huge Percherons, noisy motor bikes, and Fords and Chevrolets circa 1935. If Sunchales seems a bit sleepy and old-fashioned, it is still a far cry from the stagnant mud-and-wattle villages of rural Brazil or the Indian towns of the Andes.

The last big pre-election rally of UCRI in that part of Santa Fé was held in a neighboring town, Rafaela, and those who could went over from Sunchales to take part. The outdoor rally, or *acto publico,* is still one of the most important campaign devices in Argentine politics, especially in the interior, where television has not yet challenged "the stump" as a vote-getting technique. These affairs usually start about an hour late and bring to the platform four or five of the party's candidates for various offices

—national deputy, state legislator, mayor, city councilor—each of whom speaks for twenty or thirty minutes. In Rafaela, as at other rallies I attended, the crowd was very patient, standing three hours in the chilly night to hear the speakers out. The *acto* customarily begins with an address by a representative of the party's youth sector, who may or may not be a candidate. In Rafaela, a lawyer of about twenty-five running for the city council performed this rite. In other rallies the term "youth" was used somewhat loosely, and sometimes the representative of the younger generation turned out to be past forty; other times, older than the gubernatorial candidate!

In a non-presidential year such as 1962, maximum interest centers on the race for governor. Legislative contests are much less personal affairs than in the United States, since all deputies for a province are chosen at large from a party list. A deputy rarely bothers to go home to campaign, for if he has obtained a place on the party's list, his chief obligation is to campaign for the party anywhere he may be needed, since if it wins, he wins.

The speeches at the Rafaela *acto* were intelligent and well-informed; apart from a Latin propensity toward flowery rhetoric, they might well have created a favorable impression in any rural campaign in the United States. National and even international issues received somewhat more attention than is normal in a local campaign in rural North America because the party list system makes it necessary to defend the party's program.

Argentine law imposes a 24-hour ban on political activity the day before the election, and I used this period to talk with the young farmers, tradesmen, and professionals who were working in the Sunchales headquarters of four of the largest parties. As the guest of a UCRI candidate in his home town, I naturally started with the "militants" of his own party, but they were quite co-operative in sending me off to the command posts of their adversaries. In each headquarters I received a friendly welcome except in that of the Peronist *Laborista* Party, where the reception amid portraits and busts of Juan and Eva Peron was decidedly cool. Conversation with most of the young men of

Sunchales, for whom politics is strictly a part-time concern, quickly turned to other matters, and my new friends had as many questions for me as I for them. What was a campaign like in Tennessee or Louisiana? Why don't we have compulsory voting, as in Argentina? When will the Alliance for Progress really begin to work? Guillermo, a worker at the big Sancor creamery, wanted to take me over on his motor bike to see the plant. Daniel, a young farmer, wondered if I could stay over a few days and go duck-hunting with him. Armando, who owns and works his own medium-sized farm, asked me to come back to Sunchales to live and write, generously offering a room in his house and the use of a horse. All urged that I accompany them that evening to an *asado,* a traditional Argentine feast of meat roasted over coals in the open air and washed down with great quantities of red wine. They promised to produce Don Eduardo, one of the region's few surviving gauchos, hale and fit at eighty-six. Several hundred persons of all ages and both sexes attended the *asado* that night at a nearby park. There they forgot politics for a four-hour marathon of hearty eating, dancing, and laughter. One of my acquaintances of the afternoon presented his dark-eyed teen-age daughter, known as the prettiest girl in town, to teach me some of the *criollo** dance steps, and soon some of the crowd were demanding a sample of North American folk songs. Their enthusiasm—genuine or feigned—made up for my somewhat artless attempt to recapture the songs of college days in Tennessee; and by the end of the feast half of the *santafecinos* present were joining in the chorus of "Old Dan Tucker."

At this *asado* and continuing through similar occasions in other areas, a number of impressions regarding young people in provincial Argentina began to form in my mind. Friendly, talkative, curious, intelligent, these young men and women are extremely interested in North America and are eager to know about the latest developments there and elsewhere in the world. Most

---

* In Argentine usage, *criollo* means "local" or "native."

of them, even many who belong to extremist movements, appear well-disposed toward the United States, partly because of economic and technical progress, partly because of what they have heard of reasonably stable and democratic government. Peronist and crypto-Communist spokesmen, even when complaining bitterly about our Latin American policy or the nebulous "yankee imperialism," often appear to feel admiration as well as envy for American society. The belief is widespread that North Americans are gay, extroverted, free-spending, and somewhat naïve, but essentially just and well-meaning. Many know that Hollywood has presented an inaccurate and unfortunate picture of life in the United States, but even those who voice this opinion have an exaggerated notion of the extent of violence, racial conflict, and divorce in all parts of the country. A certain ambivalence is often present in Argentine attitudes on these matters. Tomás bitterly criticized segregation in the South and, practically in the same breath, boasted indelicately that there are few Negroes left in Argentina today. Others deplore the high divorce rate in America but appear unaware or indifferent to the high incidence of broken homes—separation or Uruguayan divorce—and illegitimacy in divorceless Argentina.

A similar ambivalence crops up in almost any discussion of the principle of "nonintervention" so honored in Latin American theories of the inter-American system, and especially so in the Plata River area. Many of the youthful supporters of Frondizi, to whose party nonintervention was sacrosanct (invoked at the Punta del Este conference on Cuba to justify Argentina's stand against excluding Cuba from the Organization of American States), now criticize the United States for not having stepped in to "save" Frondizi from the military leaders who forced him from office. Militants of the opposition, *Union Civica Radical del Pueblo* (UCRP), on the other hand, claim that a $150-million Alliance for Progress loan to Argentina announced two weeks before the March elections was an attempt to influence the outcome in favor of Frondizi. Peronists remember bitterly the anti-Peron activities of former United States Ambassador Spruille Braden in the forties, but not the help extended to Peron in the latter stages of his rule; anti-Peronists reverse the procedure.*

Despite these and many more criticisms, the "anti-yanquismo" found among young people appears more sporadic and less vehe-

---

* Juan D. Peron, an army colonel when he and a group of fellow officers joined in 1943 to overthrow the ineffective Conservative government of President Ramon Castillo, quickly consolidated a novel power base that enabled him to become, along with Getulio Vargas in Brazil, one of South America's two mass-appeal dictators. As head of the Labor Ministry, Peron courted the trade unions and made organized labor one of his new structure's three pillars, along with the army and the Catholic church. He was in control of the regime by 1944, was elected president in 1946 and again in 1951, and was ousted by military uprising in September, 1955. Peron possessed remarkable *charisma,* but in many ways his most important asset was his wife Eva, from the time of their marriage in 1945 until her death in 1952. Together they promised a new life to the *descamisado*—the "shirtless one" or common man of Argentina— and cast a demagogic spell over much of the nation. A vast program of social legislation brought minimum wage laws, compulsory retirement insurance, child labor regulation, and other projects that effected a redistribution of income. Favoritism to urban labor together with the big push Peron gave to industrialization brought a large internal migration from the provinces to Buenos Aires' suburbs. There, low-cost housing projects and the philanthropy of the Eva Peron Foundation caused the raw newcomers to look upon their benefactors as near-deities. Definitely shifting the center of power from the rural oligarchy, which had long dominated the country, to the urban middle and lower classes, Peron enjoyed an immense popularity by 1950.

After 1951 his regime slipped more and more into dictatorship as he sought to intimidate opponents by police raids, imprisonment and brutality, purges of public officials who would not join his party, and a systematic campaign against the press and eventually the church. These tactics, together with Peron's admiration for aspects of Mussolini's Fascism and his equivocal stand during World War II, led some observers to view his regime as a totalitarian dictatorship of the Nazi and Fascist variety. But although Peron's *justicialismo* ideology was a pale carbon copy of Fascism, his regime never achieved the institutional controls of a full-blown police state, nor was there a truly revolutionary restructuring of society, not even land redistribution. Populist and authoritarian, Peronism set class against class and gave the new industrial proletariat a bigger slice of the national wealth as well as a new sense of participation and status in national life.

In the process, the economy was wrecked, even though wartime sales of meat and wheat had enabled the government to accumulate huge gold reserves. Neglect of agriculture in the haste to industrialize, expensive nationalization projects, inflation, squandering, mismanagement, and outright theft all played their parts. In the fifties Peron began to slip, first in his quarrels with the church and finally with his own supporters in important sectors of the military, which toppled him in 1955's Revolution of Liberation. He was ousted, however, before the impact of his disastrous economic policies was evident or admitted by

ment than in some other areas of Latin America. In part, this may be because Argentines, who have called themselves the "Yankees of South America," found that their wealth and the cultural "manifest destiny" policy of former years earned them considerable dislike among their Latin neighbors, so that they are skittish about the shoe of criticism fitting more than one foot. In part, too, it is probably due to the nationalistic bent that popular radicalism has taken in Argentina thus far. The *criollo* nationalism that Peronism and most of the other present-day political movements have fed on is by no means immune from the appeals of anti-Americanism, but the kind it produces is less systematic than the worn bill of complaints so faithfully recited by many of the Communist-inspired protest movements in other Latin countries. In the provinces as well as in the metropolis, however, one of the most perplexing questions of today is whether the native radicalism of Peronism and its variants will continue to withstand Communist attempts to capture it.

The day after the *asado* came the election itself, held on a Sunday, as is customary. Voting is compulsory, and men and women go to separate polling places. Otherwise, most features resemble an election in the United States—secret ballots, party poll-watchers stationed near the voting booths, taverns closed for the day. This particular election was especially significant—for Sunchales as well as for all of Santa Fé. Sixteen parties were in the race to choose a new governor and seven national congressmen, and for the first time since 1954 Peronists, under the name

---

his trade union followers, and he carried their adulation with him into exile. Seven years later his movement continues to be a strong force in the country, claiming between 30 and 35 percent of the electorate. In the elections of 1957 and 1960, when Peronists were prevented from running their own candidates, they cast blank ballots of protest; but in 1958, on orders from the leader's headquarters in Madrid, they voted for Frondizi. No one seemed to know for certain what they would do when allowed to run their own candidates in 1962, but the answer was soon coming. The various Peronist parties polled more than two and one-half million votes—more than any other ticket. The one constant in the general chaos and confusion reigning within the other parties after Frondizi's overthrow has been the desire in each party—however discreetly—to court the Peronist vote.

of the *Laborista* Party, were allowed to run their own candidates. The Peronist movement had always had considerable strength in Santa Fé, and many strategists from Frondizi's UCRI, the incumbent majority party, were deeply worried over the possibility of a *Laborista* triumph. Economic development was the big issue, and the skeptics feared that Frondizi, whose austerity program had never been popular, had not produced enough tangible benefits. Others of a more conservative bent mistrusted him as a double-dealer flirting with both Peronists and the military. Still, the UCRI controlled patronage and had the best local machine, as in most of the interior provinces. Soon after the polls closed, it became apparent that UCRI had triumphed in Sunchales with the Peronists running a close second. Throughout the province the UCRI registered about 30% of the vote and the *Laboristas* about 25%. The outcome was to be even more important than I realized at the time. As a test case the Santa Fé results were crucial in shaping the electoral strategy used by Frondizi and his party for the main elections in March. To allow Peronists to run and then lick them in open fight would put the UCRI in an ideal spot, especially if, as in Santa Fé, the Peronists won second place, thereby tending to replace the People's Radicals as the minority party in Congress. The strategy didn't work in March and was the prelude to Argentina's latest time of troubles, but there was no foreboding of this as my jubilant UCRI companions drove back over the verdant Pampa to Buenos Aires.

The easy informality, ruddy outdoor complexion, and gregariousness of Santa Fé young people contrasted rather sharply with my first impression of Buenos Aires youth. This is not surprising, since the pressures of city living are everywhere noticeable in Greater Buenos Aires, where over six million inhabitants try to cope with inadequate transport systems, a severe housing shortage, the constant breakdown of public utilities, and an ever-mounting cost of living. Such problems are common in many of the world's great cities, but one aspect of urban life that seems to set Buenos Aires apart is an inescapable impression of separation and spiritual solitude. People jostle and bump each other on the streets heedlessly, and in the crowded depths of the little *colectivo* buses—which usually carry about three times their reasonable capacity of passengers—each rider seems totally unaware of the existence of his fellow transients. The Argentine writer Raul Scalabrini Ortiz characterized the *porteño* as "the man who is alone and waits." This sense of isolation amid the dinginess and gloom that comes from run-down streets and chronic power failures gives something of a serious and almost melancholy character even to the social encounters of *porteños*. Middle-class young people meet each other more often at a *confiteria* than at home, and their greetings as well as conversation are usually marked by formality and grave demeanor. Others, especially from less affluent sectors, will simply huddle for long conversations in the dark doorways that line the city's shadowy streets. There are, of course, occasions for laughter and conviviality, but even at dances the typical Argentine music—whether the *porteño* tango or the provincial *zamba*—inevitably expresses sadness, frustration, lost hopes, and nostalgia.

Family ties still are stronger in Argentina—as in most of Latin America—than in the United States, and only recently has the extended family—uniting aunts, cousins, grandmothers, and in-laws—begun to give way under the impact of apartment-living and increased mobility. The modest midtown apartment of my friend Ernesto, a young attorney, is shared not only by his wife and son but by his mother, mother-in-law, and mother-in-law's mother. On a birthday or anniversary, his seven brothers and their assorted wives and children come for a meal, hardly leaving room for any outside friends. His law partner is a cousin. A bitter complaint of the self-made managers and administrators in Argentina is that the summit is still closed to them because executive leadership in business is retained as tightly by family hands as it is by party politicians in government.

Nevertheless, there is much more mobility in Argentine society than in many other areas of Latin America. Like much of the "aristocracy" of the old Confederacy, many of the "first families" of the *estanciero* class, who gained wealth and fame in the nineteenth century, trace their origin to unknown families and penniless immigrant stock. They bequeathed twentieth-century Argentina the Jockey Club and something still called "the oligarchy," but hardly a coherent ethos or genuinely conservative tradition. Whatever the legacy, mixed as it was with a residue of frontier spirit and tidal waves of immigration toward the turn of the century, it has been subjected to powerful solvents for many years—the dominance of middle-class Radical Party politics (1916–1930) and the social upheaval that characterized the dictatorship of Juan D. Peron (1945–55). If shrill complaints and bitter dissatisfaction mark Argentine politics today, one reason is that expectations are extremely high. An open society and high material consumption are not unknowns for which newly awakened masses are suddenly groping, as in some other parts of the world. Argentines have tasted a measure of both.

Young *porteños,* like their elders, keep late hours. Although the working day—in construction, commerce, education, and many office jobs—starts little if any later than in the United States, and the siesta at midday is a thing of the past in the metropolis, the day ends considerably later. Restaurants open for dinner at eight, but nine and ten are the more popular hours for dining, and friends visit with each other far past midnight. Entire families, with young children, can be seen on the streets at 2 and even 5 A.M. A vast majority of the students at the University of Buenos Aires attend classes at night, working during the day to support themselves. Many of those whose studies have ceased work at two and sometimes three occupations to meet the squeeze between low salaries and high prices.

Gloria, an intelligent, energetic girl of twenty-three whose cultural level is as high as many an American college graduate, dropped out of high school at seventeen to support her mother and young brother. She rises at five in the morning for the long *colectivo* ride downtown, where she is a clerical employee of the city government from seven until two in the afternoon. After lunch she works several hours as secretary to a congressman, and then at home she works as a seamstress until midnight. She receives $60 monthly from her municipal employment, nominal remuneration for her political work, and an amount that varies from $40 to $80 from her dressmaking. Like many of her friends, there is little time left after work for diversion—a movie every month, an occasional Saturday night out for dinner or dancing (good restaurants and simple cabarets still maintain reasonable prices by American standards). Typical of most girls of her age who are not from very wealthy families, she may come and go at will, is highly independent, and may even return home unaccompanied after a date—something which was unthinkable a few years ago, and still is today in many other Latin areas. Gloria is a faithful Catholic and attends Mass regularly, although many young women appear to have loosened religious ties in the first flush of the new freedom. Few, however, have let "freedom" make inroads on their preoccupation with femininity. Argentine women, young and old, are generally neat and well-groomed, spend as much time as they can at the hairdresser, and when they can afford it, regale themselves with the furs and jewelry for which Buenos Aires shops are famous. They have new opportunities in business, the professions, and even politics, but the grand prize is still male admiration, marriage, and children.

If Buenos Aires young people lack many of the natural, easy social contacts that are built into the life of small towns and rural areas, their participation in formal organizational life is limited as well. Even though traditional family ties are eroding, however gradually, the growth of other types of social organization has been slow and erratic. Boy Scouts and similar groups have had difficult going and small memberships in Argentina. Youth organizations have been fostered by the Catholic church, but in size or effect they have never come close to serving the same role as the YMCA, YMHA, Father Ryan Clubs, or Epworth League in the United States. The many sporting clubs that dot the shores of the Plata River on the outskirts of Buenos Aires are usually reserved for the wealthy or for the large business organizations, which provide them for their workers. University students live at home in Buenos Aires and, unless they are active in student politics, have no campus life at all outside the classroom. Young business and professional men occasionally belong to service clubs such as the Rotary or Lions, but these are still very limited and have a bit of an elitist quality about them. Trade-union activity is divided between economic and political questions and offers little of a purely social nature. Within the framework of the organizations that exist, membership is exclusive rather than inclusive, and "joiners" of multiple clubs are exceedingly rare. This works against divided loyalties and a wider sense of community. In the case of political parties, really active members almost never belong to other organizations. It is suggestive that the expression for "fellow party member" in Argentina is *co-religionario*.

It is more difficult to generalize about the attitudes of a *porteño* than about those of young men in a small country town, but some characteristics seem to prevail regardless of political faction or economic class. The *porteño* has a quick intelligence and prides himself on being *listo* or "clever," although his impatience with detail may result in his being over-quick, forcing him to renew the operation or repeat the question at hand. Like his elders, he may display elaborate courtesy within the home or at the table, but in public he is likely to contribute to the stranger's impression of Buenos Aires as one of the world's least civil cities, where the fabled traffic observes no rules for passing or crossing intersections, and male subway passengers are notoriously indifferent to the plight of an aged or pregnant woman. He is highly individualistic in many ways, but is even more sensitive than a North American to matters of status and prestige. Keeping up with—or ahead of—the neighbors is a psychological necessity, especially in such transcendental matters as weddings and funerals. He is not lazy and believes the country as a whole must work harder to get ahead, but he loves leisure— the frequent conversational interruptions that attend almost any kind of work, the numerous national holidays, the long summer vacations. He delights in argument but, apart from the marginal scattering of hoodlums and delinquents found in any large city, is less prone to violence than his North American counterpart. His seniors still challenge each other to an occasional duel, which is illegal, but they are almost always "settled," as are traffic disputes.

More than his provincial cousins, he looks with favor or at least tolerance on little tricks or sharp practices known as *picardia criolla;* they are part of the cleverness of his city, and he has been taught to avoid being "a dope," to take advantage of things because life is short. If a pretty girl passes on the sidewalk, he probably will make a *piropo,* an exaggerated compliment, which may be poetic or crude depending on his breeding— but the old days of bottom-pinching have disappeared. Young people give the impression of eating less than their parents, but even in the relatively lean days of 1962 they were used to a rich diet of steaks, *pasta,* fruits, and wine that would seem extravagant almost anywhere in the world. The construction worker pauses at midday to broil a rich chunk of meat alongside his wheelbarrow and wash it down with a liter of Mendoza vintage. Even the university student, who is scraping and skimping on other things, will expound on the economics of underdeveloped countries over a magnificent sirloin, seemingly unaware that Argentina, at least in its habits of consumption, is exceedingly developed!

Although my observations and discussions in Buenos Aires suggested significant differences between city and countryside, they also verified certain features of experience that are common to both. On the Pampa, isolation results from the big empty lands and the distances that separate towns. In the capital and other urban areas, it has resulted from the gradual breakdown of the extended family and the erosion of church ties—the two forces that have been said to compete with the secular community for the individual's loyalties. Since this attrition has thus far not been accompanied by the growth of wider institutional loyalties (in Buenos Aires only 40% of the adults are affiliated with a formal group, and only 2% participate actively), it has produced atomization and loneliness. Even though families are getting smaller, the same old permissive-authoritarian treatment of children lingers on—youngsters accompany their parents in public far past midnight, make surly and imperious demands on their elders, yet are often summarily punished and almost never taken into family councils. Aggressiveness and extreme self-centeredness, it is true, are most noticeable in Buenos Aires; as a foreign businessman in the city aptly described it: "If four *porteños* get into an elevator, everyone thinks the other three must be going to his floor simply because that's where *he's* going." Yet these qualities exist everywhere, and somewhere in this tangle of isolation, self-centeredness, aggressiveness, and apathy must be the reason why Argentina has failed to produce a sense of community.

Obscuring her failure from the general view, and permitting a high degree of unreality to cloud the individual's picture of his ideological and institutional life, is the ever-present gap between words and facts. Over half a century ago, Augustin Alvarez warned his fellow Argentines to look for reality, not form: "Do not imagine that by playing with words you can change social conditions." But the word-play goes on. The sociologist José Enrique Miguens points out that the present generation of university students has substituted the words "planning," "collectivization," "nationalization," and "anti-imperialism" for the "liberalism," "progress," and "democracy" used by their grandfathers—but that neither the former nor the latter set has corresponded to reality in Argentina. Thus, when asking the question, "What happened to democracy in Argentina?" one must take care to distinguish between the shadow and the substance—

how much democracy existed before, and how different is the situation now?

Discussions with politically active young people have been especially interesting. Before mentioning several of them, it may be useful to summarize the post-Peron political panorama in Argentina. After the dictator's ouster in 1955 the middle-class Radical Party, which had governed the country from 1916 to 1930, emerged as the strongest non-Peronist group in the nation. During the period of General Pedro Aramburu's Provisional Government (1955–1958) the deep personal and ideological differences that divided the two wings of the Radical Party erupted into a formal split. The new parties were the UCRI, led by Arturo Frondizi, and the People's Radicals (UCRP), a slightly more conservative group. The first elections, for a constituent assembly in 1957, revealed that the People's Radicals had the edge, but in the Presidential election of 1958 Frondizi, with the help of Peronists and Communists, won office on a platform of economic nationalism similar to Peron's.

Soon after taking office, he reversed himself, began an austerity and anti-inflationary campaign, encouraged foreign investment, invited three foreign oil companies to sign contracts for development of Argentina's petroleum reserves (something even Peron had not been able to do), and received large credits from the International Monetary Fund. He put emphasis on economic development of the country and on "social peace"—surmounting the bitterness between Peronist and anti-Peronist diehards. Despite the new economic orthodoxy, much of the right continued to distrust Frondizi, believing that he was all along a Marxist wolf in Liberal fleece. The Peronists, whose own *Justicialista* Party was outlawed, felt they had been betrayed and for a time threatened indefinite disorder with bombings and violence; only by going to the armed forces for support could Frondizi survive attacks from Peronist and labor quarters. The military, in turn, hedged the president's every move and threatened him from their side. By the time he was toppled in 1962, the president had survived some three dozen actual or incipient coups. Caught in the middle, with a base of strength of only about twenty percent of the electorate in his own party, Frondizi managed to hang on by dividing his enemies and pitting them against each other—techniques he developed so well that he earned the sobriquet "the Florentine of Argentine politics."

Thus, though the paraphernalia of government included a congress and the presence of half a dozen major political parties, the legislature and parties alike had an air of unreality about them since the two chief pressure groups—organized labor and the armed forces—used "direct action" to obtain their ends. The formal machinery of the more sophisticated and circuitous route of democratic representation, with its pleading and bargaining, was more shadow than substance. Nevertheless, the party lineup at the beginning of 1962 reflected something of the spread of opinion if not the bases of power. Out of several dozen parties only six gained over 100,000 votes in the 1960 election—in an electorate of around ten million. The Conservatives, heirs of the party that governed Argentina until 1916 and again in 1932–1943, are still associated with the *estanciero* class and the older commercial-industrial interests; during the Frondizi era they had been able to control only the province of Mendoza. The Christian Democratic Party, dating from the final years of the Peron regime, is modelled after the European Catholic parties. It appeals to the liberal Catholic vote and in the early days seemed to hold considerable promise, but it has never surpassed 300,000 votes and is deeply split over cooperation with the Peronists. In the center of the spectrum are the two Radical parties, each claiming to be the legitimate descendant of Hipolito Irigoyen's middle-class reform movement of the early part of the century. Frondizi's UCRI and the rival UCRP have been fairly evenly matched since their split, each of them ranging between just under and just over two million votes in the three comparable elections. Their rivalry and the bitterly obstructionist tactics of the People's Radicals in Congress has been a major factor in the instability of recent years. The Social Democratic Party is Argentina's counterpart of the British or Scandinavian Socialists—moderate, evolutionary, but now weakened by recent splits. In 1958 the left-wing Socialists formed the Argentine Socialist Party and rolled up almost 400,000 votes, but since then even they have split into Trotskyite and pro-Soviet wings. The Communist Party, one of the largest in the hemisphere, is not outlawed, but most of its activities are banned. The Peronist *Justicialista* Party was banned after the overthrow of the dictator, and only after casting blank ballots for several years (with 1958 as an exception) did the Peronists have a chance to account for themselves at the polls, with their short-lived victory of March, 1962, when they registered over two and a half million votes.

Adding to the unreality of the political picture of 1958–1962 was the composition of the legislature. The antiquated Saenz-Pena Electoral Law awards two-thirds of a province's seats in the Congress to the front-running party, and all the rest to the second-place party. This made UCRI the majority party and UCRP practically the only opposition, despite the fact that in many provinces the two of them together received less than fifty percent of the votes.

Despite misleading superficialities of the 1962 campaign, the essential political problem of the country—never resolved during Frondizi's tenure—is still how to reconcile the "Two Revolutions." The Peron Revolution awakened organized labor to its political potential, created new expectations among millions of lower-class Argentines, and provided a new social mobility within the framework of persistent *criollo* nationalism. The Revolution of Liberation of 1955 gave voice to the sizable and extremely influential sector of Argentine society that rejects the suppression of civil and political liberties. The first revolution remains a fact of life, with about a third of the Argentine electorate still committed to the programs—and perhaps the person—of the aging leader in Madrid. So does the second revolution remain alive. The conviction that neither Peron nor Peronism shall be allowed to return to power is widely and passionately held among the remainder of Argentines, being by no means confined to the armed forces nor the *estanciero* class. The Two Revolutions confronted each other squarely after the March 18 elections. Both the cultural fabric beneath and the constitutional machinery on top proved too weak to permit adjustment of the conflict by rational, peaceful, sanctioned means. The military had the guns, and once again the politics of force prevailed. But the problem remains.

Shortly after arriving in Buenos Aires, I became acquainted with a group of university students, all of whom were identified with the "intellectual left" although they came from three different faculties—medicine, exact sciences, philosophy and letters —and belonged to different political groups. A number of them professed to be anti-American, but I encountered little difficulty in gaining an entry to the group and apparently the confidence of most of its members. In my association with them, as in later contacts with Peronist youth groups and others who were at first suspicious, it seemed to me that the key to entry and meaningful exchange was twofold. The first requirement was to be *simpatico*—friendly and reasonably flexible about doing things their way in matters of eating, hours of meeting, and the like. The second was to listen as much as possible, stressing one's desire to be objective but, in case of disagreement, stating one's point of view without hesitation. Respect is gained neither by heady irritation at what appears to be a bizarre opinion nor by unseemly accommodation in an effort to be polite.

A majority of this group belonged or were sympathetic to the *Partido Socialista Argentina de Vanguardia,* one of the four splinters of Argentine Socialism, pro-Castro and pro-Communist. Along with the Communists, the Vanguardia Socialists voted for the Peronists in the March elections. However, these students claimed to have no illusions about freedom in or infallibility of the Soviet Union. They were somewhat inconsistent when discussing the United States: they believed that the country is dominated by industrial barons in collusion with the generals of "el Pentagano" and that, despite the Alliance for Progress, it is determined to keep Latin America in a state of semicolonialism. On the other hand, they readily admitted that a considerable degree of freedom and social well-being exists in North America; and all appeared to have a certain affection for the Yankee colossus. Some had visited Cuba on Castro's guided tours; the only people suffering, according to them, were those who were formerly the exploiters. They viewed the U.S.-backed Cuban invasion attempt of 1961 and the Soviet suppression of the Hungarian revolt in 1956 as identical manifestations of big-power imperialism, the only difference being one of effectiveness. Although instruction in the social sciences is in its infancy in Argentina, most of this group had been exposed to some of the principles of social psychology and anthropology. They displayed considerable faith in the possibilities of radical "social engineering" as the only way out for Latin America. Somewhat laconic and divided in their opinions on international relations or the future course of capitalism and Communism, they appeared vigorously united on one point: in Latin America, and especially in Argentina, existing political alignments and institutions are hopelessly inadequate and evolutionary change impossible because of general nondiscipline and the intransigence of entrenched interests. Violent change and a period of authoritarianism are inevitable; the task is to utilize them for the transformation of society into a modern, secular, Socialist state. Most of these students come from "bourgeois" backgrounds, and despite their strictures against the *criollo* romanticism of Peronism, many of them shared enthusiastically in the recent revival of interest in country music and folk dancing. They impressed me as having read widely but superficially, being more interested in abstract principles than empirical data. They were surprisingly weak on details when discussing the ideas of Marx, Mao, or even Che Guevara.

One of the first Argentine Communists I met was a young woman with some talent as a minor novelist. She appeared to have the highly emotional, fuzzy-minded qualities associated with some of the romantic converts to Communism found among writers of the 1930's, yet she is apparently a genuine card-carrying party member. She claims to have been apolitical and a great admirer of the United States until 1952, when she applied for a visa to permit her to visit a relative in New York. The visa application was turned down, she says, because she had signed the Stockholm Peace Petition in 1950. Fluent in English, she then began reading about the McCarthy investigations and, embittered at what she took to be the ultimate degeneration of liberal institutions, turned to the Communist Party as a dynamic outlet for her protest. Like many leftists and Peronists, she believed that "macartismo," as it is known in Latin America, is still a potent force in American life. Like many intellectuals, she made her political affiliation on the basis of abstract and international considerations rather than the immediate situation in Argentina.

Peronists vary so widely in their thinking and background that it is risky to generalize about their philosophy, which even when formulated as *justicialismo* in Peron's day was a loose, ill-fitting garment, high on emotive symbols and low on intellectual content. A group I visited at the university in El Chaco, however, represented present-day Peronist influence among young Argentines. The meeting was impromptu, held around a cluster of drawing boards in the faculty of architecture at the university of the Northeast. This was one of the very few occasions on which I was treated rudely in Argentina. The exchange was hampered by the obvious desire of the group's leaders to score "debating points" and appear *listo* to the audience rather than have meaningful discussion. The chief spokesman, a student of about thirty with graying temples and dressed in a black leather jacket, tore immediately into a favorite theme: the invasion of Cuba proved not only that the United States is against genuine social reform in Latin America, but that the President is no more master of his house in Washington than in Buenos Aires, since surely Mr. Kennedy was pressured and tricked into the Cuban fiasco by Pentagon generals.

It is more accurate to characterize these students as neo-

Peronists, since most of them were too young to have taken an active part in politics prior to Peron's overthrow in 1955, and many were enthusiastic followers of the movement that bears his name without actually desiring the ex-dictator's return. They appeared less interested in the current quarrel between the two major Peronist factions—the trade unionists and the old machine bosses—than in a nebulous idealism, that appeals to both their sense of social justice and their nationalism. The lower-class popular base and hodgepodge collectivism of Peronism provide a leftist attraction, while the romantic appeal to *criollo* xenophobia is a strong psychological asset. Unlike Marxist leftists, youngsters attracted to Peronism encounter little incompatibility with their Catholic ties or with the hard-dying conviction that Argentina has a unique destiny that sets it—and its social revolution—apart from the rest of the world.

Young Peronists, like many other youthful Argentines, are especially enchanted with the phrase *pais subdesarollado*, "underdeveloped country." Various writers of the "national-and-popular line" (the connecting link between certain principles of Peronism, Frondizi's UCRI, the Christian Democratic Party, and others) have given the phrase popularity. Although it is used to explain a variety of needs, problems, and policies in today's Argentina—somewhat in the maner of the "class struggle" in Marxist polemics—it is not so much a part of any coherent theory as a convenient catchall concept, the nub of which seems to be that orthodox explanations of economic and political phenomena—whether liberal or Marxist—are inadequate to guide underdeveloped nations such as Argentina. The concept is extremely vague and is used to attack or defend almost anything, even to reconcile hostility toward external cooperation with widespread demands for foreign economic assistance. Some of the more thoughtful admit that most of its devotees fail to come to grips with two key questions: whether Argentina is in fact underdeveloped; and whether being developed or underdeveloped has anything to do with consumption-oriented Argentina's dilemma of how to live continuously beyond its means.

In Peronist circles, much time and energy is used in berating the villains of underdevelopment—first, the old "antinational" oligarchy with its penchant for export markets, British manners, and French culture; then, the British and American "monopolists," who sell dear and buy cheap in Latin America, attempt to exploit its natural resources, and keep the region in the bonds of economic colonialism. Young Peronists may admit that Peron was a dictator and acknowledge that he wrecked the country's economy, but their persistent psychological commitment to the movement's "national-and-popular" aspects seems far from waning. With about a third of the country's electorate and an emotional dynamism unmatched by any other large party, the future course of Peronism is crucial to Argentina. As the economic crisis following on the political chaos of 1962 deepens, there is much speculation regarding a gigantic shift to the left, at least within the trade union sector of Peronism. However, unless there is complete collapse, it seems doubtful if the workers will want to trade the gusty chorus of "Los Muchachos Peronistos" for the "Internationale."

It is as erroneous to overestimate the importance of Communist, Peronist, and left-wing Socialist strength among Argentine youth as to ignore it. In mid-1962 the proportion of extremism in youths was somewhat higher than that in the population as a whole (probably less than fifty percent) but allowance should be made for those whose conviction is marginal or for the usual percentage of university students whose radicalism fades upon entering the privileged status of professional life. During the campaign I made a particular effort to become acquainted with young men and women active in the youth sectors of the moderate political parties—Frondizi's UCRI, the opposition UCRP, the Christian Democrats, and the Conservatives. Each party has its youth branch, somewhat more formally organized than are the Young Democrats and Young Republicans in the United States and certainly more ideologically inclined, but similar in their sense of having a special mission and their enthusiasm. More often than not, the "young militant" of the party organization, at least in the interior, is not a university graduate, since university politics is a world unto itself, and the professional man who enters active politics does so somewhat later, coming directly into the major party organization.

In Resistencia, the capital of El Chaco, Raul expressed the point of view of the El Chaco UCRI youth organization, of which he is a leader. He and his colleagues worked unreservedly for Frondizi in 1958 and supported the official party platform and ticket in 1962, even though they had grave misgivings about the influence of Rogelio Frigerio, the close adviser and *éminence grise* of the Frondizi administration, who managed to have key posts throughout the government filled with his friends. Frigerio, an industrialist and alleged former Communist, preached close cooperation between the UCRI and the Peronists but, according to Raul, not by building on the bridge of common interests, but by trying to "buy" Peronist leaders and their votes and by obscuring real issues in a murky tirade of nationalist emotionalism. Raul felt hurt and confused when Frondizi openly defended Frigerio during the campaign, characterizing him as the Argentine Harry Hopkins—a man the president needs to have around in his loneliness and who doesn't want anything for himself. Raul, like other young men in the UCRI with whom I talked in this poor northern province, felt that the greatest force in Argentine politics is still radicalism and the spirit of Hipolito Irigoyen, the eccentric Radical president (1916–1922 and 1928–1930). Raul's ideas well illustrate two points: the middle-class, essentially conservative quality of radicalism in the smaller provinces, and the lingering *charisma* of Irigoyen a generation after his death.

The Young UCRI in the province of Buenos Aires—the rich "Queen Province" of the republic—is something else again. In 1962 the youthful sector took over the state organization and ran one of its own members as candidate for governor. Guillermo Acuña Anzorena, forty-one, a lawyer, one time Under Secretary of Interior and later Minister of Labor and Social Security, brought together a team of young advisers and workers to wage a vigorous and expensive campaign under the slogan *Fuerza Joven* ("Force of Youth"). Acuña had visited the United States during the presidential campaign of 1960 and had observed both Democratic and Republican machines in motion; he even patterned one of his campaign leaflets after the Nixon-Lodge throwaway showing both smiling candidates with arms upraised in the victory gesture. His campaign manager had studied the latest techniques of "hidden persuasion" and media technique, plastering every tree and telephone pole in the 280 miles between Buenos Aires and the vacationland of Mar del Plata with posters and slogans. Acuña urged the voters to put aside former passions of the Peron years and let him build part of a new Argentina based on economic development, legality, and social peace. He and his team of advisers, many of whom had been imprisoned during the dictatorship, all agreed that former Peronists should somehow be permitted to take a meaningful part in Argentina's political life, and they hoped to wean them away from extremism. Most of these hopes were shredded on the night of March 12, however, when the voters of Buenos Aires province gave nearly a half-million more ballots to the Peronist candidate than to Acuña, setting in motion the "institutional crisis" that eventually toppled Frondizi.

What to do about the roughly one-third of the Argentine electorate that remains attached to Peronist ideas and slogans is the big problem of center and conservative parties today. Only a fraction of the nation—including some of its military leaders, a segment of the business community, and the Conservative Party—is wholeheartedly committed to the idea of eliminating Peronism as such. The remainder, split into innumerable factions, seeks to transform Peronist influence and to use it, each to his own ends. Nowhere is the argument whether to lick them or join them more fundamental than within the small but influential Christian Democratic Party. This party is only about seven years old in Argentina, and in its early days it seemed capable of attracting the same kind of modern, socially conscious Catholic leadership that it has in Western Europe, Brazil, and Chile. But the growing influence within the party of those who favor coalitions with the Peronists has disgusted and driven from it many of the ablest young people, who object to the antidemocratic overtones of even neo-Peronism.

The one thing that most of the youth sectors of the center appear to have in common is a sense of disorientation and helplessness. One thinks of Latin youth as volatile, excitable, and passionate. Yet in the chaotic days of Frondizi's ouster and the months of political unrest that followed, the reaction of Argentine youth was curiously apathetic. Twice during the heat of the March crisis the UCRI Youth of Buenos Aires called for mass meetings to organize protest demonstrations. At each meeting the plans for marches and banners fizzled and were called off. In countless discussions of the coup, the country's crisis, and the distressing wave of disorder that swept Buenos Aires in mid-1962, young people told me of their shame, their mortification, and their unwillingness to put up with such conditions. Almost invariably they followed with the comment, "But what can I do as an individual? Nothing." Among a few young people, especially those who have traveled abroad, this attitude of helplessness appears to be changing. But it would seem that one of Argentina's principal disadvantages in facing the stormy years that no doubt lie ahead is the gloomy resignation shared by so many of the young men and women who will have to shape the future.

University students obviously constitute an important segment of Argentine youth. There are seven state (public) universities in the country, and together with the Catholic University of Santo Tomas in Buenos Aires they enjoy a good reputation in neighboring countries, which often send students to Argentina for advanced work. The University of Buenos Aires, founded in 1821, has over sixty thousand students enrolled, over twenty thousand of them registered in the law school alone. In Buenos Aires the university consists of nine different professional schools, each with a considerable degree of autonomy and physically scattered throughout the city, so that the notion of a "campus" is unknown. There are no university housing accommodations, and student life consists of going to class and little else. It is not rare to find a young man preparing for architecture or dentistry who hardly knows more than one or two of his fellow students on a personal basis. The quest for a professional degree usually lasts six years, but some students drag out their course work for many more, eventually becoming known as "chronic students." Tuition is free, but unless a student is from a well-to-do family, he must generally find employment, at times in two or more jobs, to support himself. At the University of the Northeast in El Chaco, over 90 percent of the students are employed full time. Besides the absence of the social clubs and hoopla that accompany most American undergraduate careers in the United States, university life is different in other respects. Student strikes are a frequent and time-honored means of political and social protest. Since the "university reform" of 1918, which took higher education out of the hands of the Catholic church, students have taken part in the governing of the institution they attend. The supreme authority of the Buenos Aires Faculty of Architecture, for example, is its fourteen-member Directive Council. Professors elect eight of their number to the council, former graduates three, and students three. A similar arrangement is used to form the all-university Superior Council, which sets university policy and can overrule the rector in case of a dispute.

University politics is stormy and complicated all through Latin America, and Argentina is no exception. Students take part in two sets of electoral contests: one for their representatives on the university councils, the other for their own student organizations. Voting in the first is compulsory, and a student may not take exams unless he has cast his ballot. Participation in student organizations, usually called *centros,* is optional, and of the five thousand architecture students in Buenos Aires, only about three thousand belong to the handful of student organizations found within each faculty. The *centros* serve several purposes: they are the avenue to representation in the important Argentine Federation of Students at the national level; locally, they provide co-operatives and canteens where the students meet to hash over world problems, drink coffee, and buy mimeographed notes for cramming. Communist and pro-Communist control over student organizations has been a problem for many years in Argentina as in other Latin American countries. Part of the problem is historical, resulting from the early identification of Communists with the reform movement, which swept university life early in the century and won its struggle for student rights and secular education in 1918. Communists exploit the continuing prestige of the *Reformista* label and cultivate a group of "chronic students" in order to maintain an organizational control far out of proportion to their real strength. Nevertheless, in the 1961 student elections in Argentina—as in a number of other Latin American countries—the Communists and extreme left lost ground to center and democratic groups. One of the most important of the latter is the humanist movement, led by liberal Catholics. *Humanistas* and other anti-Communists made important gains in several faculties of the University of Buenos Aires and in most of the provincial universities, although Communist-led groups retained control in over half of the professional schools. The elections demonstrated that center and Catholic students can win if they work together and get out the vote. Argentine students of the sixties are undoubtedly to the left—at least ideologically—of their North American counterparts, but apathy among the moderates has counted more than Communist strength in giving the extreme left its superior position.

Disorientation and apathy seem to express the mood of Argentine youth in years of crisis. Even where, as in some of the discussion among university groups, the debate is lively, the gap between words and reality robs many exchanges of meaningful social content. Professor Miguens, polling young people in six cities, found that 34% of them believed the country could go nowhere without first being "turned upside down"; 70% wanted "a strong government that can put everybody in his place." Yet very few seemed to know or care for what purpose the nation would be shaken up or just which people a new dictatorship would put in office. It may be that this apparent acceptance of extreme solutions, like the propensity to explain away Argentina's problems with the phrase "economic underdevelopment," stems more from a fascination with words than from well-reasoned conviction. Impatience with relating cause and effect may be due in part to the excessively formal methods of university instruction and the poverty of empirical research. According to Miguens, "there is scarcely a subject in which they don't teach the entire history of the discipline, what everyone in the world has said—and ceased to say—about each theme."

Nevertheless, there are a few scattered signs that a new realism may be budding in the Argentine academic community. A national research council is in the formative stage, and in economics and social studies a few clusters of serious scholars are beginning team research on a number of national problems. Some of the more thoughtful United States assistance officials and foundation representatives believe that strengthening and modernizing higher education—especially in its research aspects—may be the best contribution we can make toward the goals of stability and development in Argentina. This approach is extremely long-range and offers little possibility of the spectacular change that some Americans envisage as the relatively immediate impact of the Alliance for Progress, but it is likely to prove sounder in the end.

As of mid-1963 it is possible to combine a pessimism about Argentina's immediate political future with a degree of optimism over the country's capacity eventually to break out of stalemate and malaise. There is evidence that capable young Argentines from varied sectors of society are willing to think clearly and realistically about national problems and to articulate unorthodox views with candor. Many examples could be cited, but three young leaders I have known will serve to illustrate the point. Each of the trio—a businessman, an editorial writer, and an army officer—impressed me not only by having something important to say but also by acting without regard for personal interest.

Tomás Fillol's contribution was the publication of a prize-winning thesis he wrote for the Massachusetts Institute of Technology's School of Industrial Management in 1960,* in which he challenged beliefs cherished by most of his generation. A Swiss-trained engineer before he studied in the United States, Fillol has now returned to Argentina to manage his family's varied commercial and construction enterprises, hopeful of demonstrating the effectiveness of modern management techniques in the slow-moving Argentine economy. At a moment when almost all sectors of opinion cling to the notion that economic development is the root of all problems, Fillol's book seeks to demonstrate that "the nature of Argentina's basic problem is fundamentally . . . *social* rather than economic." In the Introduction to his brief and stimulating book he says:

An analysis of the Argentine "national character," based on a study of the value-orientation profile of the Argentine society, will demonstrate that some cultural traits of the bulk of the population are inimical to the emergence of social relationships which would enable individuals to act concertedly in the pursuit of common goals and interests. This feature, i.e., the fact that Argentines are a "conglomeration" of people rather than an organic "community," together with the fact that those same cultural traits constitute a powerful barrier to the appearance of "Western-capitalistic-like" economic initiative in the bulk of society's members is . . . a fundamental impediment retarding the nation's economic growth. . . . The viewpoint taken in this book is that the basically passive, apathetic value-orientation profile of the Argentine society must be regarded as the *critical* factor limiting the possibilities of steady, long-run economic development.

Whether Fillol's development of the Argentine national character has an adequate empirical and theoretical base, and whether

---

* Tomás R. Fillol, *Social Factors in Economic Development: The Argentine Case* (Cambridge: The M.I.T. Press, 1961).

his hope for gradual transformation through the medium of industrial relations is justified, there remains no doubt that he has produced a piece of constructive criticism that is fresh and provocative, infinitely more valuable because it comes from an Argentine. Though his point of view is not popular among his business colleagues, he is now working on a Spanish version of his book.

From the editorial pages of the distinguished newspaper *La Nacion* another young Argentine is expressing his ideas with vigor and clarity. Like Fillol, Mariano Grondono is under thirty. In his column "Political Panorama" Grondono consistently analyzes political events with a cool logic, measured style, and feel for the broad sweep of recent history that have caused some to call him the "Argentine Walter Lippmann." One of his most important contributions has been his continued insistence on the reality of the "Two Revolutions": anti-Peronists must realize that the old pre-1943 Argentina is gone forever; Peronists must accept the fact that much of the nation insists there can be no return to midnight arrests, a muzzled press, and the whims of a dictator. Grondono espouses a system of proportional representation that he believes will permit all major segments of the body politic to share in national decision-making, yet insure against Peronist control. During the months when political reform decrees were being prepared within the Guido government, he made a distasteful decision. The various drafts of the reforms were being drawn up under the direction of the military services. Grondono, a constitutional lawyer, is opposed to military dictation of the nation's political life, but he saw a chance to try to influence the political reforms for the better. Working with the army on its draft, which was close to the version adopted, Grondono chose to "walk with the devil" in order to exercise meaningful influence rather than making ineffectual criticism from outside.

The third young leader, an army colonel, must remain nameless. He deplores continued intervention by the military and is trying to convince others that it is a dead end for Argentina. It should be stressed that the Argentine Army is far from mono-lithic, and practically every political tendency or "line" can be found within it, as well as a seemingly limitless number of per-sonal ambitions and opportunistic coalitions that cut across and defy ideological lines. The views being voiced by the young colonel are not unique. But hard thinking and a measure of risk on the part of an officer who has had to make an intellectual readjustment is an encouraging sign. Like most of his colleagues, the colonel is completely disgusted with the chaotic political situation and what he sees as the bankruptcy of all the parties and former leasers. As one who has had exciting responsibilities in civil operations of military government (preparing stand-by plans for administration and even economic improvement of each prov-ince in the event of intervention), he has been fully exposed to the beguiling idea of "expert government" without interference by politicians and vested interests or all the traditional frustra-tions of democratic procedures. Yet he has come to the convic-tion that tutelary government by a progressive and patriotic military, however attractive in the Middle East or Asia, is simply not a solution for Argentina. The democratic idea, even if it has not worked well here, is too deeply implanted. Above all, any regime that bases its credentials on an act of force invites legions of would-be successors to try the same route. At a moment when there is strong pressure within the armed forces to eliminate the last traces of civilian control within the Guido government, post-pone elections again, and back off further from democracy in the name of "a period of authority which can put some order into an undisciplined country," the Colonel is trying to convince his military colleagues that this approach not only will solve no problems, but also will aggravate the pent-up resentments of a people excluded from its governance. He is also quick to scold those civilian groups opposed to the present regime who hover furtively around the military establishment looking for dissident young officers to lead a counter-*golpe* in the name of legitimacy and constitutionalism. There is no short cut to salvation, says the colonel; dreams of saviors and magic solutions must be abandoned in favor of the tedious tasks of persuasion, building an Argentine consensus, and returning to the ballot box.

The prospects for young people who think in this manner are clouded at best. Although a vast majority of Argentines complain that the country is nearing an impossible chaos and cannot possibly continue along the same path, there are no signs of immediate relief, but rather hints of increased dissension or apathy. It seems all too likely that military adventures, economic paralysis, and hypernationalism will spread. Possibly a major catharsis will be necessary before Argentines can find the minimum sense of community necessary to enable their proud nation to take the place it deserves among the prosperous democracies of this century. Meanwhile, these minority voices, like the green and spreading pampa, are among the many reasons why Argentina's future should some day be bright.